THE LOST WORK
OF
STEPHEN KING

THE LOST WORK
OF
STEPHEN KING

A Guide to
Unpublished Manuscripts,
Story Fragments,
Alternative Versions,
and Oddities

STEPHEN J. SPIGNESI

A Birch Lane Press Book
Published by Carol Publishing Group

Carol Publishing Group edition, 1999

A Birch Lane Press Book
Published by Carol Publishing Group
Birch Lane Press is a registered trademark of Carol Communications, Inc.

Editorial, sales and distribution, rights and permissions inquiries should be addressed to
Carol Publishing Group, 120 Enterprise Avenue, Secaucus, N.J. 07094

In Canada: Canadian Manda Group, One Atlantic Avenue, Suite 105, Toronto, Ontario
M6K 3E7

Carol Publishing Group books may be purchased in bulk at special discounts for sales
promotion, fund-raising, or educational purposes. Special editions can be created to
specifications. For details, contact: Special Sales Department, Carol Publishing Group,
120 Enterprise Avenue, Secaucus, N.J. 07094.

Manufactured in the United States of America
10 9 8 7 6 5 4 3 2

Library of Congress Cataloging-in-Publication Data
Spignesi, Stephen J.
    The lost work of Stephen King / Stephen J. Spignesi.
        p.   cm.
    Includes bibliographical references and index.
    ISBN 1-55972-469-2 (hc. : alk. paper)
    1. King, Stephen, 1947–   —Criticism and interpretation. 2. Horror tales,
American—History and criticism. 3. King, Stephen, 1947–   —Bibliography. I. Title.
PS3561. I483Z874   1998
813′.54—dc21   98–24116
                                          CIP

To Charlie Fried,
a cherished friend and benevolent aide-de-camp
whose inestimable help and support made this book
better than I could have made it on my own

CONTENTS

Acknowledgments

The purpose of *The Lost Work of Stephen King* is to tell Stephen King's legions of fans about what they might have missed—wonderful Stephen King writings that are not available in their local bookstore but are nonetheless very entertaining and of enormous interest.

Tracking down many of these works, some of which appeared once in one obscure forum or another and then disappeared into that place where once-written words go after they are read and forgotten, was a daunting task. I owe a great debt of thanks to many collectors of King out there who made available to me copies of some of these writings so that I could read them and write about them.

Earlier versions of a few of the chapters of *The Lost Work of Stephen King* originally appeared in my first book about Stephen King's work, *The Shape Under the Sheet: The Complete Stephen King Encyclopedia* (Popular Culture Ink.). These are mostly the chapters about the Stephen King rarities—*People, Places, and Things*; "Keyholes"; "A Possible Fairy Tale"; etc.—that I wrote about in my earlier King reference book.

The author and publisher wish to thank Tom Schultheiss of Popular Culture Ink. for his assistance in expanding these chapters and for permission to reprint selected material from *The Shape Under the Sheet* in *The Lost Work of Stephen King*.

Also, my very special thanks to Charlie Fried, a man who is one of the world's leading collectors of Stephen King material and someone who has a collection beyond the imagination of King fans. (I know, I have seen much of it.)

Also, many thanks to Tyson Blue for his wonderful chapter on *The Plant*; Dr. Michael Collings for his incredible King bibliography and for his help with the "Garbage Truck" section; George Beahm, fellow

King fan, for his unending support and friendship; Jim Cole for his terrific essay on making his movie *The Last Rung on the Ladder* and for
his ongoing friendship and support; Bev Vincent for being every King
fan on the planet's "eyes and ears"; Stu Tinker and his Betts Bookstore
for being one of the premier sources for all things King and also for selling my books; Chris Cavalier for his friendship and help with the *Glory
Days* and *Wimsey* chapters; Gary Ink and *Publishers Weekly* for their
prompt assistance in reprinting King's "My Say" essay; and my thanks
also to John White, Mike Lewis, Michelle Rein, Steven Schragis, Bruce
Bender, Meryl Earl, and especially Susan Hayes, for her special attention
and much-appreciated help.

[Horror] *is one genre that's been pretty constant all through American literature going back to the "penny dreadfuls."* Edison *made a version of* Frankenstein. *So this has always been with us. But right now in America, when things are fairly quiet, when people feel fairly confident, we live in a kind of era of good feeling where crime is down, we feel a little more freedom, I think, to explore our dark side because it's not so much with us.*

To me it's sort of interesting, in World War II, the universal monsters like Frankenstein, Wolf Man, Dracula, all disappear. There was enough real-life horror. And then, after World War II is over, you see the monsters start to come out of their dark holes again. And the biggest monster of them all was Godzilla from Japan, and he *was caused by nuclear radiation. So you have a case of the first nuclear monster originating from the only people in the history of the world who have ever had to face the atomic bomb in a real-life situation. So we see entertainment, but we also see always this working out of the real fears that are underneath.*

—Stephen King, on *Nightline*, December 10, 1997

PREFACE

THE HIDDEN WORLD OF THE LOST KING

The ideas come and they have to be let out, that's all. They just have to be let out.

—Stephen King on *60 Minutes*, February 16, 1997

I have been reading, studying, collecting, and writing about Stephen King and his work for over a decade. During this time I have had the great privilege of meeting many fellow King fans, experts, and collectors, all of whom have been extremely helpful in ways too numerous to mention.

One way I *have* been assisted, though, was by being allowed to see many rare Stephen King writings, some of which I have written about in this book. King is nothing if not prolific, and the body of his "lost work," only a fraction of which is discussed in this volume, makes very clear just how much Stephen King loves to write. King's mainstream work alone is so voluminous, and he publishes so regularly, that his "normal" output is often joked about in the media, especially on the late-night talk shows. One can only guess what these wits would say if they knew about all the *other* stuff King writes that goes unnoticed by the majority of his fans.

Some of the writings discussed in *The Lost Work of Stephen King* are so rare that many King experts have never even heard of them. As the author of *The Complete Stephen King Encyclopedia*, I was granted generous access to many of these priceless documents, and I cannot thank my sources enough. All wish to remain anonymous, but nonetheless, they know who they are.

For each piece reviewed in this book I give you a realistic assessment of your chances of finding the work. Some will be relatively easy to locate; others I tell you to not even try to find. I did not include these latter rarities to tease. This book is not meant to be a "shopper's guide" to the lesser-known work of Stephen King. Rather, we hope that *The Lost Work of Stephen King* will enhance the typical fan's understanding and appreciation of King by looking at works that illustrate the evolution of a writer and that demonstrate his early use of themes and techniques later employed so effectively in his best-known novels and short stories.

The original title of my 1990 authorized book about King's work, *The Complete Stephen King Encyclopedia,* was *The Shape Under the Sheet*, which I borrowed from King himself.

King used that phrase in his 1981 nonfiction look at the horror genre, *Danse Macabre*, to describe what the horror writer does: According to King, he takes you into a room and shows you the shape under the sheet. And what is that shape? Why, your own dead body, of course.

That metaphor is appropriate, I think, for describing the vast body of work that I am calling the *Lost Work of Stephen King,* and it looks as if I have come full circle. Once again, I hope to show my readers—and let them touch—something they have not seen before.

Don't be afraid.

Yes, this room is dark, but I think you might enjoy seeing what I have to show you.

Want to touch it?

I knew that you did.

Introduction

Welcome to Our Nightmare!

I feel a feeling which I feel you all feel.

—Bishop George Ridding

Okay, so the Stephen King works discussed in this book are not really *lost*. After all, *I* found them, right?

When we use the word *lost* to describe these writings, we mean that the typical Stephen King fan may not be aware of them or, if he or she *has* heard of them, does not know how to go about finding them.

After surveying the field and talking to King fans, I came to the conclusion that there is great interest in what can accurately be described as that hidden (or lost) body of King's work that is unavailable to the majority of his fans.

Thus this book. Here is the first comprehensive look at dozens of writings over twenty years by Stephen King that exist outside the body of his most well known work.

We look at everything, from King's early childhood writings, high school novels, and college writings to nonfiction articles about John Lennon and Rick Nelson, essays about censorship and cars, musings about Bruce Springsteen, horror movies, and being a brand name, and King's clues to a "Horrors!" crossword puzzle, not to mention Stephen King stories in which he and his family are the characters.

Stephen King has been a gigantic presence in the worlds of books, movies, and popular culture for close to twenty-five years now. Because of his prolific output, his fans eagerly look forward to the next Stephen King project.

King's achievement is unique: In addition to being a hugely popular writer whose books sell in the millions, he is also studied and collected; courses are taught about his work, and signed limited editions of his books sell for thousands of dollars.

This book you now hold in your hands is different from my earlier King tomes. It exists to steer you in the direction of King writings we know you will enjoy but may not have even heard of.

Each chapter of this book, then, begins with a definition of what the piece is, followed by the answer to the question "Chances of finding a copy?" Believe it or not, for many of these writings, those chances are pretty good. In several instances, all you need is access to a good public or university library or a mailing address for the original publisher (which is often thoughtfully provided by your humble author).

The Lost Work of Stephen King reviews and synopsizes rare King writings. However, in one case, the actual Stephen King essay ("My Say"—chapter 46) is reprinted in its entirety.

We felt that there was a real need for a book such as this. Stephen King is not only the world's most popular writer; he is also one of the few twentieth-century scribes whose work (the best of it, anyway) will be read and studied a hundred years from now.

So onward into the dark—and try not to get *too* lost, okay?

Stephen King:
A Life in the Dread Zone

1947–2000

Here is a Stephen King time line that looks at the high points of the life and work of the King of Horror.

Individual publication dates of books and release dates of movies are *not* listed (with a few exceptions), since this information can be found in "The Lost Work," "The Royal Library," and "The King of Hollywood" sections of this book. King's age at the time of the event listed is indicated in parentheses following the year(s).

1947   Stephen Edwin King is born on September 21, in Portland, Maine, at 1:30 A.M., the first and only biological child of Ruth Pillsbury King and Donald King. (King's older brother, David, had been adopted in 1945.)

1949 (2)   King's father, Donald, goes out for a pack of cigarettes and never returns.

1949–58 (2–11)   King, his mother, and brother move around, living in Scarborough, New York; Croton-on-Hudson, New York; Chicago, Illinois; West De Pere, Wisconsin; Fort Wayne, Indiana; and Stratford, Connecticut.

1958 (11)   King, his mother, and brother move to Durham, Maine. King lives in Durham until he graduates from the University of Maine in 1970.

1963 (16)   King begins high school at Lisbon Falls High School.

1966 (19)   King begins study at the University of Maine, majoring in English.

1967 (20)   King publishes "The Glass Floor," his first professional sale. He was paid thirty-five dollars.

1969–70 (21–22)   From February 1969 through May 1970, King writes "King's Garbage Truck" column for the University of Maine student newspaper, the *Maine Campus*.

1970 (22)   King graduates in May from the University of Maine with a B.S. in English. He immediately begins working at a variety of jobs, one as a laborer in an industrial laundry.

1971 (23)   King marries Tabitha Spruce on January 2. The two had met while attending the University of Maine. Their first child, Naomi Rachel, is born later this year. King begins teaching English at Hampden Academy at a salary of $6,400 a year.

1973 (26)   Joseph Hill, the Kings' first son, is born. King's mother, Ruth King, dies of ovarian cancer.

1974 (27)   *Carrie* is published. King leaves Hampden Academy. King and his family move to Boulder, Colorado. King's stay at the Stanley Hotel inspires *The Shining*.

1975 (28)   The King family returns to Maine.

1976 (29)   Brian De Palma's film adaptation of King's first novel, *Carrie*, is released. It is both a critical *and* financial success and has the added effect of helping sell, in a span of only six months, 2,250,000 copies of the paperback edition of *'Salem's Lot*, King's second book.

1977 (30)   King and his family move to England, where he meets Peter Straub. Preliminary discussions of collaborating on a novel take place. (This meeting would ultimately result in the coauthored fantasy novel *The Talisman*.) King publishes his first "Richard Bachman" novel, *Rage*. (King has been very prolific, but his publisher refuses to release more than one "Stephen King" novel a year. The only way King can publish more than one book a year is to use a pseudonym. Thus, "Richard Bachman"—Richard, in honor of legendary novelist Richard Matheson, and Bachman, for the rock band Bachman-Turner-Overdrive—was born.)

1978 (31)   The Kings' third child, Owen Phillip, is born. King serves as writer-in-residence at the University of Maine. He acts as judge for the 1977 World Fantasy Awards.

1979 (32)   King is guest of honor at the World Fantasy Convention. He receives World Fantasy Award nominations for *The Stand* and *Night Shift* (both published in 1978).

1980 (33)   King and his family move to Bangor, where they purchase a twenty-eight-room Victorian mansion. King becomes the first writer ever to have three books on the national bestseller lists simultaneously: *Firestarter, The Dead Zone,* and *The Shining.*

1981 (34)   King receives the Career Alumni Award from the University of Maine.

1982 (35)   King receives the Hugo Award for Best Nonfiction of the Year for *Danse Macabre.* He receives the World Fantasy Award for "Do the Dead Sing?" (which later appears in *Skeleton Crew* as "The Reach"). King is named Best Fiction Writer of the Year in a poll in *US* magazine.

1983 (36)   Three film adaptations of King novels are released in one year, *Christine, Cujo,* and *The Dead Zone.*

1984 (37)   King presents the guest-of-honor address, "Dr. Seuss and the Two Faces of Fantasy," at the International Conference on the Fantastic in the Arts. King appears in an American Express commercial.

1985 (38)   King acknowledges that he is "Richard Bachman" and sets another record when five of his books appear on national bestseller lists at the same time: *Skeleton Crew, The Bachman Books* (two editions), *The Talisman,* and *Thinner.* King is the guest of honor at the Third Annual World Drive-In Movie Festival and Custom Car Rally. The first issue of *Castle Rock: The Stephen King Newsletter* is published in January.

1986 (39)   King makes his directorial debut with *Maximum Overdrive* and appears as a guest VJ on MTV.

1987 (40)   King has three titles on the annual hardcover-fiction bestseller list: *The Tommyknockers, Misery,* and *The Eyes of the Dragon.* King delivers the commencement address at the University of Maine graduation ceremony on May 6.

1988 (41)   King receives the Bram Stoker Award for *Misery.*

1989 (42)   King receives Bram Stoker nominations for "The Night Flier" and "Dedication."

1990 (43)   King publishes the complete and uncut edition of *The Stand.*

1991 (44)   King is a guest at the American Booksellers Association (ABA). King's first original series for television, *Golden Years,* debuts and garners respectable ratings but is not renewed. (See "How I Created *Golden Years* . . ." in this volume.)

1992 (45)   King sues to have his name removed from an alleged "adaptation" of his *Night Shift* short story "The Lawnmower Man." He wins.

1993 (46)   A decent adaptation of *The Tommyknockers* becomes King's second TV miniseries success (after *It*). More King miniseries will soon follow.

1994 (47)   King tours the East Coast with his rock-and-roll band, the Rock Bottom Remainders. King sings lead and plays rhythm guitar. (See the chapter "The Neighborhood of the Beast.") Also, "The Man in the Black Suit" wins an O. Henry Award and a World Fantasy Award. (See chapter 72.)

1995 (48)   King wins the Bram Stoker Award for Best Novelette for "Lunch at the Gotham Café." (See chapter 72.)

1996 (49)   The year of King: King rocks the publishing industry by publishing three complete novels in one year, all of which become bestsellers. From March through August, he first publishes his Death Row serial novel *The Green Mile* in six monthly installments. Inspired by Dickens's similar publication practice, each installment sells close to 3 million copies and prompts copycat publications, including John Saul's almost-as-successful *The Blackstone Chronicles*. A couple of months later, he then publishes two new novels simultaneously—one by Stephen King *(Desperation)* and one by his alter ego, Richard Bachman *(The Regulators)*. (The fictional Bachman's widow had found the manuscript in a box somewhere and decided to allow it to be released.)

1997 (50)   King rocks the publishing industry *again* by leaving his publisher of twenty years, Viking Penguin, and moving to Simon & Schuster, where he signs a groundbreaking three-book deal in which he takes only a $2 million advance for each book but will receive substantial royalties (between 27 and 50 percent) on his books if they sell well.

1998 (51)   *Bag of Bones,* King's first Simon & Schuster novel after decades with Penguin, is published and becomes an immediate bestseller.

1999 (52)   King's fourth short-story collection is published.

2000 (53)   The third and final book of King's deal with Simon & Schuster, *On Fiction,* a nonfiction book about writing, is published.

THE LOST WORK
1956–the Present

Writing is necessary for my sanity. As a writer, I can externalize my fears and insecurities and night terrors on paper, which is what people pay shrinks a small fortune to do. In my case, they pay me for psychoanalyzing myself in print. And in the process, I'm able to "write myself sane," as that fine poet Anne Sexton puts it.

—Stephen King, *Playboy*, June 1983

1

"Jhonathan and the Witchs"

On yonder Mountain there are three witches. If you can kill them, I will give you 5,000 crowns. If you cannot do it I will have your head!

> —the King, from "Jhonathan and the Witchs"

What it is: one of the first short stories Stephen King ever wrote. (Dr. Michael Collings, in his massive bibliography, *The Work of Stephen King,* describes this piece as "the *earliest* story King wrote." [emphasis added]) King wrote this tale when he was nine years old for his Aunt Gert, who used to pay him a quarter for every story he wrote. "Naturally I inundated her!" he writes in the introduction to "Jhonathan and the Witchs."

Chances of finding a copy: excellent. The story's only appearance is in an anthology of early writings by well-known authors called *First Words,* but the book is still in print. This story is included here as one of King's "lost works" because it is likely that the majority of his fans missed its original 1993 publication and would probably want to seek it out.

First Words collected early writings from contemporary authors, including Isaac Asimov, Joyce Carol Oates, and of course, Stephen King. King's story featured a charming Christmastime photo of King, at the age of nine, posing in front of a Christmas stocking wearing a checkerboard shirt and hugging his dog, Queenie.

"Jhonathan and the Witchs" is introduced in the book by editor Paul

Mandelbaum, and in his brief introduction he quotes King from *Danse Macabre* and also cites a letter King sent to his agent accompanying the short story in which King tells how he wrote many stories for his Aunt Gert, whom he describes as his "first patron." He also notes in his letter, "By the way, one thing about the enclosed [story] should make you feel that entropy doesn't *always* apply; you'll note that at least my spelling has gotten better."

"Jhonathan and the Witchs" is 545 words long, and the first page of the manuscript is reproduced in *First Words*.

 The story is about Jhonathan, a cobbler's son, who is told by his father one day to "go and seek your fourtune."

Jhonathan sets out with the intention of asking the King for work. On his journey he saves the life of a hunted rabbit who turns out to be a "fariy" in disguise. The fairy grants Jhonathan three wishes, but he cannot think of what to wish for, so he saves them for later.

When he arrives in the kingdom, he learns that the King is in a bad mood and so orders Jhonathan to kill three witches who live on a mountain or Jhonathan will lose his own head!

At first, Jhonathan is perplexed as to how he will achieve such a task, but then he remembers his three wishes; he uses them in a genuinely clever manner and ultimately manages to kill all three witches.

The story ends with King telling his readers that "Jhonathan collected his 5,000 crowns and he and his father lived happily ever after."

"Jhonathan and the Witchs" is, as Mandelbaum acknowledges in the introduction, a classic "Grimms"-like fairy tale and truly a significant work for someone so young as well as being a sign of what was to come. After all, Jhonathan and his father live happily ever after thanks to Jhonathan's grisly murdering of three supernatural creatures.

Sounds like something out of Stephen King, doesn't it?

PUBLISHING HISTORY

1993: *First Words: Earliest Writing from Favorite Contemporary Authors*, edited by Paul Mandelbaum (hardcover; Algonquin Books of Chapel Hill, N.C.).

2

People, Places, and Things

Volume I

As they covered his body (what was left of it) and trouped away, it actually seemed that they heard laughter coming from the bottom of the well.

> —from "The Thing at the Bottom of the Well"
> in *People, Places, and Things*

What it is: a collection of eighteen one-page science-fiction and horror short stories in typescript written by Steve King and Chris Chesley—two budding writers with hopes of becoming bestselling authors—probably sometime in the late fifties.

Chances of finding a copy: impossible. There exists one original of this typed collection, and Stephen King owns it. There are a few photocopied sets of *People, Places, and Things* in the hands of a few King experts and authorities, but those are unquestionably unavailable to the average King fan.

People, Places, and Things is one of the rarest pieces of Stephen King material in existence. Douglas E. Winter describes this slim compendium as "devoted entirely to tales of horror and black irony," and as unsophisticated and juvenile as the tales are, they are nonetheless amazing examples of a nascent talent.

Stephen King and Chris Chesley's efforts here are remarkably self-assured for two teenaged writers. Most of the stories bear the unmis-

5

takable influence of *E.C. Comics,* and the majority of them are just begging to be illustrated, preferably in loud, garish tones and colors.

As noted above, *People, Places, and Things* is a collection of eighteen one-page short stories written by "Steve" King and Chris Chesley sometime in the late fifties. (Chesley and King grew up together in Durham, Maine.)

Eight of the stories were written by King, nine by Chesley, and one by the two of them. On the "cover" of this eighteen-page typed booklet is the title of the collection and the authors' names. At the bottom of the page, on two lines, is "Second Edition/Complete and Unabridged," and below that is the line "Triad Publishing Company."

Here is a complete listing of the collection's contents (Original spelling errors have been retained.)

Forward
"The Hotel at the End of the Road" (Steve King)
"Genius" (Chris Chesley)
"Top Forty, News, Weather, and Sports" (Chris Chesley)
"Bloody Child" (Chris Chesley)
"I've Got To Get Away!" (Steve King)
"The Dimension Warp" (Steve King)
"The Thing at the Bottom of the Well" (Steve King)
"Reward" (Chris Chesley)
"The Stranger" (Steve King)
"A Most Unusual Thing" (Chris Chesley)
"Gone" (Chris Chesley)
"They've Come" (Chris Chesley)
"I'm Falling" (Steve King)
"The Cursed Expedition" (Steve King)
"The Other Side of the Fog" (Steve King)
"Scared" (Chris Chesley)
"Curiousity Kills the Cat" (Chris Chesley)
"Never Look Behind You" (Steve King and Chris Chesley)

We will now take a detailed look at the foreword and nine of the stories written or coauthored by Stephen King.

FORWARD

King and Chesley pull no punches in assuring the reader that they are in for a treat: The "forward" begins: "People, Places, and Things is an extraordinary book. It is a book for people who would enjoy being pleasantly thrilled for a few moments." They then specifically "pitch" Chesley's story "Gone" and King's "I'm Falling," after which they warn the potential reader to go no further if they do not possess an imagination: "This book is not for you," they caution. The foreword concludes with the advice that "the next time you lie in bed and hear an unreasonable creak or thump, you can try and explain it away . . . but try Steve King's and Chris Chesley's explanation: People, Places, and Things."

"THE HOTEL AT THE END OF THE ROAD"

Two punks named Tommy Riviera and Kelso Black are fleeing from the cops in a high-speed chase. They take a side road (described as a "wagon track") and find an old hotel, which "looked just like a scene out of the early 1900s." The two hoods demand a room—at gunpoint—from the old hotel clerk and are given room 5. Room 5 "was barren except for an iron double bed, a cracked mirror, and soiled wallpaper." They fall asleep, and when they awake the next morning, they are paralyzed. The two punks have stumbled onto a macabre museum of the living dead and are its first additions in twenty-five years.

Comments: This "hotel at the end of the road" seems to be the great granddaddy of King's *Shining* hotel, the Overlook, and the "living mummies" in the story, King's first use of zombies. It also included King's first use of the character Kelso Black, a guy who would be whisked off to hell by Satan in a later story in this collection, "The Stranger."

There really isn't too much in the way of plot development in "Hotel," and there are a few unanswered questions, one of which is What, exactly, does the clerk do with his "nice specimens?"

For all its flaws, we can't help but be amazed by the sophisticated narrative and unstoppable storytelling powers of Stephen King, even at such an early age.

"I've Got To Get Away!"

One day Denny Phillips finds himself working on the assembly line of an "atomic factory" and decides that he and his fellow workers are prisoners and that he must try to escape. There are guards everywhere, however, and Denny is shot during his escape attempt.

Instead of being taken away by an ambulance, though, Denny is carted away in a truck with a sign on its side that reads Acme Robot Repair. Denny is really Robot Number x-238A, and for some unknown reason, he has achieved a sort of humanlike consciousness. Two weeks later he is back on the job, but once again a thought begins to race through his mind: "I've Got to Get Away!"

Comments: Here we have an early science-fiction piece by King that takes up all of a half page but is surprisingly well done. King has repeatedly used the theme of out-of-control technology in his fiction, and here he seems to be exploring ideas about machines achieving consciousness that he reworked later in "The Mangler," "Trucks," *Christine,* "Word Processor of the Gods," and *The Tommyknockers.*

A newly discovered, early Stephen King story called "The Killer," possibly from around the same period as *People, Places, and Things,* is also about a robot coming to a conscious awareness of himself, but with quite a different result. (See the chapter on "The Killer" in this volume.)

"The Dimension Warp"

This story was included in the *People, Places, and Things* table of contents but was apparently lost over the years. There is no extant information about the tale, but based on the title, it seems to have been another one of King's early forays into science fiction.

"The Thing at the Bottom of the Well"

This classic, early King short story begins with the reader's being told that "Oglethorpe Crater was an ugly, mean little wretch." Some of the tortures this little creep inflicts include sticking pins in cats and dogs, pulling the wings from flies, pulling worms apart and watching them squirm (although his fun with the worms loses its appeal when he learned that they didn't feel any pain), and tying a rope across the top of the cellar stairs so that the maid would trip and fall.

One day when Oglethorpe was out "looking for more things to torture," he spotted a well. He yelled, "Hello," down into it and heard a voice reply, "Hello, Oglethorpe. Come on down, [a]nd we'll have jolly fun."

Oglethorpe wasn't found for a month. Then, one day, he is discovered in the well. His arms and legs had been pulled out, and pins had been stuck in his eyes. As his remains are carted away, laughter can be heard drifting up from the bottom of the well.

Comments: "The Thing at the Bottom of the Well" is a very important early Stephen King story for one critical reason: It appears to be the first time King used the archetypal "thing in the sewer" monster-creature that later became Pennywise the Clown in *It.* The monster under the bed, the bogeyman in the closet—this thing at the bottom of the well appears to be the ancestral grandfather of all these fiendish bad guys.

Moreover, in this story we have King using a naturalistic theme that he would revisit later in countless other stories: Fate rules man, but we, as rational beings, have the ability to make moral choices.

Although it was fate that Oglethorpe stumbled upon the monster in the well, his earlier decisions to act in such a morally reprehensible way were his own. The universe turned in such a way as to put things right. The Wheel spun, and Crater paid the price for his terrible behavior. (See *The Dead Zone* for more on King's use of this important theme.)

"The Thing at the Bottom of the Well" is a well-told tale that hints at the caliber of writer that Stephen King was on his way to becoming.

"THE STRANGER"

"The Stranger" illustrates King's deft narrative powers, even at a young age, and also demonstrates one of his early uses of a naturalistic theme he would revisit in later, more mature works: Man possesses free will, but fate will often conspire to put things right. In this story we once again meet Kelso Black from "The Hotel at the End of the Road," only this time Kelso is holed up in an attic after having stolen fifty grand and killed a guard. He's drinking cheap whiskey from a bottle and laughing at the "dumb cops" when he's visited by a stranger "who wore a black coat and [had] a hat pulled over his eyes."

The stranger tells Black that the two of them had made an implicit pact when Kelso shot the guard. Now the stranger has come for Kelso Black. . . .

As Kelso screamed and screamed, the stranger just laughed, and in a moment the room was empty, but it smelled of brimstone.

Comments: This is another half-page story that packs an amazing wallop.

It's not clear when the story takes place, although we've already been told that Kelso Black was turned into a living mummy in "The Hotel at the End of the Road." Now, in this story, we have him being carted off to hell by Lucifer himself.

What a week Kelso's having, eh?

In any case, in this story we have King's first use of the Dark Man— a personification of evil—who would later become Randall Flagg (and other "R.F." manifestations) in *The Stand,* the *Dark Tower* series, and *The Eyes of the Dragon.*

King has not often used demons or demonic intervention as a plot device (*Night Shift*'s "Mangler" is one notable exception), but in "The Stranger" he has Satan himself come for Kelso Black.

"The Stranger" illustrates King's deft narrative powers. In a story with a grand total of 234 words, King develops his characters, gives us the background needed for the story, and delivers one "hell" of a climax.

"The Stranger" is an amazing effort for a boy in his mid-teens and a clear indication of what was to come.

"I'M FALLING"

This story was also included in the table of contents but, like "The Dimension Warp," was also lost over the years. In the foreword to the collection, though, we are told to let "Steve King's I'M FALLING transport you into a world of dreams."

"THE CURSED EXPEDITION"

Jimmy Keller and Hugh Bullford touch down on Venus and are overwhelmed by its beauty. The air is breathable, everything is "lush and green," and "the fruits were exotic and delicious." Keller was so enthusiastic about the planet that he declared, "I'm going to call it the Garden of Eden." Bullford, however, is skeptical and senses something wrong.

The morning after the landing, Bullford finds Keller dead, and it is at this point that the ground suddenly begins to open up.

Bullford analyzes a piece of the planet's soil and he learns, to his horror, that Venus is alive—*a living planet*—and at that very moment the ground opens up once again and swallows both Bullford and his ship.

The story ends with the planet "resetting" itself to "[wait] for the next victim."

Comments: Here we have a story that is ostensibly science fiction; however, like "The Jaunt," "Beachworld," and "I Am the Doorway," the science-fiction settings and trappings just serve as devices to allow King to get to the *horror* of the story. Interestingly, he uses Venus as the villain, as he would later in "I Am the Doorway."

This story is King's first use of the idea of being consumed by a living planet, which would later also prove to be the fate of Rand in *Skeleton Crew*'s "Beachworld."

The one flaw in the tale is that we're never told how Keller died. All we're told is that "there was a look of horror on [Keller's] face that Bullford never hoped to see again." Did Keller see the planet "open its mouth" during the night and become so horrified by the sight that he died of fright? Perhaps. Bullford screams at the planet: "You killed him! I know it!"

"The Cursed Expedition" is a tale that once again shows King's early use of ideas that he would later rework for future stories—stories that must be considered unique in that they show King's ability to produce undeniable horror while utilizing the specific thematic elements of science fiction.

"THE OTHER SIDE OF THE FOG"

Pete Jacobs walks out his front door and is swallowed up by a strange fog that transports him into the future, to the year 2007. He immediately runs back into the fog, trying to get back home. This time he ends up in the prehistoric past, where he is menaced by a huge brontosaurus. Pete once *again* runs back into the fog, and the story ends with our being asked to listen the next time we are caught in the fog. We may hear footsteps belonging to Pete Jacobs, "trying to find his side of the fog." The last line of the story is the plaintive plea "Help the poor guy."

Comments: This is a terrific story that would be marvelous expanded into a novel. The time-travel device is admittedly a little hackneyed, but the focus of the tale is not the travel; it's the horror of poor Pete's being thrust into a situation from which he cannot escape.

King offers no explanations for why the fog suddenly becomes a time machine, but the horror is very real, and the concept hits home: Imagine being trapped in any time but your own. Putting ordinary people in extraordinary situations has always been King's forté, and in "The Other Side of the Fog," he does a superb job of immediately thrusting us into the heart of the action. This is a smartly told story, and its narrative sophistication and strength belie the age of its author.

Just as "Night Surf" was King's "trial run" at writing *The Stand*, "The Other Side of the Fog" was clearly King's first crack at writing "The Mist."

"NEVER LOOK BEHIND YOU"

George Jacobs, who we are told had been "[picking] the people's pockets clean of money" for fifteen years, is counting money in his office one day. An old woman dressed in rags comes in and speaks to him: "Indeed a lot of money. Too bad you won't be able to spend it."

She then points her hand at him, a flash of fire blooms at his throat, and George Jacobs dies "with a final gurgle."

The story ends with the lines "That one was lucky. He didn't look behind him."

Comments: This is a story that doesn't seem to make much sense. The only interpretation this reader could come up with is that the old woman is a supernatural messenger who was sent to do away with Jacobs, a man who had been evil all his life.

The story's title and last lines would seem to indicate that her power only worked if she was looked at; thus, the warning "Never Look Behind You." If this analysis is correct, then King and Chesley seem to be telling us that the young man who was glad Jacobs was dead was *also* in danger. In a sense, he saved himself by not looking behind him, where, we must assume, the grim woman was waiting to exact her "fee."

If this interpretation jibes with the authors' intentions, it would seem to fit neatly with King's ubiquitous, naturalistic theme of man having to "pay the price" for incorrect moral judgments. (In Jacobs's case, his implied "crime" seems to be either usury or being a slumlord.)

This karmic view of the universe was very effectively developed in the Richard Bachman novel *Thinner*, in which Billy Halleck had to pay for his mistakes with the lives—and souls—of his wife and daughter.

As King said in an interview with Larry King regarding *Thinner*, "*Someone* has to eat the pie." [emphasis added].

We all *must* ultimately pay for our erroneous ways.

Interestingly, another similarity to *Thinner* in "Never Look Behind You" lies with the character of the unnamed woman who points her hand at Jacobs. The story reads: "She held up her boney hand," thus foreshadowing the *Gypsy's* bony finger scratching Halleck's cheek in the opening scene of *Thinner.*

People, Places, and Things offers a revealing look at the evolution of a master storyteller.

In his massive compendium *The Work of Stephen King: An Annotated Bibliography & Guide*," Michael Collings, one of the few others who has read *People, Places, And Things,* wrote:

> In approach, content, theme, and treatment, [these stories] suggest directions the mature King would explore in greater detail, and, since they were in fact published (even though by King himself), they represent his earliest extant attempts at reaching a specific readership. He has indicated that these stories, along with "The Star Invaders," "King's Garbage Truck," "Slade," "The Glass Floor," and others, are sufficiently flawed that he feels uncomfortable about allowing them to be reprinted.

Collings also notes: "All copies of the booklet were thought to have disappeared until one was discovered in a box of papers in King's home in 1985."

PUBLISHING HISTORY

1960: Triad Publishing Company (eighteen-page typescript booklet).
1963: Triad Publishing Company (second printing).

3

"The Killer"

Suddenly he snapped awake, and relized [sic] *he didn't know who he was, or what he was doing here, in a munitions factory.*

—The first line of King's 1960s one-page
short story "The Killer."

What it is: a one-page science-fiction story written when King was a teenager.

Chances of finding a copy: the original typescript story: Impossible. The reprint in the 1994 genre periodical *Famous Monsters of Filmland:* quite possible if you find a magazine dealer who has a copy of the issue and isn't charging a King's ransom for it. (Start with the usual sources, including Betts Bookstore and The Overlook Connection.)

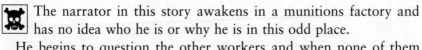 The narrator in this story awakens in a munitions factory and has no idea who he is or why he is in this odd place.

He begins to question the other workers and when none of them replies, he goes berserk and hits one "bullet-packer" in the head with the butt end of a gun. He then begins firing wildly at uniformed men, who have by now sounded an alarm and are shouting over the loud-speaker, "Killer! Killer! Killer!"

The narrator is eventually subdued with some kind of "queer energy gun" and taken away in a truck. Before he was stunned unconscious, though, he shouted, "Please! Don't shoot! Can't you see I just want to know who I am?"

The story ends with two guards watching the killer being taken away.

"One of them turns killer every now and then," one of the guards says.

"I just don't understand it," the second replies. "Take that one. What'd he say—'I just want to know who I am.' That was it. Seemed almost human. I'm beginning to think they're making these robots *too* good."

"The Killer" is about an inanimate object—a robot—becoming sentient and committing evil acts. This theme of mindless, mechanical *things* "waking up" ("Suddenly he snapped awake . . .") and becoming thinking, functioning organisms is one which King will use repeatedly in his work. What's fascinating about his employment of this leitmotif in his writing is that all of the awakened devices are *evil* when they become cognizant of themselves and their surroundings.

Other examples of this literary device in King's Directory of Dread can be found in "The Mangler" (a shirt-washing machine), "Battleground" (toy soldiers), "Trucks" (vehicles), *Christine* (a car), "The Monkey" (a toy monkey), "Word Processor of the Gods" (a word processor), *The Tommyknockers* (all types of normal household appliances, including TVs), "It Grows on You" (a house with a mind of its own), and "Chattery Teeth" (windup joke teeth).

Although King was probably in his mid-teens when he wrote "The Killer," even at that age his writing was extremely confident; it had a highly developed narrative flow; and he easily handled moving the story along, the use of dialogue, and crafting effective action scenes.

Similar in length and format to the stories in the collection *People, Places, and Things* (see the feature on that collection in this volume), "The Killer" has a surprise ending. Although the story is only one page in length, in tone and technique it comes across as something that was probably written a short time after that eclectic potpourri of juvenilia.

In fact, a story in *People, Places, and Things* called "I've Got to Get Away!" tells the story of a robot who achieves almost humanlike awareness while working on an assembly line at an "atomic factory." The robot is shot while trying to escape and is taken away in an Acme Robot Repair truck. Two weeks later, he is back on the assembly line, but it isn't long before the thought "I've got to get away" once again begins racing through his mind. "The Killer" and "I've Got to Get Away!" share similar story lines and illustrate King's teenaged fascination not only with robots but also with being trapped in an untenable situation from which there really is no escape.

"The Killer" was submitted by King to horror magnate Forrest J. Ackerman in the mid-sixties but was not published until 1994. King has admitted that discovering Forrest J. Ackerman's *Famous Monsters of Filmland* when he was a kid was a revelation. Here was a magazine devoted to the type of stuff everyone chastised him (and others like him) for enjoying. In 1982, King "returned the favor," so to speak, by writing an introduction to Ackerman's book *Mr. Monster's Movie Gold* called "The Importance of Being Forry." King was effusive in crediting "Forry" with validating his other-than-mainstream interests:

> As a kid growing up in rural Maine, my interest in horror and the fantastic wasn't looked upon with any approval whatsoever—there went young Steve King, his nose either in a lurid issue of Tales From the Vault or an even more lurid paperback of some sort or other—I had gone from Robert Bloch to Frank Belknap Long and from Long to the rest of the so-called Lovecraft Circle. I was, as far as most of my elders were concerned, eating tomatoes . . . poison fruit.

King also wrote of Ackerman's "vision":

> [Forry] stood up for a generation of kids who understood that if it was junk, it was magic junk. He has always seen the fiction of the fantastic—the stories and the cinema—as a gateway to wonder. His love of the genre is a child's wonder, untouched by the sophistication which eventually corrupts.

PUBLISHING HISTORY

ca. 1961: unpublished manuscript.
1994: *Famous Monsters of Filmland.*

4

The Aftermath

What it is: a 50,000-word science-fiction novel Stephen King wrote when he was sixteen. *The Aftermath* has never been published.

Chances of finding a copy: impossible. The manuscript of *The Aftermath* has been deposited in the Special Collections archive of the Raymond Fogler Library at the University of Maine at Orono, and access is granted only to those to whom King gives written permission. (I'd like to express my gratitude to George Beahm, one of the few who have read King's three unpublished novels at the university in their entirety. George generously made his detailed and insightful notes available to me for this feature.)

The Aftermath was the first full-length novel Stephen King ever wrote. He was in high school when he wrote it, and it has never been published. The novel takes place after an "atomic war" has destroyed a large part of the world's population.

A paramilitary organization known as the Sun Corps has risen to power, and it is the mission of one young survivor, Larry Talman, to infiltrate the Sun Corps and destroy the omniscient computer, known as DRAC (an acronym for *Digital Relay Analogue Computer*) that is controlling the organization and its activities.

Talman succeeds in destroying DRAC and sacrificing Reina Durrell, the girl he loves, in the process. After DRAC's destruction, the truth about the Sun Corps is revealed: It was actually a front for spies from the planet Deneb IV, an alien race that saw an opportunity for the domination of Earth following the atomic war. However, the Denebians

17

would be thwarted in their efforts by the Espers, a band of Terran psychics who knew of the Denebians' plans and would do everything they could to stop them.

George Beahm, in his unpublished notes for *The Aftermath*, wrote:

> In style, this is very much a "Bachman" book. . . . Despite King's youth, this first novel-length manuscript shows many of his skills: his ability to *tell a story*, an almost instinctual skill; his ability to create vivid characters, quickly and economically; his ability to develop motivation in his characters. And King Trademarks: colloquialisms in dialect; the use of brand-names; in SF, pseudoscientific language that sounds convincing.

George also made note of some of the definitive King elements that would appear in his later fiction:

> This first book shows a typical King character—an ordinary man in extraordinary situations, a standard King plot. There is rite of passage—a child's loss of innocence through experience. A child is the protagonist. The plot manifests a dark view of the world with the ultimate technological nightmare—the nuclear weapon—the catalyst. (King, a byproduct of the Fifties when bomb scares were a fact of life, would find it easy to draw on the paranoia of the times.) *The Aftermath* is a narrative that yanks the reader through the story. It begins *in medias res,* then flashes back. We later rejoin the character, changed by his experience and now realizing the truth that . . . human nature being what it is, people will always band together—but is government better than anarchy, or are they two sides of the same coin?

For a first novel, *The Aftermath* shows remarkable talent and real promise: King hits the ground running, so to speak. This early work has "wild talents," a technology out of control, global plagues, and the typical downbeat Bachman ending.

The Aftermath will likely never be published in King's lifetime, and that is probably appropriate. Make no mistake: It is embarrassing for a living writer to have to face his early, unformed works on a bookstore shelf. However, this seminal work *does* exist and should at least be acknowledged and written about, since it evinces many of the kernel images and themes that would appear in later, much more polished (and often brilliant) Stephen King novels.

PUBLISHING HISTORY

1963: unpublished manuscript.

5

"The Star Invaders"

Lord, they had locked him in a small room! It seemed even smaller than before. Jerry felt a cold sweat break out on his brow. He remembered back thirty years. He had been a kid then, a really small kid. His father had been a bear on discipline, and every time he'd done something wrong, he was locked in the closet to meditate. . . .

He had gotten to hate that closet. It was small and stuffed with clothes. The arid smell of moth-balls made him cough, and to his terrified four-year-old mind, it always seemed that a tiger crouched in the corner.

—from "The Star Invaders"

What it is: a seventeen-page short story in typescript that King wrote when he was in his teens and which he self-published as a "Gaslight Book" when he was seventeen. The text is spaced at 1 1/2 lines and the sheets measure 8 1/2 inches x 5 1/2 inches and is one of King's earliest short stories still extant.

Chances of finding a copy: impossible. "The Star Invaders" has never appeared in print. The only existing original copy of the story is owned by Stephen King.

Jerry Hiken, one of the last protectors of the beseiged planet Earth, is captured by the clawed-hand, alien Star Invaders and brutally tortured. The Star Invaders want to know where they can find Jed Pierce, the brilliant scientist who is Earth's last hope, the one man who may have a chance at defeating the alien invaders. Jed Pierce is building the Counter Weapon, the only device that may be able to defeat the extraterrestrial marauders, and the Star Invaders want to stop him.

Jerry resists as long as he can, but then the torture becomes more than he can withstand. He cracks and tells the Star Invaders the location of Jed's secret lab but then commits suicide because he cannot live with his betrayal.

The Star Invaders attack Pierce's hideout, where he has almost completed construction of the Counter Weapon. As the aliens attack, however, Pierce cannot delay implementing the Counter Weapon any longer. He fires on the invading ships, destroying vessel after vessel, ignoring the deadly consequences as his machinery dangerously overheats. Pierce manages to single-handedly destroy all of the Star Invaders' ships and then cool the atomic pile that had been feeding his weapon, narrowly averting a catastrophic nuclear meltdown.

Jed Pierce's Counter Weapon has worked, and the story ends with the inhabitants of Earth confident that they now have an effective defense against alien invaders.

There are a couple of important images and themes in "The Star Invaders."

The first is the use of imprisonment in a dark place as a device to mentally break Jerry Hiken. The Star Invaders knew that such confinement was Hiken's worst fear, and they used it to psychologically destroy him. King has a remarkably mature voice in a passage in which the Star Invaders reveal to Hiken that they know how to break him and can do it over and over again, whenever they choose to, telling him, "We can lock you in again. . . ."

In his later writings, King has repeatedly used the image of being trapped. In fact, he wrote an entire novel, *Cujo*, about precisely such a situation. There are similarly claustrophobic scenes that take place in the sewers in *It*. In *Gerald's Game*, Jessie Burlingame is trapped on her own bed in a dark room, and she may not be alone in the room. In the novel *Misery*, Paul Sheldon is held prisoner by Annie Wilkes, and in the short story "The Boogeyman," the image of something horrible hiding in a closet is used to great effect (as is a similar image in *Cujo*).

In *Carrie*, Margaret White imprisons her daughter Carrie in a closet for imagined transgressions, and in the short story "Here There Be Tygers," King uses the image of a deadly tiger crouched in the corner of a boy's bathroom, echoing back to the identical image in "The Star Invaders." Moreover, the idea of a "monster" that feeds on our worst fears was used to great effect in the character of Pennywise the Clown in *It*.

Another important image from "The Star Invaders" is the green light associated with the alien's invading ships. King would later use green fire as an image for evil in both *The Eyes of the Dragon* and *The Tommyknockers*.

"The Star Invaders" was an early science-fiction short story by King that foreshadowed themes and images he would develop in later works. It is rough and ends abruptly, but it clearly manifests the storytelling abilities King would soon perfect.

In conclusion, allow me to quote what Michael Collings wrote about this story in my King *Encyclopedia* back in 1989: "The great strength of the story is its nascent characterization, coupled with an occasional image that would resonate through much of King's fiction."

PUBLISHING HISTORY

1964: *The Star Invaders* (Triad, Inc. and Gaslight Books).

6

"I Was a Teenage Grave Robber"

*A huge, white maggot twisted on the garage floor, holding
Weinbaum with long suckers, raising him towards its
dripping, pink mouth from which horrid mewing sounds
came.*

—from chapter 8 of "I Was a Teenage Grave Robber"

What it is: Stephen King's first published story. King was eighteen
when this thriller first appeared in a 1965 issue of *Comics Review*.

Chances of finding a copy: The odds on finding an original of this
tale probably run 99 and 44/100 percent *against*. I'm sure that original
copies of the two magazines in which this story appeared exist *somewhere* (King most assuredly must have them), but just try finding one.
That one of the most important collectors of King materials on this
planet (e.g., he owns the original typed *manuscripts* of *The Plant*) has
had both appearances of this story on his "Want" list for years attests
to their rarity.

"I Was a Teenage Grave Robber," with its fabulous, classic fifties
B-movie title, is the story (in nine typed, single-spaced chapters) of
young Danny Gerad.

Gerad, a destitute orphan, is recruited by Rankin, emissary and
assistant to mad scientist Steffen Weinbaum, to work as a grave
robber.
  Danny's job will be to acquire corpses for what he later discovers are

fiendish experiments involving radioactivity and maggots. Weinbaum tells Danny, "[M]y experiments are too complicated to explain in any detail, but they concern human flesh. Dead human flesh."

Weinbaum's experiments involve exposing corpses to radioactivity, which causes the maggots on the bodies to mutate and grow into hideous monstrosities roughly the size of a double-wide trailer.

While working for Weinbaum, Danny sees a young girl running down the highway being chased by a man who is obviously drunk. Danny rescues the girl and is surprised to find out that the man chasing her is her legal guardian, Uncle David, and that he, too, had once been an employee of Weinbaum's—also in the Grave Robbing Division.

Danny and the girl, Vicki Pickford, fall in love, and one night, while they are at the movies, Danny gets a call to return to Weinbaum's Victorian mansion immediately: It's a life-or-death situation, he's told.

When Danny and Vicki arrive at the mansion, they discover that Weinbaum's maggots, as weird and pissed off as giant maggots can be, have gotten loose and are destroying Weinbaum's laboratory. Danny ultimately saves the day by burning down the mansion and saving the life of the lovely Miss Vicki at the same time. And as he flees the horrendous scene, Danny watches as Weinbaum becomes a victim of his own dark madness.

"I Was a Teenage Grave Robber" concludes with Danny musing that he had been an unwitting participant in Weinbaum's death, since in all likelihood the flesh of one of the corpses he had robbed from its grave had fed the giant maggot that ultimately devoured the mad scientist.

Interesting elements in this story foreshadow later King images and works. In this early harbinger of King's magnum opus, *It*, Danny Gerad muses about the nightmares of childhood as he enters the "Stygian blackness" of Weinbaum's garage: "All my childish fears of the dark returned. Once again I entered the realm of terror that only a child can know."

In a 1973 essay "The Horror Writer and the Ten Bears," King revealed his Top Ten list of personal fears. His number-one "bear" was "fear of the dark." (His other nine, in order from two through ten, were squishy things; deformity; snakes; rats; closed-in places; insects, especially spiders, flies, and beetles; death; others; and fear for someone else.)

This story also contained one of King's earliest uses of the image of a rat, specifically in the line "I was cut off by a sound that has haunted me through nightmares ever since, a hideous mewing sound, like that of some gigantic rat in pain." (It was actually the sound of a giant maggot that Danny was hearing.)

In this tale, King also uses the remarkably adroit and appropriately "Kingish" image of "the velvet darkness of the night."

"I Was a Teenage Grave Robber" probably embarrasses Stephen King today, but it should not. Sure, the story has some style and structure problems, but it is an important step forward for the teenaged King. In retrospect, it illustrates just how developed King's storytelling abilities were by the age of eighteen and how committed he was to *telling* those stories. By the age of eighteen, King had already written novels and short stories and was determined to someday have a writing career, which is remarkable when you consider that an awful lot of eighteen-year-olds don't do any more writing than they are required to do for school.

King was not *required* to write his stories. He wrote them because he loved to write, and that, my friends, is the difference between a *job* and a *calling*.

Everyone should be lucky enough in their own lives to be able to make that distinction. Wouldn't you agree?

PUBLISHING HISTORY

1965: *Comics Review.*
1966: *Stories of Suspense* (1966; as "In a Half-World of Terror").

7

"The Glass Floor"

In the room, a small pool of blood showed on the floor and ceiling, seeming to meet in the center, blood which hung there quietly and one could wait forever for it to drop.

—from "The Glass Floor"

What it is: an early, very Edgar Allan Poe–like short story that was Stephen King's first professional sale. (He was only nineteen when he wrote it in the summer of 1967 and twenty when it was initially published.)

Chances of finding a copy: very difficult. The original 1967 *Startling Mystery Stories* appearance is only available through the collector's market, usually at extremely high prices (several hundred dollars or more). The 1990 *Weird Tales* reprint is much less costly (usually under twenty-five dollars or so) but must also be tracked down through a used and rare book and magazine dealer. Neither of these magazines is likely to be found in libraries, so the secondary market is the only place you'll be able to find the actual complete text. Start with Betts Bookstore and The Overlook Connection (see the Sources and Resources Section) if you're interested in acquiring a copy of "The Glass Floor" in one of its appearances.

☠ Janine, the sister of Charles Wharton, has died mysteriously. Apparently against her brother's counsel, Janine had married an elderly man named Anthony Reynard and moved into his hulking

"Victorian monstrosity" of a house. Wharton arrives at the house after receiving word that his sister has died. Wharton questions Reynard about Janine's death and learns that she broke her neck when she fell off a high ladder while dusting some bookshelves. Wharton also learns that Janine has already been buried, and when he insists on seeing the room where she died, he is told that doing so is impossible; it has already been walled off and sealed for all time.

Wharton insists on knowing the truth, however, and finally Reynard's housekeeper, Louise, tells him about the room: It has a glass floor, actually a *mirrored* floor, and is rumored to be cursed.

Wharton demands that he be allowed access to the room, and Reynard reluctantly acquiesces.

Wharton trowels off the new plaster until he reaches the doorknob and then pulls open the door. He immediately sees the glass floor, and it appears to him like a "shimmering quicksilver pool." He enters the room and sees the ladder Janine fell from standing amid the room's empty bookcases, "all seeming to lean over him on the very threshold of imbalance."

The East Room then works its malefic influence on Wharton and looking down into the glass floor, he starts to feel as though he were "poised in thin air."

Wharton then loses his balance and, in a last desperate attempt to save himself, he screams out, "Reynard! I'm falling!"

Reynard comes running, but he already knows the truth. He tells Louise to get him the hook, and he drags Wharton's body out the door. He then begins the slow task of once again sealing off the East Room.

"The Glass Floor" not only feels like an Edgar Allan Poe story; King even refers to Poe in the tale. When Wharton first sees the plastered-over East Room door at the end of a long hallway, King writes that "Wharton could see the still-damp plasterer's trowel Reynard had used to wall up the doorway, and a straggling remnant of Poe's 'Black Cat' clanged through his mind: 'I had walled the monster up within the tomb'" (which is the last line of Poe's ailurophobic short story).

King's narrative voice in this story is appropriately somber; his use of language, tailored to the tone of the tale. The house is a "huge sprawling mausoleum . . ."; the housekeeper's face "hung like limp dough on her skull"; King tells us that Wharton "fancied he could smell the sweetish odor of decay emanating from the rumpled silk of the shapeless black dress she wore"; Reynard is described as "slope-shouldered, head thrust forward, eyes deeply sunken and downcast"; inside the house, Wharton's "gaze skipped from the grinning fireplace gargoyle to the dusty, empty-eyed bust of Cicero"; he felt "a thousand living yet insentient eyes [staring] at him from the darkness"; and the East Room door "swung ponderously open, shedding plaster like dead skin."

"The Glass Floor" is dark and spooky and, if anything, is a vivid example of the many horror influences King had absorbed in the years prior to writing it.

King's *Startling Mystery Stories* appearance was introduced with the following note from Robert A. W. Lowndes, the mag's editor:

> *Stephen King* has been sending us stories for some time, and we returned one of them reluctantly, since it would be far too long before we could use it, due to its length. But patience may yet bring him his due reward on that tale; meanwhile, here is a chiller whose length allowed us to get it into print much sooner.

Because it is King's first professional sale (he received thirty-five dollars for it), "The Glass Floor" rightfully holds a special place in his heart, and thus, in 1990, he allowed it to be reprinted in the horror and sci-fi quarterly *Weird Tales*. (By the way, the other Stephen King story Lowndes referred to in his editor's note was "The Night of the Tiger," which is also discussed in this volume.)

King wrote a new introduction for the *Weird Tales* appearance of "The Glass Floor" and began it by referring to the scene in James Dickey's classic novel *Deliverance* in which Griner "whangs" his hand with a tool while working on a car. When asked if he's hurt, he replies, "Naw—it ain't as bad's I thought."

King goes on to write that that is precisely how he felt after rereading "The Glass Floor." He describes the first few pages of the story as "clumsy and badly written—clearly the product of an unformed storyteller's mind." He then discusses the characters and, with thirty years' experience now informing his comments, tells us that there is a frisson of terror in Wharton's East Room scene and that it "pays off better than I remembered."

King also notes that he now sees an echo of "The Glass Floor" in his *Four Past Midnight* novella "The Library Policeman." (Interesting, eh?)

King concludes this new look at an old chestnut by admitting that the main reason he allowed it to be reprinted was to "send a message to young writers who are out there right now, trying to be published, and collecting rejection slips."

Don't give up, King says. He didn't, and we all know what *his* persistence has wrought, now, don't we?

PUBLISHING HISTORY

1967: *Startling Mystery Stories* (fall).
1990: *Weird Tales* (fall).

8

"King's Garbage Truck"

Take care of yourselves, friends.

—the last line of Stephen King's final *Maine Campus*
"Garbage Truck" column

What it is: a collection of forty-seven columns of commentary and critique totaling approximately thirty-five thousand words that King wrote from February 1969 through May 1970 for the University of Maine student newspaper, *The Maine Campus.*

Chances of finding a copy: impossible unless (1) you're willing to make a trip to the University of Maine to acquire photocopies of the columns from the reversed-image microfiche in their library and (2) the library staff will even allow "outlanders" access to their archives and equipment.

The microfiche copies of *The Maine Campus,* by the way, are reportedly the university's only surviving copies of the text. The original copies of *The Maine Campus* in which "King's Garbage Truck" and *Slade* appeared were stolen from the University's library sometime in 1988 or 1989. (*Philistines!*) The microfiche copies of *The Maine Campus* containing writings by King are now the *only* college writings by King that *might* be available to the general public. The unpublished novels and other writings that King has deposited over the years in the library's Special Collections archive have now all been sequestered, and access is limited only to those to whom Stephen King grants permission in writing.

This is the first comprehensive and detailed look at all of "Steve" King's forty-seven University of Maine "Garbage Truck" columns.

These early writings of King's are very important, and there is a great deal in these columns that presages images and themes that King will use later in his novels and short stories. These columns also provide us with a vivid and revealing look at what life was like on a college campus in the late sixties. King's "Garbage Truck" writings very effectively re-create the truly unique sensibility of the times.

Most interestingly, there are also several instances of Stephen King's defiantly individual and memorable use of language in these columns.

The opening line of King's May 8, 1969, column, for instance—"Want me to tell you a bad thing?"—is classic King, as are the opening lines of his June 12, 1969, column—"Boom! and all at once it's summer."—and, most notably, his December 4, 1969, column: "It's a little bit frightening to wake up in the middle of the night and realize that you may be the only one on earth that realizes why the world is in so much trouble."

Any of these could easily serve as the opening line of a Stephen King short story or novel, and it is just one more indication of Stephen King's gift that his narrative voice in the "Garbage Truck" columns is incredibly mature, insightful, and confident, at a time when King was just a twenty-two-year-old college student writing a column in a campus newspaper while also juggling classes and all the other responsibilities (and, of course, pleasures!) of university life.

FEBRUARY 20, 1969 (642 words)
First line: *"The Goddard College Dancers, seven students from a small liberal arts school in Vermont, put on a program called* Why We Dance *last Sunday night in Hauck Auditorium."*

King reviews a dance troupe that performed at the University of Maine, noting that the artistry "ranged from the very good to the astonishingly awful." King particularly liked a final image in which flames were projected onto the body of a dancer, noting that the impact was "almost numbing."

King uses the second half of his column to recommend that his readers head to the Hauck Auditorium on the twenty-eighth to catch an unedited screening of *Hush . . . Hush, Sweet Charlotte,* assuring film fans that "if you think you saw it on TV, you're wrong." He then lambastes the edited ABC-TV version, accusing the censors of being "smarty-pants" who would outlaw Halloween if they could.

King singles out Bette Davis's performance in the film and describes her as someone who can "scare the hell out of you." He especially liked the scene in which Davis crawls down a staircase letting out "the most godawful sounds."

He also mentions Agnes Moorehead and Joseph Cotten, and in a line that reflects just how tuned in to pop culture King was (and, of course, still is), he says he kept expecting Joseph Cotten to pull out a bottle of aspirin and start his "spiel." (Apparently, Cotten was doing aspirin commercials at the time, and the ads must have been running on TV *a lot.*)

King concludes the column with another suggestion that everyone go see *Hush . . . Hush, Sweet Charlotte* ("If you're big on spooky movies, go see it"), cautioning that we may not have Bette Davis around to enjoy much longer, "especially at three packs a day."

FEBRUARY 27, 1969 (515 words)
First line: *"You have to feel sorry for William Shakespeare."*

Even though this second "Garbage Truck" column is mostly a review of Franco Zeffirelli's film *Romeo and Juliet,* King uses the opportunity of reviewing a Shakespeare movie to make some salient points about how Shakespeare is taught—and mistaught—in modern academia.

King notes that the student usually approaches Shakespeare "in the same way porcupines make love—very cautiously." He writes that the bard has been "inspected, perfected, elected and resurrected" and that after all of the critical studies and annotated editions, the student soon quakes at the mere thought of studying Shakespeare, whom he now perceives as "God's step-brother."

But Shakespeare was only writing about "the same old things," King notes, including "sex, murder, love, honor, draft-dodgers, kings, commoners, fat men, skinny men, idiots and saints."

King then bravely states something that, for this reader, has always been obvious: The Elizabethan dialect used in Shakespeare's plays is "just more trouble than it's worth." That is exactly the same thought I had while screening Kenneth Branaugh's sprawling full-text adaptation of Shakespeare's *Hamlet* for my 1997 book *The Robin Williams Scrap-*

book. (Robin played Osric, a royal courtier.) King admits that after a period of listening to Shakespeare, many students just "drop out" and go "read Raymond Chandler."

However, this *Romeo and Juliet* (by Franco Zeffirelli, "an Italian director you've never heard of") is different, King assures his readers. Romeo and Juliet are hot-blooded teenagers who make out, fight, cry, and act pretty much like teenagers have acted since God created the teen years.

Shakespeare is the *real* hero of this movie, King concludes, telling his readers to check it out at the Westgate Cinema in Bangor. "You owe it to your hormones."

Note: Romeo and Juliet was Zeffirelli's breakout film, for he did not, in 1969, have the recognition and reputation he enjoys today (thus explaining King's comment about Zeffirelli's being someone most people had never heard of). Subsequent notable films by Zeffirelli include *Jesus of Nazareth* (1976), *The Champ* (1979), *Endless Love* (1981), and *Jane Eyre* (1996).

MARCH 6, 1969 (515 words)
First line: *"If you watch TV at all lately, you've probably noticed a new trend in entertainment—the cheapie game show."*

This is a very funny—and brutally sarcastic—column in which King skewers American television with a ferocity that makes it clear that he was completely fed up with the garbage being produced by the major networks in the late sixties.

King notes that the game shows being aired in 1969—*The Dating Game, The Newlywed Game, The Baby Game, Dream House*—were mostly geared for "young swingers" and that there was nothing for the "Geritol drinking, Lawrence Welk–watching Americans over thirty." (*Good heavens!*)

King then suggests five game-show concepts for this ancient crowd:

1. *The Middle-Aged Game:* Hosted by Bud Collyer, contestants have to try and tie their shoelaces without bending their knees and then guess which cigarette has been soaked in acid. The grand prize is a trip to a Betty Crocker Bake-Off.

2. *The Brutality Game:* Reflecting the tenor of the times (and King's liberal sensibility in certain sociocultural situations), King has this show hosted by Chicago mayor "Dick" Daley. The show pits forty Chicago

cops against an audience of "pacifists, hippies, college professors, and ethnic minority groups."

3. *The Divorce Game:* Hosted by Zsa Zsa Gabor, this show has three divorced couples discuss child custody, alimony, mental cruelty, and other elements of the typical divorce. The studio audience votes for their favorite couple.

4. *The Wife-Swapping Game:* This game is hosted by Dr. Joyce Brothers and is essentially nothing more than a mass orgy, with audience participation.

5. *The Burial Game:* This show is hosted by Vincent Price and has a quintessential "Stephen King" flavor. Three people compete to be the first to bury a dead friend. The grand prize is a lifetime membership in the American Mortician's Association.

King concludes the column by encouraging the networks to consider these ideas and try to come up with even better ones: "There's new ground to be broken here," he tells the studio execs. "I'm sure you can manure it thoroughly, with no trouble at all."

MARCH 13, 1969 (690 words)
First line: *"There's a Plot afoot."*

The "Plot" King refers to is the attempt (by critics, professors, film producers, record-company executives, etc.) to eliminate mediocrity (and to King it is clearly *beloved* mediocrity) in the arts. In a defense of "second-class material" and as an attempt to sabotage such a dire scheme, King declares "National Mediocrity Week."

To celebrate this event, King recommends seeing a mediocre movie (he suggests *Born Wild*), listening to a mediocre record (Tammy Wynette's *Stand by Your Man* is King's choice), and reading a mediocre novel. (His pick is William Goldman's *Boys and Girls Together.*)

"Help make 'National Mediocrity Week' a success," King concludes. "If worse comes to worse, you can always go to an SDS meeting."

MARCH 20, 1969 (670 words)
First line: *"I am soliciting."*

What is Steve King soliciting? Not his readers' bodies, he assures them. No, he wants their *minds* and their *memories.*

This is one of King's most important "Garbage Truck" columns. It is blatantly autobiographical, and King is very forthcoming about his memories of childhood.

"I've always been very big on playing 'Do you remember . . . ,' " King writes. And remember he does, including a reference to "how you felt when you heard the Russians had put this funny little ball called Sputnik into orbit," an incident he will revisit in *Danse Macabre*, his 1981 nonfiction look at the horror genre.

King also remembers *American Bandstand* and Robert Stack as Elliot Ness on *The Untouchables* and Elvis: "I can remember going to see him at the Community Theater (my brother held my hand crossing the streets). . . ." King is referring here to his brother, David King, to whom he will later dedicate his novel *Cujo*, writing, "This book is for my brother, David, who held my hand crossing West Broad Street. . . ."

King also remembers Davy Crockett hats, Wiffle balls, and especially, hula hoops. He writes that "the bitterest moment of my tenth year came when my hula-hoop rolled out into the street and got squashed by an unfeeling oil-truck." (In King's 1983 novel *Pet Sematary*, little Gage Creed will die after being run down by a most assuredly "unfeeling" ten-wheeler.)

King also remembers playing Rock-Breaks-Scissors for hours and concludes this column by asking his readers to remember things that turned them on before "pot, Marshall McLuhan, and Jimi Hendrix" and to mail their recollections to him at the Maine campus. "It might be fun."

MARCH 27, 1969 (600 words)
First line: *"This was a pretty good week."*

Why was it a good week? Because King received many responses to his March 20 request for memories. It "restores your faith in human nature," he writes, that so many people remembered so much about growing up. "Apparently I'm not the only one who was listening to Top Forty while Paul McCartney was still playing washtub for a Liverpool skiffle group."

The rest of the column is a nostalgic look back at the fifties and includes King's own recollections of the period as well as some of the things his readers recalled, such as *Gunsmoke, Inner Sanctum,* Saturday matinees, the *Rocket Man* serial, Hitchcock movies, and "low rubbers that your mother made you wear all winter and half the spring."

He concludes this column with a paragraph that could very easily have come from his novel *It*:

Somehow everything seems to get just a little dirtier and more self-ish as we get older. It's good to remember other times, once in a while. We'll have to do it again some time.

APRIL 10, 1969 (580 words)
First line: *"You say it's been a bad week?"*

King's solution if you *have* had a bad week? Go see Peter O'Toole in *The Lion in Winter*. He gives the flick a rave review and also uses the opportunity to describe the Academy Awards as "that annual fool's clambake."

This week, King also reviews the new William Castle–produced film *The Riot* (it will eventually be retitled as *Riot*), starring Jim Brown and Gene Hackman, describing it as "an odd mishmash of vulgarity, inanity, and a few sparkling scenes that seem hopelessly wasted." King suggests watching the Paul Muni classic *I Am a Fugitive from a Chain Gang* instead. "You can catch that one some night on the late show. Free."

APRIL 17, 1969 (740 words)
First line: *"I was in Fun City this weekend for the first time in four years, and it's a strange scene for a country boy who grew up in a small Maine town where there are more graveyards than people."*

As a college-newspaper columnist, King was one of a group of students invited to New York by United Artists for advance screenings of two new films, *Popi* and *If It's Tuesday, It Must Be Belgium*.

King devotes most of this column to reviews of these two movies (he liked *Popi*; hated *Tuesday*), and because these films are now nowhere to be found on the landscape of American pop culture (except in some dusty corner of your local video rental store), this material is now quite dated.

Where King *really* shines, though, is in his final few lines about the essence of New York and why he likes Maine just fine. This is truly marvelous writing and, again, could easily be plugged into any of King's works of fiction: "A hollow-eyed Indian girl with purple-dyed hair gave me a flower on Seventh Avenue, but it was plastic. People seem to look at your shoes before they glance at your face. You can get seven TV channels, but the air smells bad. At the risk of sounding hopelessly rustic, I like it better up here. The flowers grow for real, and besides, my shoes have holes in them."

Indeed.

APRIL 24, 1969 (690 words)
First line: *"As President Emeritus of this* [several words obscured and illegible in the reversed-image microfiche] *Nitty Gritty Up Tight Society for a Campus with More Cools (which we lovingly refer to as the N. G. U. T. S. C. M. C.—pronounced Nuhgutsmick, for all you linguists out there), I have the happy duty of announcing that we have decided to call a general student strike next week."*

In this very funny column, King calls for a general student strike unless certain demands are met. First, he wants more black literature and black-history courses as well as courses geared to other minority groups. King suggests courses on the History of Plumbing, the Art of Mandarin Fingernail Growing, and a seminar on "Why Macy's Doesn't Tell Gimbel's."

King also wants birth-control vending machines in every dorm (slogan: "A Pill for Every Jill"); the abolishment of curfews, on-call limo service at all the girls' dorms, and free motel rooms.

King also wants to ban the bookstore and, finally, to abolish the university completely. Why? Because as part of the "sinister military-industrial educational complex," the university contributes to pollution, inflation, and eye disease.

King has always been a very astute social analyst, and columns such as this one dramatically demonstrate that even at the age of twenty-two he was paying attention and making judgments. His sharp and focused writing also shows that he possessed the skills to articulate—in an amusing way—the many problems he saw and just could not keep quiet about.

MAY 1, 1969 (600 words)
First line: *"SS-1 was the course number of the first special seminar taught here at Maine, during the '68 Fall semester."*

This column is about poetry. King starts off by praising University of Maine professors Burton Hatlen and Jim Bishop (two well-known names to King fans) and the contemporary-poetry course they cotaught.

King then shifts his attention to a young poet named Ron Loewinsohn, whom he describes as "one of the best of the contemporary poets." King writes that Loewinsohn is "a juicy poet, real and alive, with guts and energy." He tells his readers that Loewinsohn will be reading at the university in a few days and recommends that all attend.

King also used this column to review a recent reading of "older" poets, including Howard Nemerov, Constance Hunting, and Richard Wilbur, noting the differences between "old-line" writers and the new breed, like Loewinsohn.

With a deft and mature style and tone, King writes, "Instead of goose-fishes, poems for the insomniac, and Stravinsky concerts, we have the scent of death like fresh-churned butter, sweat labor, glazed eye desire, and, in Loewinsohn's own words, 'Invention out of all that!' "

MAY 8, 1969 (914 words)
First line: *"Want me to tell you a bad thing?"*

Stephen King must have shook up the University of Maine establishment with his "Garbage Truck" columns, especially when he wrote a column like this one. One cannot help but wonder if the academic community had any idea just *how good* a writer King actually was from his weekly efforts in the *Maine Campus*.

What is the "bad thing" King writes about in the first line of this column? It is waking up in the middle of the night, lighting a cigarette, and wondering "what the hell you are doing in this place."

This is a very important column, one that contains images and seminal ideas that appear in later King works, including "Paranoid: A Chant," "Cain Rose Up," and many others. It also demonstrates—and foretells—the engaging narrative style King fans will later find so appealing.

King senses—he *reads* it like a book—an apathy and an angst permeating the campus and personalizes the frustration and stress of college life in this essay with a few pointed characterizations.

He begins the story of one of his "desperate" characters by telling us,

"I have a memory that has always haunted me." This memory is of a fellow student, a girl, suddenly bursting into tears one Saturday night during dinner, leaping up from the table and running out of the room. People were stunned, but only for a moment, and the next thing King knew, someone had stolen the girl's dessert. No one sought to help this tortured soul, and in no time at all, everyone started talking again as though nothing had happened.

King admits that college life is a "pressure-cooker" but reveals that what scares him the most is that this pressure doesn't end with graduation.

King then imagines (predicts?) the futures of two typical students— Sally Socialite and Harry Harried.

Sally will marry, have kids, gain weight, watch soap operas, "and one morning she will wake up forty, wondering whether she did it all on her own or if she was raped into it."

Harry Harried is so highly strung, King writes, that "whatever you do, don't startle him." King paints an even bleaker picture for Harry. He will graduate with painfully earned honors, go to work as an insurance adjuster or an engineer or a computer programmer, get married, buy a car he can't afford, and have his first heart attack at thirty-five.

"And when he wakes up after the second coronary, the big one—*if* he wakes up—he'll look at the tube coming out of his arm and wonder what made him want to work himself to death so he could afford more life insurance."

How many twenty-one-year-olds do *you* know who have such a fully realized, relentlessly cynical, and brutally pessimistic vision of their future as King details here?

King then talks about the coping devices available—drinking, hostility in class, dropping out—noting that "you might even start looking at the Stevens Hall tower and wondering—just *wondering,* mind you— how nice it might be to climb up here and pick off a few people."

How nice *would* this kind of "target shooting" be? Read King's short story "Cain Rose Up" and you'll find out.

King concludes this dark rumination with the revelation that for him coping involves putting on Bob Dylan singing "Ballad of a Thin Man." He also says that he'd like to know who stole the hysterical girl's dessert: "Maybe he's the guy we want to get to. He may be the only well-adjusted one left."

MAY 15, 1969 (715 words)
First line: *"Ugly."*

This column consists of four scenes from an antiwar rally King participated in at the University of Maine. All of the scenes are introduced by a single word: "Ugly."

The first scene takes place as King marches behind a banner that reads: End the War. He and his like-minded fellow students are jeered at, insulted, and an attempt is made to tear down their banner. Someone throws an egg at them that splatters on the road. "A kid in Biafra would have been glad to see it," King writes. "He won't." King then gets punched in the stomach, which "surprises me more than it hurts." He admits that he wants to hit somebody, that he wants to cry. This scene ends with the plaintive line "I wonder what is happening to me."

The second scene takes place at the same march; only now the eggs have been joined by rocks. A girl walking next to King gets hit in the chest with an egg. "Her voice is strange," King writes as she tells him that someone *threw something at her*—in *Orono, Maine*. Things like that just *don't happen* in such a place.

The third scene is a confrontation between fraternity members and the antiwar protesters. "Behind them," King writes, "I see Gestapo figures burning books and Jews."

The final "ugly" scene is at the conclusion of the march as they all watch a skit. Speakers talk about the war and about dope, and then an army vet gets up and asserts that the war could be won in six months but that "the boys over there don't want to come home." Somebody plays Sgt. Barry Sadler's "The Ballad of the Green Beret" from a dorm window. King wonders if his son will "have to kill somebody in the name of national pride." King concludes this week's column by noting that the last things on his mind are that somebody punched him and the image of splattered egg in the road and on a girl's blouse.

"Ugly."

MAY 22, 1969 (780 words)
First line: *"I've always been fond of clichés, and one of my favorite is, 'If you can't say something nice, don't say anything at all.'"*

This column consists solely of King's strong condemnation of Steve Hughes, a man who had been nominated for a position on the University of Maine's board of trustees and who King believed was facile, manipulative, and prone to political tantrums if he didn't get his way. (I guess he didn't follow the advice of that cliché, eh?)

JUNE 12, 1969 (518 words)
First line: *"Boom! and all at once it's summer."*

This column is King's appreciation of summer. "The nice thing about summer," he writes, "is that things go slower." The first example he cites of what is possible in this slow, hot season is, "If you've got an ulcer, you can treat it right." Hmm.

King also teases his readers with some of his upcoming "Garbage Truck" column topics (movies and music top the list) and admits that there will also be "a lot of other stuff which I haven't thought about yet mainly because I haven't done much thinking at all since I stepped out the door after my last final."

King also effectively evokes the memories of winter by describing the snow and slush of the previous February and then offering some suggestions as to how to forget about all that. ("Sit on the porch with a coolerful of beer and get stoned.")

King concludes this column by telling his readers, "There's nothing like summer. Winter is going to land on your back with a great big thump along about November 15th, but right now it's iced tea weather."

JUNE 20, 1969 (528 words)
First line: *"People have been telling me for years that I've got a sympathetic face."*

This is a funny column in which King reprints some of the "Dear Stevie" letters he supposedly began receiving after he started writing the "Garbage Truck" column.

King reprints letters from five correspondents, "Fuzzy in Bangor," "Upset Wife," "The Stranger," "Worried Mom," and "Bangor Daily."

Sixteen-year-old "Fuzzy" wants to know if she can get pregnant from French kissing. King's reply: French kissing only causes pregnancy when done by a Frenchman.

"Upset Wife" is afraid that her raised-on-a-farm husband wants to have her mother put to sleep because she broke her leg; and "The Stranger" wants to perform unnatural sex acts. King suggests that "Upset Wife" bring her mother to a vet and tells "The Stranger" to look for enough "unnatural" girls.

King concludes this week's installment by telling his readers, "No more letters. I just can't stand all this grief."

JUNE 27, 1969 (878 words)
First line: *"It's summer, and you're hot."*

This week, twenty-one-year-old college newspaper columnist Stephen King—the Maine writer who will eventually be known around the world as the author of dozens of creepy horror novels, including *'Salem's Lot*—reviews horror novels, making this "Garbage Truck" entry a significant milestone in King's early autobiographical writings.

He offers several novels as part of "King's Kure to Beat the Heat," since it was hot as blazes when he wrote this column. "Your summer-weight Arrow shirt is hanging on you like a sack [and y]our deodorant has gone on strike."

The books King reviews are *The Dead Beat* by Robert Bloch, *The Shrinking Man* by Richard Matheson, *The Coffin Things* by Michael Avalione, and *Dracula* by Bram Stoker.

Since King has acknowledged both Bloch and Matheson as personal favorites and influences, it isn't surprising that he not only gives each of their books rave reviews; he also speaks with an informed passion about these legends' work. His enthusiasm is contagious.

Since King's superlative novel *'Salem's Lot* is his own personal, contemporary spin on the vampire mythos, it is also not surprising that he describes Stoker's classic *Dracula* as a "monsterpiece." For *The Dead Beat*, King wrote: "A kind of jolly graveyard humor counterpoints the terror. . . ." He describes *The Shrinking Man* as a "tour-de-force," noting that Richard Matheson writes about "a special kind of noonday horror." King describes *The Coffin Things* as a "deadly little gem" that is "as poisonous a piece of black humor as ever has come your way." Regarding *Dracula*, he warns his readers not to "read it where anyone can creep up behind you and say Boo."

"So now you know how to beat the heat," King concludes. "Curl up beside your favorite headstone and cool it. Just get home before dark."

JULY 4, 1969 (790 words)
First line: *"I was thumbing through a stack of old records last week at the home of a girl who has graduated from Bobby Rydell and chewing gum to Jethro Tull and Tareytons."*

Stephen King discusses the influence of the Beatles, essentially coming to the conclusion that the Fabs revolutionized pop music and put the beat that "made rock-and-roll juicy" back into the music.

This is a fairly perceptive analysis of a group that still existed as a group back in 1969, but King seems to assign too much gravitas—and also thinks it better than it really is—to the Beatles' (actually John and Yoko's) latest single, "The Ballad of John and Yoko," a decent rocker but not a song warranting the kind of praise King awards it.

JULY 11, 1969 (1,000 words)
First line: *"The man's name is Neil Armstrong."*

This column is ostensibly about the July 1969 *Apollo* walk on the moon, but what it's really about is fear.

King's essay reads like a short story—a *Stephen King* short story—and it all boils down to one unavoidable question: What if there is something waiting for us out there, on the moon, in the dark?

King writes that there is a voice in the attic of his mind that asks this question, and he also tells of a horrifying dream in which he sees the *Apollo* astronauts mugging for the camera and then suddenly everything changes as one terrified astronaut face floats by his eyes. "A huge, tideless wind has swept down on them and their puny ship, a cyclopean gale from no place that is sweeping them off their neatly computerized orbit and into the gaping germless map of deep space itself."

King muses that perhaps one of man's biggest fears is that we are, as a species, just a little bit *too* inquisitive.

King concludes this evocative column by wistfully thinking, "[T]he guy in the attic notwithstanding, I only hope there is nothing waiting for us in the dark."

JULY 18, 1969 (880 words)
First line: *"The time has come, folks, the day you've all been waiting for—today is the day we give out the coveted Gritty Awards."*

In this column, Steve King competes with the Academy Awards by doling out his own Nitty Gritty Up Tight Society for a Campus with More Cools (the NGUTSCMC) movie awards. He was apparently inspired (infuriated might be a better word) by the awarding of the 1968 Best Picture Oscar to a movie "about a kid shoplifter (set to music, yet)." King obviously did not feel that *Oliver!* was worthy of the accolade and so decided to remedy the situation by the awarding of his own honors.

To make things more interesting, King invents his own categories, including "Best Line Delivered by a Male Actor" and "Best Line Delivered by a Female Actor." The winners were Mickey Rooney's "Looks like I just shot the priest" from *The Last Mile* and Marla English's naive inquiry—"Is something the matter, John?"—to Lon Chaney Jr. as he transforms into a werewolf in [*Face of the Screaming*] *Werewolf!*

King also picks the Best Lousy Movie (*The Good, the Bad, and the Ugly*) and the Lousiest Lousy Movie (*Vixen*, Russ Meyer's "ode to pneumatic breasts," which King describes watching as "fun in a nauseating sort of way—like falling naked into a swimming pool full of salad oil").

For Most Nauseating Actor and Actress, King picks Elizabeth Taylor and Michael J. Pollard, respectively, describing Taylor as "looking like she just crawled back into the land of the living after spending two weeks with a sex-crazed python."

King then shifts gears and lists nine of Hollywood's *greatest* offerings (leaving the tenth choice to the reader).

His picks are very interesting and make for an eclectic and stimulating at-home film festival. If you'd like to experience the flicks Stephen King was watching when he was a twenty-one-year-old college student, then go out and rent *Romeo and Juliet* (1968); *Point Blank* (1967); *The Hustler* (1961); *Psycho* (1960); *The Last Mile* (1959); *Picnic* (1955); *Rebel Without a Cause* (1955); *High Noon* (1952); and *Mildred Pierce* (1945).

Interestingly, King writes of *The Last Mile*: "Hardly anyone remembers this violent little classic about one man's final revolt on death row." Twenty-five years later, King would write his *own* death-row story, the six-part serialized novel *The Green Mile*.

Stephen King obviously remembered, wouldn't you say?

JULY 25, 1969 (950 words)
First line: *"The university's annual Freshman Orientation program, that amiable orgy of tourism, lectures, scheduling, and general all-around rubber-necking has been in full swing now for the last six weeks or so, and the casual observer hardly knows whether to be amused, skeptical, or envious."*

In this column, King writes evocatively about what it is like to be a freshman at college.

King remembers *his* first days on campus at the University of Maine, "clean-shaven, neatly dressed, and as green as apples in August," and describes himself as "a tired old hack of 21-going-on-seventy."

King also writes about his first date, humorously remembering shaving "three times in twenty minutes, and that was just to call her up and ask her."

King describes the typical freshmen as "wide-eyed, trusting souls" and admits that "they make me feel like I've been through the mill."

King concludes this warm remembrance by suggesting that his readers give the incoming freshmen a break because, he reminds them, "we were all young once."

AUGUST 1, 1969 (790 words)
First line: *"I think that of all the people on earth that I would most not want to be, the one who would cop the prize would be Pope Paul."*

This is a very serious column about birth control and abortion. When he wrote this column (he was twenty-one at the time), Stephen King was anti–birth control and proabortion.

Now how, you are probably wondering, does that make any sense at all?

King defends his position eloquently. "I think birth control demeans the act of sex and makes it fundamentally purposeless." He describes sterilized sex as akin to driving a car at a high speed—in neutral. He makes the point that the poor (the ones who could *really* use it) are not using birth control; it's the well-off, "the people who could afford three [kids] and have one."

King then defends Norman Mailer's position regarding birth control and abortion. Mailer is dead set against birth control but completely in favor of legalized abortion with no restrictions. This makes sense to King. Why? "If you become pregnant . . . and abortion is legal, then you KNOW what you are doing—committing an act of murder, which you may consider justified. The morals of the act are clearly delineated for you to grapple with."

Birth control, King believes, only kills a *potential* child, thus neatly obscuring the moral issues involved in such decisions.

King does not discuss these kinds of issues these days in nonfiction forums. He tackles serious moral matters in his novels and stories, but it is hard to know how much of what his characters think is also what *he* believes.

Nevertheless, this early glimpse at King wrestling with such life-and-death concerns was important enough that the editors of the *Maine Campus* chose only *this* column to run twice of all of King's "Garbage Truck" columns to date.

AUGUST 8, 1969 (930 words)
First line: *"Last week-end I spent about an hour leafing through some back issues of the CAMPUS, glancing at some of the stuff I'd written for the Garbage Truck over the last five or six months."*

King uses this column to thank a slew of people who supported him in his "Garbage Truck" efforts and in his college studies.

King fans will not recognize most of the people King thanks, but there are three worth noting and whose names serious King fans probably *will* recognize.

King thanks his English professor Carroll Terrell, who, he tells us, understands almost everything.

He also thanks James (Jim) Bishop, of the English Department, for explaining Faulkner's *Hamlet* to him over the phone one Sunday.

And King thanks his English professor Burton Hatlen, "one of the few faculty members . . . who refuses to teach out of comic books."

All of these men played important roles in King's development as a writer and have been interviewed about King by writers and biographers in the years since King's graduation from the University of Maine.

King concludes this column by noting that someone had recently told him that they enjoyed his columns but found him "overly cynical." King writes that he did not mean to come across that way and apologizes if he did. The people he thanked, he writes, are sufficient reason for his *not* being cynical, and after all, he asks, "anyone who likes the Pope can't be all bad, right?"

SEPTEMBER 18, 1969 (780 words)
First line: *"And here we all are again, in our places, with bright shiny faces."*

This column is basically a "Hello, suckers" column dedicated to the university's incoming freshmen. If read by any of them on their first day on campus, it might have made them stop unpacking, put on their coats, and run back home to Mama.

By 1969, King was a jaded and weary upperclassman, and in this week's installment, he spells out what being a freshman in college is really all about.

The pluses, he tells his readers, include the fact that these naive newcomers are now, for all intents and purposes, almost totally on their own. There are no parents to hassle them about their clothes, and they won't "have to pop a peppermint" every time they smoke a cigarette. They can wear funny clothes if they want to, and they are finally away from their annoying siblings.

The ultimate point King eloquently makes is that all this freedom comes with a price: He calls it the Suckership Dues. These dues boil down to some irrefutable facts of college Life: Any weaknesses a frosh may have (sensitive stomach, emotional disturbances) will get worse; and any regrettable character flaws (drinking, smoking, etc.) will be gleefully indulged for at least the next four years.

King tells his readers that two out of every fifteen thousand college students will commit suicide and that one in six of them will emerge from their college "experience" with some kind of mental disturbance.

King concludes this sober (yet funny) diatribe by advising incoming freshmen to not worry about flunking out. "Worry about staying in and keeping your mind right," he tells them. College can, he assures them, be a "fantastically rewarding experience," even if the university does its "friendly level best to mess you up."

In hindsight, I sincerely wish Stephen King had been writing a column in *my* student newspaper the year *I* started college. He might have saved my beleaguered mother a few sleepless nights—and a lot of money.

Oh, well.

September 25, 1969
(Reprint of King's August 1, 1969, column)

October 3, 1969 (550 words)
First line: *"A funny thing happened to me on my way to class a couple of days ago."*

There were several student groups on campus during King's university years, and he uses this week's column to rant a little about their cliquishness and blatant exclusivity. "Groups on campus," he writes, "who can understand them?"

His main point is that being a member of these groups has nothing to do with merit or achievements, and he cleverly concludes his blast against their elitist mind-set with the following: "I know a perfectly wonderful girl who is an Eagle [a student group]—when I first saw the little blue star stuck on her forehead, I asked her what it was for. She grinned and told me she'd gotten an A in spelling. Myself, I wish that was true. Then anybody that was deserving would get one and no one would have to flaunt them."

OCTOBER 9, 1969 (750 words)
First line: *"By now, you've probably read at least a dozen reviews of* Easy Rider, *the new Peter Fonda movie."*

This column starts out as a review of the generation-defining movie *Easy Rider,* but as is often the case when Stephen King starts thinking out loud on paper, it turns into something much more than just a simple movie review.

King astutely interprets *Easy Rider* within a larger context, and his perspective provides a very vivid snapshot of what the American cultural landscape looked like back in the late sixties, as seen from a university campus. Today the term "generation gap" has a quaintly archaic ring to it. In 1969 this "gap" was serious business, Jack.

"*Easy Rider,*" King writes, "states a purely American situation in purely American terms. And for me, at least, the most startling thing about the picture was the way it points up the gap between the generations in America today."

King rightly notes that the three thematic linchpins on which the movie turns are sex, drugs, and violence.

Describing the scenes involving the casual and repeated use of drugs in the movie (Fonda and Hopper's heroin-financed trip cross-country, the marijuana usage, the classic "graveyard/acid trip" scene), King writes: "If you aren't into the drug scene, this calm acceptance comes as a neck-snapping surprise." What King recognized as revolutionary about *Easy Rider* was that drug use was presented as a given in the movie: "Nobody preaches drugs in *Easy Rider*; drugs are just there." As

many others realized when the movie was first released,
radical about *Easy Rider* was that it not only showed th
drug use in America; it came to what King describes as "the
conclusion . . . that [drugs were] here to stay."

The violence in *Easy Rider* is also more than just bloodshed and
mayhem, and one scene in the movie in particular seems to have influenced a later Stephen King story. King pointedly describes the diner
scene in which blue-collar workers taunt and bait the long-haired
Hopper and Jack Nicholson, calling them the "purtiest girls" they ever
saw. King talks about the "tension and impending violence" in this
scene and how this kind of hassle is familiar to any young person who
has long hair who hazards entering anyplace where he is clearly the
outsider.

Almost a decade later, in 1978, King would publish his brilliant short
story "Nona" in a horror anthology called *Shadows*. In this dark tale,
the unnamed Narrator, a college student hitchhiking west, stops on a
cold, snowy night at a truck-stop diner called Joe's Good Eats. The heat
in the place and a Merle Haggard song playing on the jukebox were the
first two things that struck the young man upon entering Joe's.

In the story "Nona," it isn't long before a trucker makes a crack
about Christ coming back. Another one plays "A Boy Named Sue" on
the jukebox, and, finally, the Narrator is confronted by a Neanderthal
who asks him if he actually is "a fella." The scene in *Easy Rider* plus
King's *own* experiences as a "longhair" in the sixties seem to have influenced this gripping scene.

In his column, King then moves on to a discussion of the use of sex
in the movie. He notes that Hopper and Nicholson have to deliberately
adjust their thinking when they visit a whorehouse, for *they have never
had to pay for sex before*. The movie, King writes, does not preach the
fact that "free love" (there's another of those archaic terms) was everywhere by this time; it simply presents Nicholson and Hopper's dilemma
and leaves it to the audience to deal with the realities of the situation.

King concludes his review by baldly stating: "Most adults aren't
going to like *Easy Rider*." He was, of course, correct. Adults in the sixties were shocked by the film, while kids were bemused and puzzled
by their reactions.

Easy Rider ends with Hopper and Nicholson getting shot to death on
their motorcycle by a couple of rednecks in a pickup truck. King writes

that as he was leaving the theater after seeing *Easy Rider,* he overheard two cops talking about how the only part of the movie they liked was the ending. He admits wanting to run away and hide after hearing this reaction, and his last suggestion to his readers is that they owe it to themselves to see the film.

Overall, this is one of King's most important "Garbage Truck" columns and one that still has relevance today.

OCTOBER 16, 1969 (680 words)
First line: *"It has been suggested to me by a lot of people, from Chancellor McNeil, from faculty members, from student senators, and from the general run of the student body, that this is a pretty apathetic campus."*

In this column, King tries to rally his fellow students into picketing a local grocery store that is selling California grapes.

King urges a boycott of the Columbia Market because the grape pickers in California have been striking for better working conditions and many of the farmers have replaced them with illegal Mexican workers ("scab labor") and have used terrorism against Mexican-American labor leaders.

King's anger against the apathetic attitudes of many of his classmates is evident in this week's installment, and he hurls equal amounts of sarcasm and indignation at everyone, from "Miss Co-Ed" to the owner of the market, who, King writes, "looks like a fat cat."

King concludes his diatribe by opining that the university's ideals are "nothing but bullshit" if people don't act on them.

OCTOBER 23, 1969 (684 words)
First line: *"Well, a part of me went into hibernation last week."*

Why did a part of Steve King go into hibernation? Because the World Series was over and his beloved game of baseball had gone to sleep for another year, until spring training brought out the boys of summer once again.

After a loving discussion of some of his favorite past seasons, King concludes this affectionate reminiscence by admitting, "During the fourth game, somebody held up a sign at Shea that expressed my feel-

ings toward not only the Mets and the World Series, but to
baseball as a whole. The sign said: WHEEEEEEEEE!! It's th.
I feel when I have a slice of Mom's apple pie with milk, c
little kids say the Pledge of Allegiance. It's part of a tradition. .
thing in this dirty old world that's just good." (See the chapter o.1 King's
contribution to the 1991 *World Series Souvenir Scorebook*, "Perfect
Games, Shared Memories.")

OCTOBER 30, 1969 (990 words)
First line: *"Friends and neighbors, we here at the Nitty Gritty Up Tight
Society for a Campus with More Cools (NGUTSCMC—you all remem-
ber us—right?) are starting to get a little worried."*

Steve King was obviously quite pleased with the way things were
going on campus when he wrote this column, and so he decided to
single out the worthy people and notable events by pretending to be a
paranoid nut who sees deception, corruption, and depravity in everything going on at the University.

He begins with the school's new dean of students, ranting that
"anyone who is consistently fair with students must be planning something." (He reveals that one of the members of his "Up Tight Society"
will soon plant a bomb of ripe olives and Breck hair spray in the dean's
car, which, upon detonation, will drive the Dean into "a massive mental
breakdown.")

King then discusses David Bright, the editor of the *Maine Campus*
and a well-known name to King fans. (Bright is the name of a character in both *The Dead Zone* and *The Tommyknockers*.)

The faculty of the English Department is next up in the sights of
King's literary gun. He describes the "subversive" work of these people,
revealing that they are actually planning a poetry festival and that they
want to teach more black authors at the university as well as Norman
Mailer's *Armies of the Night* and John Steinbeck's "Commie manifesto"
In Dubious Battle. King writes that he would like to hold a competing
poetry festival which would feature the work of Rod McKuen and
Stephen King.

This was a funny column in which King doles out some well-
deserved praise while upholding the idiotic tenets of his imaginary
"Society," all of which make for a very entertaining column.

NOVEMBER 6, 1969 (782 words)

First line: *"In the short course of this year I've already managed to alienate the Maine freshmen and the organized flabs on campus (Owls, Eagles, etc.); now I'm going to see if I can alienate the rest of you by picking what I consider were the best singles and albums of the year— and the worst."*

Stephen King as record reviewer.

King's picks for best album are not surprising, but reading his reviews is like taking a trip back in time: The Beatles' *Abbey Road* and Bob Dylan's *Nashville Skyline* are now universally honored as brilliant musical archetypes as well as being acknowledged as evocative icons of a lost time. Thus, it is a cultural *jolt* to read commentary on these works written when they were *new releases.*

King's picks for best singles of the years are the Beatles' "Ballad of John and Yoko"; Simon and Garfunkel's "The Boxer"; Credence Clearwater Revival's "Green River"; and, surprise, surprise, "Sugar, Sugar" by the Archies.

King defends liking this teenybopper hit by reminding his readers that the song *does* make you smile when you hear it and then asks, "What, precisely, is wrong with that?"

King *really* hated Blood, Sweat and Tears when he was in college and picks their self-titled album as one of the worst of the year. He pulls no punches: "Bad jazz, bad rock, bad lyrics." Ouch. King also picks their single off the album, "And When I Die," as one of the worst of the year. (The song itself is actually a pretty good Laura Nyro composition. I guess King just hated what Blood, Sweat and Tears did with it.)

King's other choices for worst album were *Electronic Music* by George Harrison and the soundtrack to the movie *Wild in the Streets.* ("Don't listen to it after you eat," King tells his readers. "You'll whoops your cookies for sure."

King's two other worst singles were "Cherry Hill Park" by Billy Joe Royal and "Where's the Playground, Susie?" by Glen Campbell, noting that he thinks it's time Campbell went back to Alabama.

King concludes this highly opinionated but very funny column with the plea "Don't lynch me too high, huh?"

NOVEMBER 13, 1969 (818 words)
First line: *"The subject this week is cops."*

This week's installment is probably the most important "Garbage Truck" column Stephen King ever wrote.

Why? Because it is an incredibly passionate, scathingly angry, and sublimely intelligent defense of cops.

King starts off by checking off for his readers the people who do *not* like cops. This group includes the New Left, the Supreme Court, jaywalkers, people who can't get their tickets fixed, and taxpayers.

Who *does* like the cops? "Well, I do," King states with pride, admitting that "mostly it's the New Left that ticks me off." King does not like the cartoons in underground newspapers that show cops as pigs in uniforms beating people up. He also doesn't like people who defend Huey Newton, "who shot one." King describes these "whiners" as "idiots who prate insane nonsense about . . . 'fascist pigs' and 'racist gunslingers.' "

King then details the specifics of the life of a New York City cop. A cop makes $8,500 a year, King tells us, and out of that has to come his uniforms, shoes, and accessories. "For this incredible fortune," he notes, "your average cop is faced with the garbage of humanity."

King then describes some of the scum of the earth that cops have to deal with on a daily basis, including mothers who beat their kids and dump them in the trash, blacks who loot "for the greater glory of the struggle," and whites who loot "to show their support."

King also lists the "piggy" things cops do, like arresting heroin dealers, firing their weapons at people who are shooting at them, using Mace to break up race riots, standing all-night stakeouts, and covering up dead bodies after accidents, and for all this they have lousy insurance, lousy vacations, lousy pensions, and they have to work holidays.

"It's a dirty old world," King writes, and blasts the New Lefters, who "exist with their heads in the rosy clouds of Marxism, socialism, liberalism, urban reform, racial reform, world reform, and spiritual reform."

King describes cops as "the people who stand between you and the chaos of an insane society."

This "Garbage Truck" column should be reprinted and posted on the bulletin boards of every precinct station house and public building in the United States. Back in the late sixties, when King was writing these columns, there was a strong anticop sentiment throughout the land, and it was because the United States was being rocked by a tidal wave of social and cultural upheaval and the cops often found themselves in the uncomfortable position of having to restrain and oftentimes arrest their friends and neighbors. Things are somewhat different now, but there is still a faction of society that thinks any and all police presence and authority are too much.

This is, of course, nonsense, and as King reminds us in this column, cops are the only people "trying . . . to make sure that the rest of us aren't robbed, raped, kidnapped, conned or killed."

This "Garbage Truck" column contains anything but.

DECEMBER 4, 1969 (770 words)
First line: *"It's a little bit frightening to wake up in the middle of the night and realize that you may be the only one on earth that realizes why the world is in so much trouble."*

This is a funny column in which King blames all the problems of the world on not drinking enough plain water.

"[We] drink milk, beer, chocolate frappers, egg-nogs, Coca-Cola, Pepsi-Cola, RC cola, root beer, cider, Haig & Haig, Kool-Aid, Za-Rex," he raves.

All of this beverage intake is not enough, he states. Why? Because we have no idea what all the "strange components" in these drinks are doing to our urinary tracts.

He asserts that we are all being contaminated by these unknown substances and that they are "generally screwing up the waterworks."

King then posits the end of the world due to urinary tract malfunction. He suggests that if President Nixon were ever called upon to make an important decision during a time when his urinary tract is screwed up, the ICBMs would start flying, and the world would end in a nuclear holocaust.

Maybe we should ban all beverages but water, he muses, suggesting that clean bladders and urinary tracts may ultimately bring about world peace.

Well, it *is* something to think about, wouldn't you say?

DECEMBER 11, 1969 (590 words)
First line: *"Okay, folks, because absolutely nobody asked for it, here it is."*

This was Steve King's first annual Trivia Contest, in which he asked seven questions in three categories: Television Trivia, Movie Trivia, and Recorded Trivia.

Players had to answer all the questions in all three categories to enter, and first prize was an "all-expense-paid tour of Veazie [a small Maine town], conducted by me, with a final stop at my apartment, where I will regale you with anecdotes out of my colorful past, such as the GE sit-in, an account of my past love-affairs, my opinion on the state of world affairs and the major heads of state."

Second prize was a hamburger (an *all-expenses-paid* hamburger) with King at Farnsworth Cafe. Third prize was a trip to the Bangor Public Library, where King promised he would "goose the librarian of your choice."

King's questions indicate a wide-ranging knowledge of TV, movies, and music—pop culture at its most pervasive.

A couple of King's TV questions (actually, the only ones I could answer) were: "What was the Fugitive's real name?" (see the chapter on King's introduction to *The Fugitive Recaptured*); and "Who was the host of a daytime quiz show called *Seven Keys*?" (Dr. Richard Kimble and Jack Narz).

His movie questions included, "Who played the werewolf in *I Was a Teenage Werewolf*?" and "Who played the sexy girl next door in *Picnic*?" (Michael Landon and Kim Novak).

King's trivia questions about records included, "Who sang 'Party Lights'?" and "Who was the dean of the Kollege of Musical Knowledge?" (Claudine Clark and Kay Kyser.)

King promised the answers in the next week's *Maine Campus*, but ultimately this "first annual" contest was also King's last, since he graduated five months later.

DECEMBER 18, 1969 (884 words)
First line: *"There are strange things in the world."*

Strange things—unexplained oddities, weird disappearances, bizarre phenomena—were on Steve King's mind when he wrote this week's column.

He starts off by regaling his readers with the stories of several odd occurrences, including the disappearance in the 1890s of both Judge Crater and writer Ambrose Bierce, the 1936 rain of frogs on dustbowl Oklahoma (see "Rainy Season" in *Nightmares and Dreamscapes*), the 1947 UFO sighting that resulted in a dead air force pilot, the giant five-foot-across floating red eye that scared the bejesus out of a bunch of Boy Scouts and their scoutmaster in 1949, and the 1964 Amityville horror incident on Long Island.

King also talks about the 1800s disappearance of a group of Shakers from Jeremiah's Lot, noting that the "town remains uninhabited to this day." (Sound familiar? See "One for the Road" in *Night Shift*.)

King then reveals that he himself had an accurate death premonition that clearly shook him to his soul. It seems that the night before a high school friend of his died in a car accident, King had a dream of "a hideous man with a scarred face hanging from a black gibbet against a green sky." The hanged man had a card around his neck that had King's friend's name on it. (Yikes!)

King then discusses Shirley Jackson's hypothesis that "houses live and that some . . . are psychotic and are apt to kill anyone who sets foot inside their door." King also muses about witch cults and Charles Manson, a psycho who believed he was Satan.

But then King steps back and plays devil's advocate: "But of course it's all nonsense," he writes, but we know he doesn't mean it. King does admit that he would love to know where Judge Crater and Ambrose Bierce went and where the frogs came from, cautioning, though, that "if I found out I might never be quite the same." King muses that perhaps there's a rip in the fabric of our world and that sometimes "things cross back and forth." Maybe the people in the lunatic asylums (who see strange things on a regular basis) "only got halfway through," he suggests.

This is one of King's best "Garbage Truck" columns because it is the only one that *truly* foreshadows the mesmerizing writer he would become. It reads like some of the best of King's fiction, and I, for one, ended up wishing it were at least twice its length.

JANUARY 8, 1970 (794 words)
First line: *"So there are your 60's."*

In this "Farewell to a Decade" column, King reflects on what he sees as an all-encompassing madness permeating American culture, a widespread insanity epitomized by violence and sexual aberration in the movies, relentlessly violent and aggressive art, political hysteria and an extremism bordering on madness, and a "sick and angry" tone to humor.

In this depressing column, King seemed to be quite worried about the way things were going, and he concluded his diatribe thusly: "The next ten years may be even more interesting. If we're lucky, maybe there will even be somebody left hanging around to write about them."

JANUARY 15, 1970 (805 words)
First line: *"I, Stephen Edwin King, being of sound mind and body . . ."*

This is a funny, yet biting column in which King makes some telling points about his years at the University of Maine and also about his thoughts on everything from politics to conscience. King uses the form of a last will and testament to praise and skewer some ripe targets.

He blasts the university's English Department for not teaching him to read or write creatively and thanks them for staying out of his way.

He praises the *Maine Campus* and Dr. Goodfriend of the Chemistry Department. ("Anyone who can make such terrible puns must be a Gentleman, a Scholar, and a Humanitarian.")

To the "Emancipated woman of the seventies," King snidely bequeaths "nothing—if she's so smart, let her get it herself."

King leaves Andy Warhol and the makers of *I Am Curious Yellow,* "one bucket of warm spit each."

He leaves Alfred Hitchcock the wish that "he will stop making lousy spy movies like *Torn Curtain* and *Topaz*."

To all of his friends with "long hair, weird clothes, and strange jewelry," King leaves the "reminder that all of that doesn't mean a damn thing if you don't grow it on the inside as well."

The most significant codicil of this spurious last will and testament is the one in which King expresses his feelings about the state of modern American literature: "To Norman Mailer, Philip Roth, and John Updike," he writes, "I bequeath the hope that they will eventually learn to write like me."

Now *that's* what I call confidence, wouldn't you say?

FEBRUARY 5, 1970 (762 words)
First line: *"The subject this week, my friends, is the Boob Tube."*

King takes on television in this column, and overall, it ain't pretty to watch.

He does like some things about the network TV programming of the period, specifically the *ABC Movie of the Week* (singling out *The Ballad of Jody, The Silent Gun,* and *The Immortal* as worthy efforts, while blasting *Honeymoon with a Stranger* and *The Over-the-Hill Bunch* as unwatchable); and he also likes the prime-time series *Then Came Bronson, Gunsmoke, Mannix,* and *Ironside.*

King then levels both barrels on what he does *not* like about TV (which he describes as "wet and sick and fat"), specifically citing *The Courtship of Eddie's Father, Bewitched,* and *The Flying Nun* as particularly execrable examples.

King also uses this column to lament the loss of some shows he felt were really superb examples of what this "marvelous invention" could produce, naming *Thriller, The Naked City, You Bet Your Life, The 87th Precinct,* and appropriately, *The Twilight Zone.*

He concludes this week's installment with a warning to the networks: "You guys better wise up or pretty soon nobody is going to watch you but those Nielsen families."

King was only reviewing the offerings on *three channels.* Wouldn't you just love to know what he thinks about cable?

FEBRUARY 12, 1970 (676 words)
First line: *"If you're a conservative and a* Bangor Daily News *reader, or even if you're not, gather 'round."*

In this week's installment, King angrily blasts what he sees as a pervasive societal hypocrisy regarding America's perception of its young people.

Make no doubt about it: King is *pissed* in this column. "I'm getting awful damn sick of hearing stupid comments about the young," he begins.

He then takes on Nixon's "silent majority," a group he believes "are silent because they are too stupid to read or write," and describes them as a "vapid wasteland of fools [and] bigots."

King cannot understand how hair became such an important issue to so many people. (This was the sixties, remember, when long hair was considered a perverse affectation that branded the wearer as a Communist or, worse, a homosexual.)

He also points out the hypocrisy of those who consider drugs, specifically pot and hash, a horrible scourge but think nothing of drinking themselves into oblivion every night of the week.

King concludes this cautionary rant by noting that "at a time when society needs its young more than ever before—the new ideas, the new lifestyles, the fresh approach—this same society seems hysterically bent on perpetuating its own mordant mould."

Right on.

FEBRUARY 19, 1970 (649 words)
First line: *"Flowers this week for MUAB, the Memorial Union Activities Board."*

The Memorial Union Activities Board was the university group that booked cultural events for the student body, including movies, dances, and visiting dance troupes.

This week, King praises the board for a horror-film festival currently in progress, and it is fascinating to read college writings by the future King of Horror in which he discusses the classic fright flicks of all time.

He mentions the original 1931 *Dracula*, starring Bela Lugosi, admitting he was "delighted" to have finally seen it and that now he knows why "it has spawned so many imitations." He specifically cites Dwight Frye, a former leading man who played Renfield in the film. Decades later, in his short story "The Night Flier," King would name his own vampire character "Dwight Renfield" as a tribute to this 1931 film.

King then mentions *Frankenstein,* starring Boris Karloff; *The Hunchback of Notre Dame,* starring Charles Laughton; *Frankenstein Meets the Werewolf* ("not very good but a lot of fun"), Vincent Price's *Pit and the Pendulum,* and the movie he describes as "one of the most frightening (and artful) movies ever made," *The Haunting.*

King concludes the column by suggesting a future festival of old gangster movies (with Edward G. Robinson, James Cagney, etc.) as well as a festival of classic Westerns.

FEBRUARY 26, 1970 (532 words)
First line: *"Two years ago an excellent actor by the name of George Kennedy won an Academy Award for Best Supporting Actor in a Paul Newman movie called* Cool Hand Luke *('What we have here is a failure to communicate')."*

King devotes this entire column to a favorable review of the new George Kennedy film, ... *tick* ... *tick* ... *tick* ..., calling it "part of a dying breed—just a plain old good movie."

... *tick* ... *tick* ... *tick* ... also starred Jim Brown, Fredric March, Lynn Carlin, Don Stroud, Clifton James, and Janet MacLachlan. It was directed by Ralph Nelson (*Requiem for a Heavyweight; Charly*) and has never been released on tape or disc for home video.

MARCH 19, 1970 (687 words)
First line: *"The other day I came across a letter I wrote last February 26th, which was the day of The Big Snowstorm of '69."*

This is a critically important column because it gives us an intense and vivid glimpse of the superb writer Steve King had already become, even though he was still four years away from publishing his first novel.

Almost the entire column consists of a letter King wrote—but never mailed—to a girl named Maureen.

"All this snow," he begins. "It sets off strange thoughts in the head— or at least in my head, which is always filled with middling strange thoughts."

King then paints an evocative word picture of people stranded in The Den (a campus gathering place) as the snow continues to pile up and the power eventually fails. These passages remind us of scenes from both *The Shining* and *The Stand,* and they feature King writing passages of powerful, lyrical fiction within the structure of a letter to a friend. "The record on the jukebox dies—guitars, drums, and organ elongating, deepening, dying," he writes.

"Morbid, but oddly beautiful," he tells Maureen. "Big world out there, big dark, little us. Very little."

The final paragraph of this column is especially revealing: "In a lot of my writing I've been worried about the morbid, about Things that Lurk. Maybe those things—my big snowstorm, for instance, are only part of an urge to externalize the internal monster in us all."

He then quotes W. H. Auden, who wrote, "We are all children in a happy wood / Who have never been happy nor wise nor good," and concludes that we are all wandering through "our haunted woodland ... knowing that here there be Tygers. ..."

Two years earlier, in the spring of 1968, King had published his chilling short story "Here There Be Tygers" in *Ubris,* the University of Maine's literary magazine. The image obviously still haunted him.

King ends the column, though, on an up note, reminding his readers that spring was on its way and that they can all "worry about the Tygers some other time."

MARCH 26, 1970 (889 words)
First line: *"I've been student teaching for the last eight weeks, and I've been out of touch."*

In this column, King offers some suggestions for improving the university, the most important of which was the abolishment of required courses: "Students hate requirements," he wrote. "Most merely go through the motions, get their Cs, and try to forget the whole thing." He also opines that required courses are "generally a waste of time, money, and intelligence."

APRIL 9, 1970 (515 words)
First line: *"Have you ever thought how exciting some of those boring TV shows would be with a few campus personalities to liven them up?"*

King imagines some contemporary TV shows—*Then Came Bronson, The Nanny and the Professor, The Courtship of Eddie's Father, Room 222, Combat!, Adam 12, Peyton Place, The Fugitive, and Lassie*—but with University of Maine faculty members as the stars.

This was probably hysterical to the readers for whom it was originally intended, but if you do not know the people involved (as none of us late-1990s readers do), you just won't get the joke.

APRIL 16, 1970 (787 words)
First line: *"Last year, in May, Dick Mieland and I were handing out flyers in the Memorial Union just prior to the Rally for Free Speech (that rally, you may remember, followed the March to End the War, when eggs and other objects were thrown)."*

King discusses democracy and what it means to live in a truly free society in this week's installment. The column was inspired by an incident in which an old lady called King a "scummy radical bastard" when he tried to hand her a leaflet announcing a Rally for Free Speech.

King defines himself politically here, proudly declaring, "I have always been a conservative and I remain a conservative," but admitting that he registered as an independent because of his feeling that "the Republican Party has disowned me."

He then discusses at length his belief that the United States is first and foremost a country of individuals and that "the individual is the most important item on the agenda." He makes the point that people should be totally responsible for their moral views and decisions without allowing groups like B'nai B'rith, the Daughters of the American Revolution, or the Catholic church to tell them how to think—or vote.

He concludes by admitting: "I wish people would stop messing around with me."

The column illustrates very dramatically the volatile segmenting of our country back in the late sixties and early seventies, the friction caused by the Vietnam War, and the societal animus toward young people (like King), who not only felt that they had the *right* to speak their minds about what they saw going on in America and in the world but that they had a *duty* to do so, even if people judged them "scummy radical bastards" because of it.

APRIL 30, 1970 (717 words)
First line: *"Well, folks, it looks like that season again."*

King discusses the art of girl watching, calling it the "most difficult and demanding of all American sports," noting that May is the "prime month" for this particular endeavor.

MAY 7, 1970 (957 words)
First line: *"Well, this is almost it—the garbage truck is almost out of gas."*

In this penultimate "Garbage Truck" column, King writes that he has only three or four columns to go, but he actually ended up writing only one more.

King uses this week's column to discuss "Where We Are At," using recent world history as a benchmark paralleling his own personal growth. There are some revealing insights into King's childhood and development as a writer in this column, which is important because in it King talks about the Russian satellite *Sputnik*, stating that he was "waiting in the barber shop to get a haircut when that happened." Eleven years later, in *Danse Macabre*, King would write that he was in a movie theater in Stratford, Connecticut, in 1957 when the theater manager stopped the picture to announce to the audience that the Russians had put *Sputnik* into orbit over their heads. The *Danse Macabre* account of this incident is rich with specific detail, and it is obvious that King remembered, upon reflection, that he was in the theater and not the barbershop when *Sputnik* was launched. This "correction" illustrates what a difficult task it is to write accurate biography: Sometimes even the people who lived the events cannot remember them correctly.

King notes that fear was a constant during his childhood—fear of the Russians, fear of the government, fear of the unknown—and he smoothly discusses pivotal events of the period that helped define him: *Sputnik,* the Hungarian Revolution, the shooting down of Gary Powers's spy plane.

King notes that these were "some of the formative factors in the education of an American" and promises to talk more the following week about post-1962 events.

King's next column would be his farewell column, appearing two weeks later, on May 21. He never got to finish his review of America's recent past for the "Garbage Truck," although he *did* complete it (in a sense) a decade later in his 1981 book *Danse Macabre,* which not only surveyed the horror field up to that year but also offered insightful commentary on societal changes from the fifties through the end of the seventies.

MAY 21, 1970 (486 words)
First line: *"A blessed (?) event announced to the University of Maine at Orono."*

This was King's final column before his graduation from the university on June 5, 1970.

He wrote it as a spurious birth announcement and included his weight (207 pounds 6 ounces); his height (six feet three inches—noting, "I didn't know they piled it that high, either!"); his complexion ("hairy"); his favorite color (blue, although, he writes, black is probably more appropriate after a period in which Bobby Kennedy and Martin Luther King were assassinated and America entered Cambodia and Laos); and his favorite films (*They Shoot Horses, Don't They?, Bonnie and Clyde, M*A*S*H, The Wild Angels, Attack of the Giant Leeches,* and *The Ballad of Cable Hogue*).

King also muses about his "future prospects," which he concludes

are "hazy, although either nuclear annihilation or environmental stran-
gulation seem to be definite possibilities."

He also notes: "The boy has shown evidence of some talent,
although at this point it is impossible to tell if he is just a flash in the
pan or if he has real possibilities."

King concludes his final column with three pieces of advice to the
"general body politic": "Live peace," "Love a neighbor today," and "If
the establishment doesn't like it, then screw 'em."

His last line?

See the epigraph to this chapter.

Steve King's "Garbage Truck" columns, when read in their entirety
(something very few people will ever actually be able to do), provide a
revealing look at a brilliant college student, a committed young writer,
and a devoted patriot.

A few years ago, King reportedly forbade the University of Maine to
reprint these columns in a new edition that they wanted to publish and
sell to raise money for the school. One source I spoke to about these
writings told me that King was embarrassed by them and that he did
not want them widely disseminated.

That's understandable, since most writers cringe when they read their
early stuff.

But *Stephen* King (no longer "Steve" except to his friends) is now an
important American literary figure. Thus, these "Garbage Truck"
columns are also an important literary artifact; they are integral writings
that illustrate the evolution of a writer from a twenty-two-year-old college kid to the world's bestselling novelist.

PUBLISHING HISTORY

1969–70: *Maine Campus* (February 20, 1969–May 21, 1970).

9

Sword in the Darkness

Michigan Circle, in the theater district, is quiet and deserted. The marquees are unlit, the discotheques empty and shuttered. Pigeons poke through the gutters. One happens on the fragmentary stub of a marijuana joint, shakes it half-heartedly, and pounces on the bright glitter of a chewing-gum wrapper.

—from chapter 1 of *Sword in the Darkness*

What it is: the longest of the unpublished Stephen King novels on deposit at the University of Maine.

Chances of finding a copy: impossible. The manuscript of *Sword in the Darkness* has been deposited in the Special Collections archive, the Raymond Fogler Library, at the University of Maine at Orono, and access is granted only to those to whom King gives written permission. (Grateful appreciation goes to George Beahm, one of the few who have read King's three unpublished novels at the university in their entirety.)

Sword in the Darkness is a 150,000 word, 485-page, double-spaced manuscript in elite typeface that King wrote when he was a sophomore in college.

It is ostensibly the story of a race riot in a big city called Harding, but it is actually about a high school boy named Arnie Kalowski (a prototype for *Christine*'s Arnie Cunningham, it could be said) who sees his mother and sister die early on in the novel and must then care for his father, who suffers a nervous breakdown and becomes more and more catatonic as the story progresses.

As the story unfolds, Arnie watches the underside of life in Harding get sleazier, beginning with the goings-on in his own high school.

Sword in the Darkness, which ends with an enormous race riot in Harding, is about racism, violence, incest, deceit, blackmail, and lust and was Stephen King's somewhat naive attempt to write a story about things of which he had no direct knowledge. King grew up in a small town of nine hundred people and had never actually even *witnessed* a race riot, let alone participated in one.

In *Stephen King: The Art of Darkness,* Douglas E. Winter commented on this mighty effort from King:

> Heavily indebted to the *Harrison High* novels of sometime horror novelist John Farris—who, along with Don Robertson, author of *The Greatest Thing Since Sliced Bread* (1965), *Paradise Falls* (1968), and other novels (including *The Ideal, Genuine Man,* published by King's own Philtrum Press in 1987), was a major influence upon the maturing King—this lengthy tale of a race riot at an urban high school was rejected an even dozen times on Publishers' Row. King reflects: "I had lost my girlfriend of four years, and this book seemed to be constantly, ceaselessly pawing over that relationship and trying to make some sense of it. And that doesn't make for good fiction."

Sword in the Darkness is not an overt supernatural or horror novel, although there is a scene in chapter 83 that seems to foretell later scenes in *The Stand* and other more mature King works:

> *And then another black shape shouldered in, and this was Satan, come to retrieve his black and tortured spirit. Satan with gigantic quicksilver eyes, Satan with a gigantic squat phallus in both hands.*

Even though King considers *Sword in the Darkness* a "failed" novel (a "badly busted flush" is how he describes it), there are still some very interesting characters in the work, including:

> *Henry Coolidge,* a high school principal sexually obsessed with his blonde niece, Kit Longtin.

Kit Longtin, a hot, young thing King describes as a "professional seductress": She keeps careful track in a diary of how many times she has had sex. When the novel begins, Kit had logged 175 carnal encounters with just under fifty guys.

Arnie Kalowski, the student who wants a relationship with the lovely Janet Cross, but finds himself drawn to the irresistible Kit Longtin.

The race riot in *Sword in the Darkness* (which was also known for a time as *Babylon Here*) does not begin until 400 pages into a 485 page book. The riot itself is unconvincing, although one of its instigators is a guy named Slade—the name King would use again later in the *Maine Campus* serialization of his comic novella *Slade.* (See the chapter on *Slade.*)

His most sexually explicit work to date at the time, *Sword in the Darkness* was an enormous undertaking for a student barely twenty-five years of age, and even though it will likely never be published, it does give hints of the writer Stephen King would soon become.

PUBLISHING HISTORY

1970: unpublished manuscript (completed April 30).

10

"A Possible Fairy Tale"

The following little piece is fictional—a fairy tale, if you like.

—from "A Possible Fairy Tale"

What it is: an anti–Vietnam War essay that King wrote in 1970 when he was a student at the University of Maine.

Chances of finding a copy: probably impossible. This essay appeared in the *Maine Campus*'s special publication, the *Paper,* and has never been reprinted. After the theft of the original copies of the *Maine Campus* from the university's library, there is the possibility that a copy of "A Possible Fairy Tale" is not even archived at the library anymore.

On Friday, May 8, 1970, the University of Maine's student newspaper, the *Maine Campus,* published the second edition of a special publication called the *Paper.*

The *Paper* was an attempt by some students to call attention to the war in Vietnam and to the Nixon administration's refusal to acknowledge the strong resistance of many Americans to our involvement.

The front page of the paper had a peace sign as part of its masthead, and the entire front page was taken up by photos of an antiwar rally.

Of interest to Stephen King fans is the presence of an essay by King in the paper as well as his listing as one of the people who participated in the actual publication of the paper by writing for it and donating his time to make it a reality.

The student staff of the *Paper* consisted of "David Bright, Russ Van Arsdale, Mark Leslie, Steve Rubinoff, Jeff Strout, Ken Weider, Roy

Krantz, Steve King, Pam Murphy, Peggy Howard, Mary Ellen Gordon, Margie Rode, Bob Haskell and many others."

David Bright, a college friend of Stephen King's, is mentioned by name as a character in both *The Dead Zone* and *The Tommyknockers* and was the editor in chief of the *Paper* (and the *Maine Campus*). Bright authored the publication's leadoff editorial called "We Call the Shots," which urged students (during this period when the military draft was still in existence) to give long thought to whether they actually *did* have a military obligation after college.

Stephen King's contribution appeared on page 5 of the newspaper. It ran approximately six hundred words and described an imaginary end to the war in Vietnam within a ten-day span, with the war ultimately ending completely on May 18, 1970. The essay began:

> *The following little piece is fictional—a fairy tale, if you like. But fairy tales do come true. Witness our space program as one example. Or the airplane as another. So let's say that it's only a piece of fiction right now. So many people have been trying to turn "once upon a time" into "happily ever after" lately that maybe—just maybe—it can all come true.*

King then begins a chronology of events that would result in the complete end of the Vietnam War within ten days. All the events of King's chronology were the direct result of the efforts of "the people."

Here is a paraphrased rundown of the eleven war-ending events the way King imagined them happening:

1. Friday, May 8, 1970: The University of Maine joins the nation-wide campus strikes against the war in Vietnam.
2. Saturday, May 9: One million people participate in an antiwar sit-in at the White House.
3. Sunday, May 10: The White House sit-in swells to an astonishing 1.2 million people.
4. Monday, May 11: The campus strikes continue; all the members of the Teamsters Union decide to strike until President Nixon withdraws our troops from Cambodia.
5. Tuesday, May 12: National Guard troops refuse to enter the Berkeley campus; twelve platoons of army troops and marines refuse to go to Cambodia.

6. Wednesday, May 13: The members of the United Auto Workers union join the nationwide strikes; there are calls for Vice President Spiro Agnew's impeachment.

7. Thursday, May 14: President Nixon addresses the nation and pleads for support. Rail workers join the strikes, while the sit-in around the White House grows to 2 million people. Democratic senator Eugene McCarthy, who had been strongly opposing the Vietnam War since 1968, describes the activities so far as "a groove."

8. Friday, May 15: A bill is expected to pass the House today forbidding President Nixon to spend any more money in Southeast Asia.

9. Saturday, May 16: Postal workers, dockworkers, and some federal government employees join the nationwide strikes. There is talk that articles of impeachment against Spiro Agnew will be drawn up by Thursday, May 21.

10. Sunday, May 17: President Nixon tells the nation that he is withdrawing 500,000 troops from Vietnam and that the Cambodia invasion is over.

11. Monday, May 18: Soviet premier Aleksey Kosygin "calls Nixon . . . [and] congratulates him on 'an act of sanity and humanity.' " The two leaders decide on a summit "to discuss complete disarmament."

King then ends his "fairy tale" with this:

So there's your fairy tale, complete with happily-ever-after ending. It would be nice if things could turn out that way, but I doubt if they will. But then, there was the story of Icarus, the boy who wanted to fly. That was a fairy tale once, too. Perhaps man could fly in other ways.
Let's all hope so.

This piece, plus King's involvement in the strikes, the rallies, and the newspaper, illustrates just how deeply committed he was to the antiwar effort. King was an activist and used his talent with words to try to persuade others to give peace a chance.

King's fairy tale did not come true as he imagined it, not even one of the "events," but eventually we did get out of Vietnam, and Stephen

King's voice, along with those of countless other like-minded people, helped achieve the end of what may have been the least popular war in American history. Some wars are real "crowd pleasers," you know? The Persian Gulf War, the first one to be given a prime-time slot on TV, was one of them. Vietnam was not.

A cease-fire in Vietnam on January 28, 1973, ended our direct involvement in Southeast Asia. The last U.S. troops left Vietnam on March 29 of that year, but we continued to bomb Cambodia while retrieving American prisoners of war.

American battle deaths for the Vietnam War totaled 56,000 lives.

Publishing History

1970: *The Paper* (a special publication of the *Maine Campus*; May 8).

11

Slade

*Slade is in some ways the most revealing of King's uncollected
early works, especially as it shows King reveling in the joy
of storytelling. It is an engaging explosion of off-the-wall
humor, literary pastiche, and cultural criticism masquerading
as a Western—the adventures of Slade and his quest for Miss
Polly Peachtree of Paduka.*

—Dr. Michael Collings, The Work of Stephen King

*"Slade!" she cried, jumping to her feet and running to him.
"I'm saved. Thank heaven! . . . You came just in time!"*

*"Damn right," Slade gritted. "I always do. Steve King
sees to that."*

—from chapter 6 of Slade

What it is: an eight-installment, 6,500-word comedic novella (a
parody of the traditional western) by "Steve" King that King wrote
while attending the University of Maine and which was published in
the *Maine Campus* during his final semester and in the summer following his graduation.

Chances of finding a copy: impossible unless you're willing to make
a trip to the University of Maine to acquire photocopies of the novella
from the reversed-image microfiche in their library. (Which, by the way,
is the only surviving university copy of the text. The original copies of

the *Maine Campus* in which *Slade* appeared were stolen from the university's library sometime in 1988 or 1989. Moreover, as discussed in chapter 8, the microfiche copies of the *Maine Campus* containing writings by King are now the *only* college writings by King available to the public.)

Not many twenty-three-year-old writers can effectively maintain a sardonic, yet genuinely funny, sense of humor in their writing. Stephen King was one who could.

Slade is "Comedy by Stephen King." It is about Jack Slade, a gunslinger with a grim face and "two sinister .45s." (Slade's guns are *always* described as "sinister"). As our story begins, Slade is in mourning for his lost love, Miss Polly Peachtree of Paduka, Illinois, who has been killed in an untimely accident: A flaming Montgolfier balloon crashed into her barn as she was milking her cows.

Always politically minded, King used *Slade* as a forum for a few well-placed digs at the then-reigning political and social hierarchy. There are characters in *Slade* named Hunchback Fred Agnew (the "most detested killer" in the American Southwest); Hoagy Carmichael (Dead Steer Spring's deputy sheriff); Mose Hart (Miss Sandra Dawson's top hand on the Bar-T Ranch); Sunrise Jackson (one of Sam Columbine's gunmen); John "Quick Draw" Mitchell (another of Sam Columbine's gunmen); Big Frank Nixon (yet *another* of Sam Columbine's gunmen); Shifty Ron Ziegfield (and *another*), and perhaps the funniest characterization, Slade's "huge black stallion" Stokely.

Slade is silly, but King knows it and has an enormous amount of fun with its good-natured foolishness. There was probably a certain amount of giddiness in King that spring and summer; he was graduating from college, and it was only two short years after 1968's Summer of Love. There was *nothing*—and there has been nothing since—like a college campus in the late sixties and seventies. No wonder baby boomers are so nostalgic about their past.

Here is a look at each of the eight installments of *Slade*. [*Note:* All quoted excerpts from Stephen King's *Slade* are from the 1985 transcription by Michael Collings, which was made from photocopies provided by the Raymond Fogler Library, Special Collections, at the University of Maine at Orono and provided to me by Stephen King. Special thanks to Stephen King, Stephanie Leonard, Shirley Sonderegger, Dr. Michael Collings, and the staff at the University of Maine's library for their assistance with this feature. Also, for more information, see my earlier book *The Complete Stephen King Encyclopedia* for an alphabetical concordance of the people, places, and things of *Slade,* as well as all of Stephen King's "To Be Continued" notes from the serial.]

CHAPTER 1

Jack Slade rides into Dead Steer Springs dressed all in black and enters the Brass Cuspidor Saloon. In the saloon is John "The Backshooter" Parkman, one of nasty Sam Columbine's top gunmen. Parkman asks Slade what he's doing in town and Slade admits that he is working for Sandra Dawson of the Bar-T Ranch. (Everybody knew that the nasty Columbine was trying to force Miss Dawson off her land.) Parkman then tells Slade that he himself is working for Columbine, and also tells him he can "go to hell if you don't like the sound of it, Pard." Slade shouts at Parkman to "fill yore hand," and chapter 1 comes to a tense conclusion.

CHAPTER 2

Chapter 2 begins with the shoot-out between Backshooter Parkman and Jack Slade in the Brass Cuspidor Saloon. Before Backshooter can even draw his guns, Slade shoots the slimy worm six times in the heart. Slade then goes behind the bar to pour himself a shot of Digger's Rye (a 190-proof whiskey that in a later chapter inexplicably changes itself into an even more potent 206-proof booze). As he's standing behind the bar, a beautiful blonde introduces herself as Miss Sandra Dawson and kisses him smack on the lips when she learns that he has done away with Backshooter Parkman. Miss Dawson tells Slade that Sam Columbine wants her land so that he can resell it later at a huge profit to the Great Southwestern Railroad when they start building a branch line through her ranch. "Can you help me?" Miss Dawson asks Slade, to which he replies that he can, but cautions her not to "get yore bowels in an uproar." At this point in the story, the bartender bursts into the bar with terrible news: The Bar-T Ranch is on fire! Slade immediately springs into action, and chapter 2 concludes with the man in black furiously riding Stokely out to Sandra Dawson's burning ranch.

CHAPTER 3

When Slade arrives at the Bar-T, he finds three of Sam Columbine's men—Sunrise Jackson, Shifty Jack Mulloy, and Doc Logan—"laughing evilly" as they watch the bunkhouse burn. Slade gets into a gunfight with Columbine's men after Shifty Jack calls him a "Republican skunk," whereupon Slade blows away Sunrise Jackson and Shifty Jack. Someone comes running out of the ranch house, and Slade draws his sinister .45s and blasts away, mistakenly killing Miss Dawson's Chinese cook, Sing-Loo. "Well," he muses, "I guess you can't win them all." Slade then reaches for one of his "famous" (they're *always* "famous") Mexican cigars but changes his mind and rolls a joint instead. He then rides back into town where he learns that Sam Columbine has kidnapped Miss Sandra Dawson!

CHAPTER 4

Slade returns to Dead Steer Springs and rents a hotel room so he can get a good night's sleep before he sets out to rescue Miss Sandra Dawson. Slade is exhausted: "Since I got to this damn town I have had to blast three gunslingers and one Chinese cook, and I'm mighty tired." After requesting some Solarcaine for the blisters on his trigger finger, Slade takes a second-floor hotel room in which he undresses, puts his boots back on again, and gets into bed. Hunchback Fred Agnew then sneaks into Slade's room and puts a twelve-foot python named Sadie Hawkins in bed with Slade. Slade awakens when he hears "the faint hiss of scales on the sheet," leaps out of bed and shoots Hunchback Fred: "His sinister career was at an end." Slade then dresses, straps on his gunbelt, and chapter 4 ends with him heading out to the Columbine ranch "grimly determined to find Sam Columbine and put a crimp in his style once and for all!"

CHAPTER 5

Slade stops at the Brass Cuspidor where he tells Mose Hart that Hunchback Fred Agnew is dead. Hart is stunned: "There was talk that he might be the next vice president of the American Southwest." Slade then demands a mixed drink he "ain't never had before," and the bartender fixes him three zombies, drinks so potent that the bartender had stopped serving them. Slade downs three beer steins full of zombies,

and chapter 5 ends with the gunslinger being arrested for public intox-
ication and being hauled off to the Dead Steer Springs jail.

CHAPTER 6

King used almost the entire text of chapter 6 to good-naturedly rant
and rave against the editorial staff of the *Maine Campus* for censoring
what he described as "a pretty damn good love scene" from his ongoing story.

This is a very funny chapter that King also uses to throw a little dig
at the schizophrenic, hypocritical mindset of American culture that considers violence A-OK, but insists that sex be taboo. King tells his readers that instead of the love scene he has decided to insert a "more
wholesome, All-American ending."

This new, more acceptable ending? Instead of embracing Sandra after
she swoons into his arms in grateful appreciation for saving her life,
Slade clubs her over the head with one of his sinister .45s.

CHAPTER 7

Slade heads for the Mexican border, where Sam Columbine is torturing
the customs men with the help of his "A-No.-1 Top Gun," Pinky Lee,
who got his nickname during the Civil War when he rode with Captain
Quantrill and his Regulators. Slade ties Stokely to a parking meter, and
sneaks up on the grisly scene.

At one point, Slade hides behind a "giant bottle of mayonnaise that
had been air-dropped a month before after the worst flood disaster in
American Southwest history (why drop mayonnaise after a flood disaster? none of your damn business)." Slade then puts a bullet through
Pinky's head, and this chapter ends with Slade storming down the hill
to finally have it out with Sam Columbine.

CHAPTER 8

As Slade advances on Columbine, the dastardly villain convinces Slade
that they should holster their weapons and have a duel like real men
instead of just shooting it out. Slade agrees, but then someone screams,
"Wait!" It is Miss Sandra Dawson! She gives Slade some incredible
news: She is really his lost love Miss Polly Peachtree. She has had amne-
sia all this time but now knows who she really is. She pulls off her

blonde wig and Slade sees that she is, indeed, the dead Miss Polly Peachtree of Paduka.

As they embrace, Sam Columbine sneaks up behind them and shoots Slade three times in the back. "Thank God!" Polly whispers to Sam. "Not only was he killing everybody, but he was queerer than a three-dollar bill." But just when they think it's over, Slade sits up and blasts them both. His bulletproof underwear has saved his life. Slade is sad over Polly's death, though, and he throws away his cigar and lights a joint instead.

Chapter 8 ties up all of *Slade*'s loose ends and concludes with Slade and his one true love—Stokely the horse—"riding off into the sunset, in search of new adventures."

The end, for now. . . .

Publishing History

1970: The *Maine Campus* (June 11, p. 4; June 18, p. 4; June 25, p. 5; July 2, pp. 5, 7; July 9, pp. 5, 7; July 23, p. 5; July 30, p. 6; August 6, p. 5).
1985: Transcription by Michael Collings (July 29; bound and privately printed typescript transcription of all eight episodes of *Slade*).

12

"Squad D"

Please don't think I killed your son—all of your sons—by taking their picture.

> —from Josh Bortman's letter to his squad
> members' families in "Squad D"

What it is: an eleven-page, 2,000-word unpublished Stephen King short story that exists only in manuscript form. It was written by King for Harlan Ellison's *Last Dangerous Visions* anthology, a collection originally scheduled for publication in the late seventies.

Chances of finding a copy: in its existing form, your chances are zero. If it is ever published in Harlan Ellison's *Last Dangerous Visions* anthology, it may or may not resemble the manuscript version originally submitted to Ellison.

It is very difficult to talk about an unpublished story. There are many reasons, but probably the most significant one is that when, and if, the story ever does appear in print, what you finally read may bear little or no resemblance to the original version.

In a 1989 interview with George Beahm for the first edition of *The Stephen King Companion*, Harlan Ellison had this to say about the story:

> Stephen sent me a story for *Last Dangerous Visions* that needs to be rewritten. The problem is, when you say, I'm going to talk to Stephen about rewriting, I'm going to make suggestions, it sounds

as if you are trying to blow your own horn: Well, here I am, the smart, clever fellow who is going to teach Stephen King how to write. Well, I don't mean any such thing as that. What I mean is that I was sent a short story, and I think there's a lot more in it than Stephen had time to develop. The story deserves better, the work deserves better, and Stephen's reputation deserves better.

In a 1989 telephone conversation with King expert Tyson Blue, Ellison said this about "Squad D":

The story is currently in preparation. When it appears, it will not be in the form it is in now, and a story should not be critiqued until it's in its final form. Other persons who have discussed the story before this have jumped the gun.

Taking all this into consideration, then, the question ultimately remains, is it valid to talk about the story as it now exists (in what some—especially Harlan Ellison—consider a first-draft version), or should discussion of the piece wait until it is in its final form and published—assuming, of course, that it will someday *be* published?

It has been eight years since I originally wrote about "Squad D" in my Stephen King encyclopedia, and during this period, nothing has changed. *Last Dangerous Visions* has not been published; "Squad D" has not appeared anywhere else; and neither Stephen King nor Harlan Ellison has commented publicly on the status of either the story or the anthology. (In a December 1997 interview with Tom Snyder on Snyder's late-night talk show, Ellison did reply cryptically, "Keep watching the skies," when the subject of *Last Dangerous Visions* came up.)

When King wrote "Squad D" and submitted it to Harlan Ellison, he obviously felt it was ready for publication, which is enough to confirm that the story is worthy of seeing print in the form in which it was written. Whether or not it is ultimately published as is or in a substantially revised version, it is valid to discuss the existing incarnation of "Squad D."

The decision to revise or not to revise "Squad D" is ultimately between Harlan Ellison and Stephen King.

I am a fan of Harlan Ellison's. I consider his short story "The Whimper of Whipped Dogs" a masterpiece, and I believe that *Slippage,* his 1997 collection, is one of the most entertaining—and important—

single-author compilations of the past few decades. Ellison's nonfiction is insightful and astute, and there is no doubt that he is one of the keenest observers of contemporary culture and twentieth-century American literature writing today. He is fiercely intelligent, he has a red-hot mind, and if you stand close enough to that skull of his, you'll get blisters. However, I am a *bigger* fan of Stephen King's. I have always respected his judgment when it comes to writers and writing. Open any page of *Danse Macabre* and you will find books worth tracking down and reading, movies worth watching, writers and directors worth paying attention to. King has steered many of us in the direction of artists we may have overlooked; thus, many of us King fans hold great store (rightly) in King's opinions. Don Robertson, Joseph Payne Brennan, Jim Thompson, and many other writers are on the list of "King Recommendations"; it is therefore my feeling that if King felt "Squad D" was worthy of being read by his readers, then I defer to his judgment and feel it is justifiable to fill you all in on his original version of the tale.

"Squad D" is a touching and sad story that seems to stand just fine as is, even though Ellison feels it could be better. He's probably right, but only because of King's talent and the certainty that if he *did* decide to rewrite the story, it would more than likely become even more powerful.

In its current version, though, it is a very moving story of redemption. King authority Michael Collings (one of the few others who have read this version of the story), in his book *The Shorter Works of Stephen King,* had this to say about "Squad D":

> "Squad D" is a story of guilt and forgiveness, of peace growing out of turmoil. Josh Bortman finds the peace he has sought, among his only friends. Dale Clewson becomes reconciled to his son's death—and to the tragedy that took the lives of too many sons.
>
> While not a particularly "dangerous" vision, "Squad D" does deserve to be seen. With "The Reach," it is one of King's most penetrating statements on the relationship of life and death—and the tenuous border separating them.

"Squad D" has attained an almost mythical reputation among King fans: It is the story that was supposed to be published but has not been; it is the story that Harlan Ellison refuses to publish as is; it is one of Stephen King's only attempts at writing about the Vietnam War.

Dale Clewson is the father of Billy Clewson, a young soldier killed in Vietnam while crossing a bridge that had been booby-trapped by the Vietcong. Billy was a member of D Squad, which had ten members, nine of whom were killed that day on the bridge.

The tenth member of the squad, Josh Bortman, of Castle Rock, Maine (a town certain to be familiar to King fans), was in the hospital that day with bleeding hemorrhoids and was thus spared a fiery death.

From his hospital bed, Josh writes letters to each surviving family, and with the letter, he encloses a photograph—enlarged and framed—of the nine squad members killed. Josh had not been with his squad when the picture was taken or when they all died.

Eleven years and one day after Squad D was wiped out, Josh Bortman's image suddenly appears in the Squad D picture, finally completing the ten-man squad. When Dale Clewson sees the tenth man suddenly appear in the picture, he questions his own senses: Weren't there always nine men in the picture?

Dale decides to call Josh, his son's friend and the only survivor of Squad D, only to find out that Josh had finally found a way to catch up with his friends: He had hanged himself the day before in the garage.

PUBLISHING HISTORY

Late 1970s: never published.

13

"The Blue Air Compressor"

Oh, Gerald, this is such a bad story. I don't blame you for using a pen-name. It's—it's abominable!

—Mrs. Leighton, "The Blue Air Compressor"

What it is: a gruesome horror short story King wrote when he was in college and then revised a decade later for a reprint in *Heavy Metal*.

Chances of finding a copy: the 1971 *Onan* version is only available (at a high price) from rare- and used-book dealers. The 1981 *Heavy Metal* version might still be available from the right used-magazine dealer.

Writer Gerald Nately rents a cottage by the sea that is owned by an incredibly obese woman named Mrs. Leighton. When he first lays eyes on her, Gerald thinks to himself, "This woman is so goddam fucking big and old she looks like oh jesus christ print dress she must be six-six and *fat* my god shes fat as a hog. . . ."

Nately becomes so obsessed with Mrs. Leighton's corpulence that he tries writing about her in a short story he initially titles "The Hog." Mrs. Leighton reads the story and takes great delight in mocking Nately mercilessly for his failure to truly capture her enormity: "You haven't made me *big* enough, Gerald. That's the trouble. I'm too big for you. Perhaps Poe, or Dostoyevsky, or Melville . . . but not *you*, Gerald. Not even under your royal pen name. Not *you*. Not *you*."

Gerald becomes so enraged with her ridicule that he kills her, using one of Stephen King's most inventive forms of literary execution. Gerald offs Mrs. Leighton by shoving the hose of a blue air compressor down her throat and "overinflating" her until she explodes. He then cuts up what's left of her body and buries the pieces in the sand beneath a toolshed. Nately later kills himself in Kowloon by cutting off his own head with an ivory-figured guillotine.

The story owes its plotline to a similarly themed *E.C. Comics* story, and "The Blue Air Compressor" marks one of the first times (if not *the* first) King placed himself—by name, as the writer—in a story. "My own name, of course, is Steve King, and you'll pardon my intrusion on your mind," he tells his readers.

He then defines "Rule One for All Writers," which is: "The teller is not worth a tin tinker's fart when compared to the listener." In later years, King would hone this sentiment: "It is the tale, not he who tells it." Even while in college, King was already developing an artistic ideology in which the storyteller is absolutely secondary to the story itself.

King mentions his own real-world work along with that of Poe's (and fictitious author Nately's) as representative of the type of writing in which Freudian symbols (locked rooms, empty mansions, etc.) are apt to run rampant.

In the *Heavy Metal* version of this story, King has Nately kill Mrs. Leighton with a Winchester rifle first and *then* overinflate her until she explodes.

In this odd story, King, during one of his authorial interruptions of the tale, tells us that he remembers coming up with the three dominant images of "The Blue Air Compressor"—"ivory guillotine Kowloon; twisted woman of shadows, like a pig; some big house"—during an early-morning English class taught by Carroll F. Terrell, an important figure in King's life and career.

PUBLISHING HISTORY

1971: *Onan* (January; University of Maine student literary magazine).
1981: *Heavy Metal* (July).

14

"The Hardcase Speaks"

I'll put the hoodoo on you, I can do it, it comes in a can.

—from "The Hardcase Speaks"

What it is: a sixty-six-line free-verse poem by "Stephan King" that was published in a literary magazine that also included works by Jim Bishop, Burton Hatlen, Tabitha King, and James Lewissohn, four writers publicly associated with Stephen King. Michael Collings included "The Hardcase Speaks" in his annotated bibliography *The Work of Stephen King,* despite the anomalous spelling of King's first name, because of the presence of the other writers in the journal (all connected to King in some manner) and also because of the writing style and imagery used throughout the poem.

Chances of finding a copy: probably impossible. *Contraband 2* was an extremely obscure publication, and the only chance of finding a copy of the issue with King's appearance is at the University of Maine, but unless you're a student there, you will probably not be granted the kind of access necessary to track down any existing copies of this journal in their archives.

"The Hardcase Speaks" is written in irregular block paragraphs and has a harsh and brutal tone reminiscent of other King writings and characters.

There are several images in this work that shriek "Stephen King," including a critical one from *It*: "virgins pedaling bikes with playing cards affixed to the rear spokes with clothespins." (Mike Hanlon bought Bill Denbrough a deck of Bicycle playing cards for Silver's wheels in *It*.)

There is also the image of a dismembered woman in the poem ("Strawberry Spring" comes immediately to mind) and the graffiti "Stop Me Before I Kill Again," written in "her juice" on the wall above her body.

The poem also mentions Utica, a town King has often jokingly referred to as the place where all of his ideas came from, and there is a reference to saving "corn for murderers," suggesting imagery from "Children of the Corn."

The poem mentions Chuck Berry ("Maybelline" by Chuck Berry was one of Dennis Guilder's imagined songs on Christine's demonic playlist in *Christine*); and the line "I could gun you down with magic nose bullets" suggests "The Ballad of the Flexible Bullet," from *Skeleton Crew*.

Perhaps the most important "Stephen King" images in "The Hardcase Speaks" are contained in these lines:

> *bore a little hole in your head sez I insert a candle*
> *light a light for Charlie Starkwether* [sic] *and*
> *let your little light shine shine shine*

This stanza contains three seminal images that appear in King's later works. The first is "bore a little hole in your head." This image will be fully realized in the excerpt from *The Tommyknockers*, "The Revelations of 'Becka Paulson," when 'Becka shoots herself in the forehead and later pokes a pencil in the hole and pushes its eraser against her brain.

The second extremely important reference in this stanza is the mention of Charlie Starkweather, the madman who killed ten people in 1958 and who was electrocuted for the murders the following year. In *The Stand*, Randall Flagg remembers going to high school with Charlie Starkweather, and later, in *The Stand: The Complete and Uncut Edition*, Trashcan Man travels across America with The Kid, "who looked like Baby Elvis" and is a reincarnation of Charlie Starkweather. (We are told that The Kid is a reincarnation of Starkweather by Douglas Winter—who ought to know—on page 192 of the paperback edition of *Stephen King: The Art of Darkness*.)

Another revealing image in this stanza is, of course, the thrice-repeated use of the word "shine." Stephen King's novel *The Shining* was originally titled *The Shine* but was changed before publication because of its possible offensive racial connotations.

There are many other "Kingish" images in the remaining lines of this poem, and they are evocative ("Learn to do magic like me") and often gross ("buy some plastic puke at Atlantic City").

The poem concludes with the line "Go now. I think you are ready." This echoes the tone of many of the lines of "Paranoid: A Chant" from *Skeleton Crew,* especially the lines "Listen—/listen/do listen:/you must listen."

"The Hardcase Speaks" is King writing in that odd and dark (yet somewhat one-dimensional and limited) persona of the paranoid madman he periodically used when he was writing during his college years (and shortly thereafter). He seemed to be very interested in getting inside the mind of the sniper and the serial killer. It is a testament to his genius that even now, decades later, these works still chill and frighten, even though King has moved on to deeper, more complex characters.

King continues to explore the dark side of human nature, but now he has the maturity to help us understand those characters a little better.

PUBLISHING HISTORY

1971: *Contraband 2* (December 1, Contraband Press; a literary magazine published in Portland, Maine, and edited by Bruce Holsapple and Michael Barriault).

15

Blaze

George always said that if you were a dummy you were a dummy and there was no shame in it but you had to recognize it.

—from chapter 1 of *Blaze*

What it is: a 50,000-word novel King wrote around the same time he was writing *Second Coming* (which would later be published as *'Salem's Lot*). King has described *Blaze* as a "literary imitation" of John Steinbeck's 1937 novel *Of Mice and Men*.

Chances of finding a copy: impossible. The manuscript of *Blaze* has been deposited in the Special Collections archive, the Raymond Fogler Library, at the University of Maine at Orono, and access is granted only to those to whom King gives written permission.

Blaze tells the story of an abused, mildly retarded, three-hundred-pound man—Claiborne Blaisdell Jr.—who kidnaps an infant and holds him hostage for $1 million. Blaze ultimately falls in love with the child and is shot to death by the police while trying to flee with the baby across a frozen lake.

Blaze receives his instructions from George Rockley, his partner in crime, who *we* learn in chapter 1 has been dead for three months as the story begins in a snowy bar parking lot in Maine. Even after his death, George serves as Blaze's mentor and inner guide, but Blaze does not realize that George is dead until chapter 18:

"Christ, George, are you in my head?"
"I always was, asshole. Now GO!"

George's ghostly presence in the novel (which, of course, can be interpreted as a wholly psychological hallucination on Blaze's part) is the
only hint of a paranormal theme in *Blaze,* and the novel is more of a
Richard Bachman–like crime novel than a Stephen Kingish tale of vampires and other demonic creations.

The book also tells the story of Blaze's childhood through a series of
flashbacks in chapters 3, 8, 11, 15, 17, and 19. Through these flashbacks we learn that Blaze was physically abused by his father when he
was a child. In one especially ghastly scene, Blaze is thrown down a
flight of stairs by his dad—three times in a row—as he sits watching
his Saturday morning cartoons. Blaze was in the second grade when
this took place, and it isn't long before he is taken away from his abusive father and placed in a home. He remains institutionalized until he
is sixteen and then leaves the home and meets George Rockley in
Boston.

Blaze is flawed but entertaining and exciting. It's a bit far-fetched to
believe, for instance, that a grossly obese, retarded man could effectively
care for an infant for an extended period of time, even though King does
include a scene in chapter 6 in which Blaze spends $221.55 on supplies
at the Baby Shoppe before he performs the actual kidnapping.

The novel has a downbeat ending typical of a Bachman tale, concluding with an especially violent scene in which Blaze is shot to death
by the police as he stands thigh-deep in the icy waters of a frozen lake
after he has fallen through the thin ice, while still holding the helpless
infant in his arms. He is shot by the police six times with .38-caliber
bullets. The first three hit him in the right calf, the back of the knee,
and the right hip. The fourth bullet shatters Blaze's spinal column, and
the fifth hits him in the back of the neck. The sixth and final shot "blew
the back of his head off."

Blaze ends with an epilogue in which the parents of kidnapped infant
Joseph Gerard II hold a press conference to announce that the baby is
fine and that they are leaving for a much-needed vacation after their terrible ordeal. King then takes us to Blaze's grave site and then returns to
the kidnapped baby. Apparently, Blaze did make an impact on the
infant: King writes that as his parents watch him, the baby sees "the
wrong face" peering down at him in his crib. "They were all the wrong

faces," we are told. "He knew; their foreheads were wrong."

King has written about *Blaze* in the afterword of *Different Seasons*, noting that "[*Blaze*] had been written immediately after *Carrie*, during the six-month period when the first draft of *Carrie* was sitting in a desk drawer, mellowing. . . ." He also admitted that "some of the pages of *Blaze* had been typed on the reverse side of milk-bills."

Just before *Carrie* was published, King sent Bill Thompson, his new editor, two manuscripts, both of which he wanted Thompson to consider as his second novel. They were *Blaze* and *Second Coming*, and Thompson felt that *Second Coming* was the stronger effort. *Second Coming* was eventually published as *'Salem's Lot*, and *Blaze* went back into the drawer. The manuscript ultimately ended up in the Special Collections archive at the University of Maine, and King has not indicated any desire to resurrect it.

Blaze could be a terrific book if King ever did choose to revise it and correct some of its narrative problems, but for now it only exists in its original, unpublished form, and all we can do is read *about* it.

PUBLISHING HISTORY

1973: unpublished manuscript (completed February 15).

16

"Weeds"

What it is: Stephen King's original text version of the short story he later adapted as the "Lonesome Death of Jordy Verrill" segment of his movie *Creepshow.*

Chances of finding a copy: extremely difficult but not impossible. This text version of "Weeds" only appeared in print twice, both times in raunchy men's magazines that are never archived in libraries and which rarely survive long enough to enter the collectors' market. I have occasionally seen offered for sale (at between twenty-five and fifty dollars) copies of the issue of *Cavalier* in which the story first appeared. Try the usual sources (Betts Bookstore, The Overlook Connection, etc.) if you are determined to acquire an original appearance of this tale.

"Weeds" was introduced in its *Cavalier* appearance by the headline "More Than a Green Thumb . . . Will Be Necessary to Stop the Weeds: A chilling new story by the author of *Carrie* and *'Salem's Lot*."
 "Weeds" is richer and less comic than its *Creepshow* adaptation. Comparing the two is fascinating because it shows how King (and *Creepshow* director George Romero) used the more visual, over-the-top elements of the original story to create both the movie and the simultaneously published comic adaptation while ignoring the story components that only worked as part of the longer text version.
 "Weeds" runs close to six thousand words, and its length allows King to flesh out Jordy Verrill more than he was able to do in the greatly abbreviated cinematic adaptation, which, by necessity, gives us a broadly drawn caricature of Jordy Verrill, a farmer who is a shit-kicking lunkhead. The *Creepshow* version of the story also gives a

much larger role to Jordy's dead father, a character who is only referred to in passing in the short story.

The story is classic sci-fi/horror:

A meteor from outer space lands on Jordy Verrill's New Hampshire farm one Fourth of July evening. The meteor contains a sentient, vegetative alien life-form that begins to propagate by growing weeds on anything it touches. It can feed on the earth, thrives when given water, and within hours after it has landed, it is already blooming. Witless Jordy touches the meteor and begins to change into a walking plant. When he is literally nothing but a green monster, he puts himself out of his misery by blowing his own head off with a shotgun. The story ends with a weather forecast calling for rain. The last lines of the short story consist of the thoughts of the alien weeds:

> *Jordy-food.*
> A fine planet, a wet planet. A ripe planet.
> *Cleaves Mills-food.*
> The weeds began to grow toward town.

King also had some fun with the *Creepshow* adaptation by changing the name of Jordy's banker from Mr. Warren to "Mr. Bilkmore" and adding a TV evangelist named "Reverend Fleece U. White" (of the Church of the Holy Shrinking Purse). King also made "Weeds" a "Castle Rock" story by revealing in the *Creepshow* segment that Jordy's doctor came from Castle Rock, Maine.

"Weeds" is richer and less comic than its *Creepshow* adaptation (in which King himself played the unforgettable Jordy Verrill). The *Creepshow* segment also did not include a really fine chunk of characterization, specifically King's description of Jordy's "three types of thinking":

> *For Jordy there were three types of thinking: plain thinking, like what you were going to have for supper or the best way to pull a motor with his old and balky chain-fall; work thinking; and Big Thinking. Big Thinking was like . . . . what he was going to do about this meteor.*

Jordy Verrill seems to be a distant relative of *Cujo*'s Castle Rock mechanic Joe Camber, and "Weeds" also shows the influence of King's earlier drive through the cornfields of Nebraska, an experience he has often talked about in interviews and which also inspired his *Night Shift* story "Children of the Corn." Jordy's thoughts about the corn and his memories of his father's bringing him out on the porch one night to hear the corn grow have a very "Children of the Corn" feel to them.

"Weeds" is from that era in King's career (early- to mid-seventies) when he was still publishing short fiction in the men's magazines of the period, those breast-obsessed journals that would run his tales alongside ads for 8-mm stag films, such as *Tijuana 8-page Sex Comics* and *Peter Pumps*. During this very productive period, King produced several notable short stories, many of which were ultimately collected in *Night Shift*. (His *Skeleton Crew* short stories were from the early eighties, when King had "graduated" to magazines like *Redbook, Twilight Zone, Ellery Queen's Mystery Magazine, Yankee,* and *Playboy.*)

Unfortunately, "Weeds" has never been reprinted in any of King's short-story collections, so the only way you'll be able to read it will be by buying one of the magazines in which it originally appeared.

PUBLISHING HISTORY

1976: *Cavalier* (May).
1979: *Nugget* (April).

17

"The Cat From Hell"

The cat was forcing its way into his mouth, flattening its body, squirming, working itself further and further in. He could feel his jaws creaking wider and wider to admit it.

—from "The Cat From Hell"

What it is: a feline-themed horror short story Stephen King wrote "to order" for Nye Willden's *Cavalier* magazine. Willden sent King a photo of a cat and wanted him to write the first five hundred words of a story. Willden's idea was to run a contest and let the reader complete the tale. King was in a creative zone when he started the story, though, and so he completed it. Willden *did* run only the first five hundred words in *Cavalier* but a couple of months later published the whole story in the magazine, along with the reader-completed version. (King's opening ended with the hit man initially meeting his feline "victim." The final story runs close to seven thousand words.)

Chances of finding a copy: for the completed story, the chances are good. "The Cat From Hell" has been reprinted several times over the years (although never in one of King's collections), and one of the collections listed below in "Publishing History" should be relatively easy to find. (*Magicats!,* even though it was originally published in 1984, will probably be the easiest anthology to find. I recently saw the Ace mass-market paperback at a Barnes & Noble.) Finding a copy of the issue of *Cavalier* with the first five hundred words of the story, however, will be considerably more difficult, if not impossible. The June 1977 issue, containing the entire story, can run upwards of fifty dollars or more; the issue with the partial story may be even more costly. Start with the usual sources.

☠ A hit man named Halston takes on an odd assignment—a murder commissioned by a dying old man named Drogan who has made a fortune in the pharmaceutical business. His success, however, has come at a price: the lives of fifteen thousand cats killed during experiments to perfect a painkiller for the terminally ill.

One day, Drogan tells Halston, a stray cat showed up at his door. It wasn't long before three people in his house were dead. Drogan fears for his own life now, and thus has called in Halston to kill the cat. It is obvious that Drogan believes the cat is some kind of feline emissary sent to exact karmic revenge on him for killing so many of his cousins.

Halston takes the job (the fee, after all, *is* twelve grand—the same amount Halston got for killing a person) and plans on taking the kitty out into the country, snapping its neck, burying it, and then bringing the tail to Drogan.

Things do not go as planned, however, and Halston ends up in a car crash when the cat attacks him as he's driving it to its death. Halston is pinned in the front seat, and the cat ravages him by clawing his face, digging into his testicles, and ultimately worming its way into Halston's mouth and all the way down into his stomach. A farmer comes upon Halston's body and is just in time to see the cat clawing and biting its way out of Halston's stomach: "The cat forced its body out and stretched in obscene languor."

The cat from hell then runs off into a field, "and then it was gone." The farmer tells a reporter that the cat ran away as "if it had unfinished business." The cat, of course, *did* have unfinished business. It was on its way to finish off Drogan and complete the avenging of his buddies' deaths.

"The Cat From Hell" is a short horror classic. King quickly establishes a complete history for every character in the tale and fully develops the story line in what is one of his briefer and quicker-paced tales.

Interestingly, the scene in which Sam the killer cat eats its way out of Halston's stomach would be echoed a couple of years later in the movie *Alien* when one of the alien creatures chews and claws its way out of a crewman's stomach.

Coincidence? Or could writer Dan O'Bannon and director Ridley

Scott have been influenced by the almost identical scene in King's short story?

Just asking.

"CAT FROM HELL"

During the years when I was first married, my sales to Cavalier *helped my wife and I to keep our heads above water—my full-time job at that time was washing hotel sheets in an industrial laundry.*

—from "Cat From Hell"

What it is: Stephen King's brief nonfiction article about how his story "The Cat From Hell" came to be.

Chances of finding a copy: extremely difficult, since this mini-essay has only appeared in an issue of *Castle Rock* and has never been reprinted. You will have to seek out an original *Castle Rock* from one of the usual dealers in order to acquire a copy of the piece.

In this brief background essay about how "The Cat From Hell" came to be, King defends editor Nye Willden and *Cavalier* magazine against charges that the magazine was nothing but a cheesecake rag which existed solely to run pictures of naked, big-breasted women.

Frankly, I did not know that *Cavalier* had run early fiction by Ernest Hemingway, Erskine Caldwell, and Mickey Spillane. I thought Stephen King was the most famous writer they had ever published, and I was thrilled to learn that I was wrong.

King then relates how editor Nye Willden asked him to write a story based on a photograph of a cat with a half-black, half-white face and that he was "tickled" by the idea. "It put me for the first time in my life in the illustrator's position; the artwork was not created to reflect the story, but the story was to be created to reflect the artwork."

King also liked the idea because he initially thought he would not have to "tie up my own loose ends," since he was only being asked to write the first five hundred words of the story.

Of course, King did end up writing the entire tale because, he reveals, he came up with the idea for an ending inspired by Edgar Allan Poe's "Black Cat" and also "because I saw so clearly how to."

King concludes this interesting essay by noting that it was the only time he ever "wrote a story to order—and from a photograph at that."

It turns out that "The Cat From Hell" was only the *first time* King would write a story to order. In 1982 he wrote "Skybar" for a special publication, and in 1986 he came up with "For The Birds" for another "themed" tome. (See the features on those two stories.)

PUBLISHING HISTORY

"The Cat From Hell" (story)

1977: *Cavalier* (first five hundred words only; March).

1977: *Cavalier* (June).

1978: *Tales of Unknown Horror* (Peter Haining, editor; New American Library paperback).

1978: *Year's Finest Fantasy* (Terry Carr, editor; Berkley hardcover).

1979: *Year's Finest Fantasy* (Terry Carr, editor; Berkley paperback).

1984: *Magicats!* (Jack Dann and Gardner Dozois, editors; Ace Books paperback).

1996: *Twists of the Tale: An Anthology of Cat Horror* (Ellen Datlow, editor; Dell paperback).

"Cat From Hell" (article)

1985: *Castle Rock: The Stephen King Newsletter* (June).

18

Wimsey

*"The rain's beastly, isn't it?" Lord Peter Wimsey said
drearily, looking out the window to his right.*

—the opening line of Stephen King's
proposed *Wimsey* novel

What it is: fifteen pages of manuscript in typescript consisting of the
first chapter (fourteen pages) and the first page of the second chapter of
a proposed "Lord Peter Wimsey" novel Stephen King was thinking of
writing in 1977.

Chances of finding a copy: impossible. These pages have never
appeared for sale in the secondary market, and there aren't more than
a half-dozen collectors who possess copies.

In the summer of 1977, Stephen King and then-editor Bill Thompson
(he bought *Carrie*, remember?) discussed the possibility of King's writing a novel using British novelist Dorothy Sayers's character of Detective Lord Peter Wimsey.

This was at a time when King was preparing for a fall move to England for a year's stay that ended up lasting only three months. King and
his family ended up renting a furnished house at Mourlands, 87 Aldershot Road, Fleet Hants, in the county of Hampshire, for fifty pounds a
week. (This relocation—"abridged" as it ultimately was—would result in
King's collaboration with Peter Straub on *The Talisman*.)

King apparently planned this move specifically to write a novel with
a British setting.

King's publisher, New American Library (NAL), issued a press release that said that King had temporarily relocated to England to write an English novel. "With its history of eerie writers and its penchant for mystery, England should help Stephen King produce a novel even more bloodcurdling than his previous ones—a novel that will only go to prove his title of 'Master of the Modern Horror Novel.' "

The NAL press release notwithstanding, if "Wimsey" was the novel he hoped to write while in England, King was planning on writing a *mystery,* not a horror, novel.

King sent the first chapter and the first page of the second chapter of this contemplated novel to Thompson for his review. To date, none of this material has ever appeared in print.

King has always had an affinity for British mysteries, and in 1987 he published his own original Sherlock Holmes story, "The Doctor's Case," which appeared in his collection *Nightmares & Dreamscapes* after its initial appearance in the anthology *The New Adventures of Sherlock Holmes.*

Lord Peter Wimsey and his faithful manservant, Bunter, are on their way, in Lord Peter's Bentley, to Sir Patrick Wayne's estate on the day before Halloween. Rain is coming down in torrents, and the fog has begun to creep up, making driving even more difficult. (This opening chapter contains a glaring error that would have undoubtedly been caught by King during revisions: King has Bunter driving a Bentley with the steering wheel on the *left side* of the vehicle; in England, the steering wheel, of course, is on the *right.*)

Lord Wimsey is depressed: His beloved Harriet has died during the German blitz of England; his friend Salcomb "Sally" Hardy has also recently died; Miss Climpson, a beloved member of his office staff, is suffering through her final days in a hospital; and now he is on his way to a dinner party he most definitely does not want to attend.

As they drive through the English countryside on a potholed road also dotted with shell craters, the two men cross a terribly rickety bridge, and Lord Wimsey asks Bunter to pull over so he can relieve himself. While waiting for his master, Bunter hears Lord Wimsey urgently call to him. Bunter ventures out into the rain, where he learns that Lord Wimsey has discovered that the supports on one side of the bridge they just crossed have been cut halfway through with a hatchet.

Suspicious now, they get back into the car and continue on their way to Sir Patrick's estate. Suddenly, Bunter announces to Lord Wimsey that their vehicle no longer has any braking power. The two men end up crashing into a tree, and the first chapter comes to a violent conclusion.

In chapter 2, Lord Wimsey, who was thrown from the vehicle upon impact, awakens with a terrible pain in his head and rainwater in his eyes. He is shocked to see the Bentley smashed against an elm tree, steam rising up out of its crumpled engine. Thunder rumbles, and Lord Wimsey calls out to Bunter.

And that is where these pages end.

It is a shame that Stephen King did not publish this work. (Notice that I did not say *complete* this work. King may very well have his entire *Wimsey* novel sitting in a drawer somewhere.) King deftly sets the stage for what will clearly be a thrilling tale of mystery, and he is very skilled at evoking the feel of a rain-soaked British countryside as well as the narrative sensibility of the best British mysteries.

I guess for now we will have to be content with King's aforementioned Sherlock Holmes story if we want a dose of the British King.

PUBLISHING HISTORY

1977: unpublished manuscript.

FURTHER READING

Dorothy L. Sayers's *Lord Peter Wimsey* novels and short-story collections include *Whose Body?* (1923); *Strong Poison* (1930); *Clouds of Witness* (1926); *Unnatural Death* (1927); *Lord Peter Views the Body* (1927); *The Five Red Herrings* (1931); *Have His Carcase* (1931); *Murder Must Advertise* (1933); *The Nine Tailors* (1934); *Gaudy Night* (1935); and *Busman's Honeymoon* (1937).

19

"The Night of the Tiger"

*So I became a roustabout, helping put up tents and take
them down, spreading sawdust, cleaning cages, and
sometimes selling cotton candy when the regular salesman
had to go away and bark for Chips Baily, who had malaria
and sometimes had to go someplace far away and holler.*

—from "The Night of the Tiger"

What it is: an early short story set at a circus and involving a supernatural battle of wills between two men and a tiger.

Chances of finding a copy: pretty good. The paperback *Magazine of
Fantasy & Science Fiction* collections should still be available from St.
Martin's; the Underwood-Miller hardcover is probably still available
from the usual dealers and sources. The original 1978 *Magazine of Fantasy & Science Fiction* appearance of the story will be considerably
more difficult to find.

King wrote this atmospheric tale when he was in his late teens, around
the same time he wrote "The Glass Floor," the story which was his first
professional sale. (See the feature on "The Glass Floor" in this volume.)

"The Night of the Tiger" was rejected due to its length by the editor
of *Startling Mystery Stories* (where "The Glass Floor" appeared), and it
would not be published for more than another decade, when it finally
appeared in 1978 in the *Magazine of Fantasy & Science Fiction*.

King has written that he believes "Night of the Tiger" is the better of
the two stories, and I agree with him. The story does have a few prob-

lems and inconsistencies, but overall it is quite an exciting tale and one that is astonishingly mature for a writer less than twenty years old. King's skill at describing the oppressive heat and an approaching storm and using its almost-demonic winds and the frightening colors of the sky as a metaphor for the increasing tension between the two main characters is very dramatic and told with a very confident narrative voice.

Eddie Johnston, a young roustabout for the Farnum & Williams' All-American 3-Ring Circus and Side Show, relates the story of Jason Indrasil, the circus's cruel and explosive tiger tamer, and his ongoing, mysterious feud with the taciturn Mr. Legere, a dark and moody character who follows the circus from town to town and who seems to watch over the circus's star attraction, a magnificent tiger named Green Terror.

The hatred Indrasil and Legere feel for each other is palpable, and everyone in the circus waits for the final confrontation between the two men, a battle royal which they all sense is inevitable.

One night, during a terrible storm that breaks a brutal heat wave, the two men face off during a tornado. The next morning, the bodies of Green Terror and a *second* tiger are found on the circus grounds. Mr. Indrasil has disappeared, and Mr. Legere is nowhere to be found. The circus folk are horrified and bewildered to discover that the second tiger—the one no one had ever seen before—has a long scar on the back of its neck, the same kind of scar the missing Indrasil had. Eddie remembers Mr. Legere shouting at Indrasil above the raging storm, "When a man and an animal live in the same shell, Indrasil, the instincts determine the mould!"

Trying to understand what has happened, Eddie remembers back to when Legere had told him that he was a sort of "policeman." Eddie also remembers how Green Terror seemed to be able to understand Legere's unspoken commands—and how he obeyed him.

We are left believing that Indrasil was really a tiger that had been able to take on the form of a man, that Green Terror was his enemy, and that Mr. Legere was Green Terror's "guardian," so to speak, and thus Indrasil's enemy.

"The Night of the Tiger" is Stephen King's take on reverse zoanthropy, the belief that a person has been transformed into an animal. It is an exciting tale and one well worth seeking out.

PUBLISHING HISTORY

1978: *Magazine of Fantasy & Science Fiction* (February).

1979: *The Year's Best Horror Stories, Series VII* (Gerald W. Page, editor; Daw trade paperback).

1988: *The Best Horror Stories from The Magazine of Fantasy & Science Fiction* (Edward L. Ferman and Anne Jordan, editors; St. Martin's Press mass-market paperback).

1989: *The Best Horror Stories from The Magazine of Fantasy & Science Fiction* (Edward L. Ferman and Anne Jordan, editors; St. Martin's Press mass-market paperback).

1992: *Horrorstory, Volume Three: The Year's Best Horror Stories VII; The Year's Best Horror Stories VIII; The Year's Best Horror Stories IX* (Karl Edward Wagner and Gerald W. Page, editors; Underwood-Miller hardcover).

20

"Man With a Belly"

"A man with a belly," she whispered into the darkness just before Bracken dropped off. "I am his belly. I am his guts. I am his honor."

—from "Man With a Belly"

What it is: a very rare King short story about a Sicilian Don who hires a hit man to rape his disrespectful wife.

Chances of finding a copy: extremely difficult, since "Man With a Belly" has only appeared in print twice and neither of the men's magazines where it was published (the raunchy journals *Cavalier* and *Gent*) are archived in libraries. You may be able to find one or both of the actual magazines through the usual dealers (Betts Bookstore, The Overlook Connection, etc.), but if they have a copy of either, it will be expensive (expect to pay fifty dollars or more for each mag). Since King has never reprinted the story in any of his collections, finding an original issue of these magazines is the only way you'll be able to read this gripping and very effective crime story.

The first appearance of "Man With a Belly" was in the December 1978 issue of *Cavalier* magazine. (In the seventies, as a way of making extra money and also getting his name in print, King published several short stories in somewhat "low rent" men's magazines, including many that ultimately appeared in his first collection, *Night Shift*.)

The cover of this issue of *Cavalier* listed some of the features within. They included: "Faking It: Did She or Didn't She?"; "Down Mammary

Lane With Three 'Big' D-Licious Stories"; and—of most interest to us King fans—"A New Macabre Tale by the Author of *Carrie*." In addition to numerous pictorial layouts of *astonishingly* well endowed women, this issue also boasted a serious article about the new Yukon pipeline that had originally appeared in the *Wall Street Journal*. Talk about a schizophrenic editorial policy, eh?

"Man With a Belly" is Stephen King as crime writer. (Other King stories of this period and genre include "The Fifth Quarter," "The Ledge," and "The Wedding Gig.")

"Man With a Belly" is a Sicilian idiom for a man with an "iron fist inside the glove." In other words, a man with balls, *cojones*, a stand-up guy.

John Bracken is a hit man who is very good at his job. One day he gets a call from Benito Torreos, the right-hand man—the *consigliere*—of crime lord Vito Correzente. (Stephen King no doubt read the early-seventies' classic *The Godfather* and paid close attention to the subsequent *Godfather* movies. "Man With a Belly" shows the obvious influence of Mario Puzo's and Francis Ford Coppola's American Mafia masterpieces.)

Torreos tells Bracken that his boss has a job for him if he wants it. Bracken tells Torreos he is available, and the next day he meets with crime lord Don Correzente.

"I want you to make a hit," Correzente tells Bracken. The fee, Bracken learns, is thirty thousand before and twenty thousand after. Bracken immediately grows suspicious. This is much too high a price for a run-of-the-mill rubout.

But then Correzente tells Bracken, "You doan have to make no bones." This means that no one has to die.

Bracken learns that Correzente wants him to rape his wife, Mrs. Norma Correzente, a white Protestant trophy who has a very heavy gambling problem. Norma White Correzente was a "fine, aristocratic-looking woman with dark hair, a self-confident way of moving, and sleek body lines." Correzente had married Norma because "of an itch." He wanted her body, her youth, and her bloodline. Norma wanted Don Vito's money. Once Norma was legally Mrs. Correzente, she indulged her gambling compulsion to the tune of almost ten thousand a week at the tables.

This was unbearable for the elderly crime lord: "Don Vittorio was being laughed at. It could not be borne."

So he hired John Bracken. "He had struck upon the solution because it was fitting. It was cure, object lesson, and vengeance all in one."

Bracken accepts the job and, after two weeks of preparation, grabs Norma as she is walking through a park by pretending to be a loser junkie slouching on a bench.

The rape is brutal: Norma fights back viciously, and both she and Bracken end up bloodied and bruised.

Bracken fulfills his contract, and when he is finished, he tells Norma Correzente what he was told to say, reciting from memory. "I am told to tell you that this is how your husband pays a debt to his honor. I am told to tell you that he is a man with a belly. I am told to tell you that all debts are paid and there is honor again."

However, as Bracken gets up off the ground to leave, Mrs. Correzente says, "Wait."

She then offers Bracken *twice* what her husband paid him to do a job for *her*.

Norma wants Bracken to make her pregnant so that she can hit Don Vito with the ultimate dishonor: He wants an heir, and she will allow him to believe that he was virile enough to make a son, but then, after the baby is born, she tells Bracken, "at the right time, I will kill him with the truth."

Bracken takes *this* job as well and spends the next ten weeks living in Norma's secret second apartment, having sex with her repeatedly until she becomes pregnant. For this, his fee is one hundred thousand dollars.

Nine months later, Bracken receives another call from the *consigliere*. Don Vito wants to see him. Norma is no more, having died during childbirth, and the Don now wants to ask Bracken a single question.

Bracken knows he must obey this summons or he will be dead within days.

Bracken visits Don Vito, who is now on his deathbed. The Don tells Bracken that his new son, who is ill but alive in an incubator, has blue eyes and that "there is no blue-eyed Sicilian."

Bracken asks him what his question is, and the Don replies, "I have ask my question."

Bracken knows what the Don is asking: Did he—an old man in failing health—make a son? Or did Bracken double-cross the Don and "do a job" for Norma, thereby insulting the Don and putting a "stain on his pride"?

Bracken sees deeper, however, and knows that the Don is more concerned about dying with his "belly" than in exacting revenge on Bracken. So Bracken does what he knows he must. He says to the Don, "How stupid you are. Death has made you senile. I have my own belly. Do you think I would take my own leavings? . . . The baby's eyes will go brown. Too bad you won't see it."

Bracken then leaves Don Vittorio to his death and returns to Palm Springs, confident that he acted like a man with a belly and also did his jobs—both of them—like the professional he was.

"Man With a Belly" has not appeared in print since 1979, nor has it been adapted for the movies.

Publishing History

1978: *Cavalier* (December).
1979: *Gent* (November/December).

21

"The King Family and the Wicked Witch"

On the Secret Road in the town of Bridgton, there lived a wicked witch. Her name was Witch Hazel.

—from "The King Family and the Wicked Witch"

What it is: a short story King wrote for his children in 1977 and which he gave in January 1978 to a college friend who was then the editor of a Kansas newspaper, the *Flint*.

Chances of finding a copy: probably impossible. I have not been able to track down the newspaper in which this piece was originally published, leading me to believe that they have ceased publication. Thus, back issues are probably nonexistent except in a few libraries around the, I presume, Manhattan, Kansas, area, since there is a display ad in the text for a Manhattan business. King insider and authority Douglas E. Winter remembered this piece appearing in a Kansas publication, and his recollection, plus the ad for the Manhattan Moped shop on the same page as King's text, made me conclude that the *Flint* was published in Kansas. I may be wrong, since I have not been able to confirm this.

This charming children's story was published for the first and only time in 1978 in (presumably) the Kansas *Flint* and was introduced with the following editor's note:

> Stephen King and I went to college together. No, we were not the best of friends, but we did share a few brews together at

University Motor Inn. We did work for the school newspaper at the same time. No, Steve and I are not best friends. But I sure am glad he "made it." He worked hard and believed in himself. After eight million book sales, it's hard to remember him as a typically broke student. We all knew he'd make it though.

Last January I wrote of a visit with Steve over the Holiday vacation. We talked about his books, *Carrie, 'Salem's Lot, The Shining,* and the soon to be released, *The Stand.* We talked about how Stanley Kubrick wants to do the film versions of his new books. We didn't talk about the past much though. We talked of the future—his kids, FLINT . . .

He gave me a copy of a story he had written for his children. We almost ran it then, but there was much concern on the staff as to how it would be received by our readers. We didn't run it. Well, we've debated long enough. It's too cute for you not to read it! We made the final decision after spending an evening watching TV last week. There were at least 57 more offensive things said, not to mention all the murders, rapes, and wars . . . we decided to let you be the judge. If some of you parents might be offended by the word "fart," you'd better not read it—but don't stop your kids, they'll love it!

According to my research, this story was originally titled "The King Family and the Farting Cookie." In my *Complete Stephen King Encyclopedia,* Douglas Winter mentioned a story with that title and admitted to having held a copy of it in his hands. It is likely that the title was changed so that the word "farting" would not be in a family newspaper's headline.

So what is this legendary tale about?

"The King Family and the Wicked Witch" is a *very* funny story which has as its main characters Stephen and Tabitha King and their two children, Naomi and Joe. (The Kings' third child, Owen, would be born in 1978.)

☠ Once upon a time, a very wicked witch named Witch Hazel lived on the Secret Road in Bridgton, Maine. This witch was very wicked indeed and had once changed a Prince from the Kingdom of New Hampshire into a woodchuck. We're talkin' *mean:* She had also changed a little kid's favorite kitty into a pile of whipped cream and especially liked to turn baby carriages into big piles of horse turds while the mommies shopped.

This wicked witch hated the King family. "There was a daddy who wrote books. There was a mommy who wrote poems and cooked food. There was a girl named Naomi who was six years old. . . . There was a boy named Joe who was four years old."

Witch Hazel hated the Kings because they were happy. She decided to get even with them by putting four terrible curses on them that she would hide in four cookies. She dressed up, and on the pretext of getting some of the daddy's books autographed, she went to their house. As she was leaving, she gave them each a cookie, which they all eagerly ate.

These were cursed cookies, and when they ate them, dreadful things happened. The daddy's nose turned into a banana, and when he tried to write, all he could type was the word banana. The mommy's hands turned into milk bottles, and "she could not even pick her nose." When Joe and Naomi ate their cookies, they started to cry and could not stop.

The happiest family in Bridgton was now the saddest family, and Witch Hazel was delighted.

A month after eating the cookies, the King family came upon a woodchuck caught in a trap in the woods near their home. They all worked together to free it. Daddy squeezed some banana oil out of his nose to loosen the trap, Mommy gave the woodchuck some milk to drink from her hands, and Joe and Naomi pulled open the trap.

As soon as he was released, the spell on the woodchuck was broken, and he became once again the Prince of New Hampshire. He then used the power he had as Prince to break Witch Hazel's spells, and the Kings were all changed back to normal.

They all wanted to teach Witch Hazel a lesson, and so the Kings and the Prince baked a magic cookie using a special spell the Prince knew. They then dressed up as itinerant orange pickers from California and went to Witch Hazel's house to sell her the cookie.

As they had expected she would, the wicked witch stole the cookie and ate it up. The cookie had three-hundred-year-old baked beans from New Hampshire in it, and before Witch Hazel could cast another spell, she began farting. Her first fart blew all the fur off her cat, Basta; blew out all the windows of her house; and sent her flying up into the air like a rocket.

"Brrrrrrappp!" went the second fart, and this one knocked down her house and the Bridgton Trading Post. "You could see Dom Cardozi sitting on the toilet where he had been pooping."

Witch Hazel cut another fart that smelled like "two million egg salad sandwiches" and flew up into the sky, never to be seen again. (That night, Barbara Walters reported that a 747 had sighted a "UFW"—an "Unidentified Flying Witch" over Bridgton.)

And the Kings lived happily ever after, but the daddy never again used the word "banana" in his books.

"The King Family and the Wicked Witch" is very funny and contains some real-life King family details. King mentions the family's red Cadillac and blue truck, and he writes that the mommy was writing poems and cooking. Today Tabitha King is an established novelist in her own right, but back in the late seventies, she was obviously busy raising their kids and running the household.

There are also a couple of "Kingish" images in this brief children's tale. King writes that the witch would see the mommy reading Joe a story and "her bony fingers would itch to cast a spell." In *Thinner,* the Gypsy man's bony fingers *do* cast a terrible spell on Billy Halleck. Also, the character of Dom Cardozi in this story could be seen as yet another *Thinner* foreshadowing, this time in the character of Italian mobster Richard Ginelli.

This tale is King writing to entertain his kids, something we can be certain he has done since they were old enough to be read to. This stuff usually never sees print—except in rare instances when King specifically gives someone a story and permission to print it, as he did with this tale. (Of course, the exception to this is the novel *The Eyes of the Dragon,* which King wrote for his daughter, Naomi, but which he planned from the beginning on publishing.)

"The King Family and the Wicked Witch" may be a tad scatological, but I'll bet his kids absolutely loved it. After all, there is *nothing* like a good fart joke to crack up a six-year-old, right?

PUBLISHING HISTORY

1978: *Flint* (Kansas).

22

"On Becoming a Brand Name"

Being a brand name is all right. Trying to be a writer,
trying to fill the blank sheet in an honorable and truthful
way, is better. And if those two things ever change places
on me (and it can happen with a creepy, unobtrusive ease),
I'm in a lot of trouble.

—from "On Becoming a Brand Name"

What it is: an entertaining nonfiction essay in which King ruminates about how quickly he became known almost exclusively as a horror writer after the publication of *Carrie* and *'Salem's Lot*. King also provides biographical details about his early life as a writer and discusses the creation of his first several novels.

Chances of finding a copy: difficult if you want to own an *original* appearance of the piece, since both editions of *Fear Itself* are out of print and the rare *Adelina* appearance will be even more difficult to locate. The good news, though, is that because *Fear Itself* was a collection of serious literary criticism about King's work (and, by extension, the entire horror genre), it was purchased for circulation (and reference) by many libraries when it was initially published and may still be on the shelves at a library in your area.

This important, introspective essay by King was written when King seemed to still be somewhat awed and humbled by his sudden, breathtaking success in the field of horror fiction and film. Which is not to say that he still isn't amazed by his worldwide achievements (my guess

111

would be, how could he *not* be?), but after two or so decades of nothing but huge earnings and number-one bestsellers, the "surprise factor" is probably somewhat muted.

What is very interesting to the King fan in this piece is King's chronicling of his writing career from his high school years through *The Stand*. King coyly refrains from naming his early novels, instead referring to them as Book 1 through Book 7. This was intentional. At the time he wrote this essay, he was publishing paperback originals using the name "Richard Bachman," and his pseudonym had not yet been discovered.

King gives a little info about each book, and from his hints (and details found elsewhere) we can make some pretty good guesses as to what books he was talking about.

King writes, "I wrote my first novel when I was a freshman in college and submitted it to a first novel competition. . . . I thought the book had an outside chance, and I was enormously proud to have fathered such a wonderful creation at the age of nineteen." This novel was *The Long Walk,* and it was rejected with a standard "Dear Contributor" note. Ironically, *The Long Walk* is now considered one of King's strongest works, with a gripping premise and realistic characters.

King describes Book 2 as "a 500-page novel about a race riot in a major (but fictional) American city." Entitled *Sword in the Darkness,* it, too, was rejected, this time by *twelve* different publishers. King describes *Sword in the Darkness* as "a badly busted flush."

King sent Book 3—*Getting It On*—to "the Editor of *The Parallax View*" at Doubleday and for a time actually had hope that they might buy the book. The novel was ultimately rejected (after three rewrites) and was later published as *Rage* under King's Richard Bachman pseudonym.

Book 4, we now know, was *The Running Man,* initially rejected by both Doubleday and Ace Books and later published as a Bachman book. King tells us: "Writing it was a fantastic, white-hot experience; the book was written in one month, the bulk of it in the one week of winter vacation." Several years later, in his essay " 'Ever Et Raw Meat' " (see the feature on that essay in this volume), King would write, "*The Running Man* (published under the name Richard Bachman) was written in four days during a snowy February vacation when I was teaching high school." In "Brand Name," he writes of *The Running Man*: "The book, unfortunately, was not fantastic."

Book 5 was *Carrie,* and in "Brand Name," King writes of its circuitous path to publication, remembering how he threw away the first few pages of the story and how his wife, Tabitha, fished them out of the trash, read them, and encouraged him to go on with the story.

King describes Book 6 as a "psychological suspense novel." According to Douglas Winter in *Stephen King: The Art of Darkness,* it was the still-unpublished novel *Blaze.*

Book 7 was *'Salem's Lot* (originally titled *Second Coming*), and King tells the story of how a dinner-table conversation with his wife and their longtime friend Chris Chesley about Bram Stoker's *Dracula* generated the idea of a vampire story set in modern America. (See my *Complete Stephen King Encyclopedia* for an interview with Chris Chesley in which he discusses this conversation but self-effacingly refuses to take any credit for inspiring King's novel.)

All this bibliographic info aside, though, what's most engaging about "On Becoming a Brand Name" is King's very appealing conversational tone and the undeniable feeling that he is speaking directly to *you,* and nobody else, as he recounts some of the details of his early career and how he became a brand name.

King talks about the production mix-up that led to the publication of the paperback edition of *Carrie* without his name or the title of the book on its cover. He also talks about doing the mandatory "Author Tour" and being asked to give an autograph while sitting on a toilet bowl in Pittsburgh.

King also discusses what being a "brand name" means and makes the point that perhaps such a sobriquet should not necessarily be considered a negative assessment of a writer's "worth":

Perhaps the first brand name writer was Charles Dickens. In America people used to line the docks when the ship bearing the next installment of Little Dorritt *or* Oliver Twist *was due.*

Picking up this thought an astonishing sixteen years later, King writes in the foreword to his 1996 serialized bestseller *The Green Mile:*

Dicken's serialized novels were immensely popular; so popular, in fact, that one of them precipitated a tragedy in Baltimore. A large group of Dickens fans crowded onto a waterfront dock, anticipating the arrival of an English ship with copies of the final installment of The Old Curiosity Shop *on board. According to the story, several would-be readers were jostled into the water and drowned.*

"On Becoming a Brand Name" is the "nonfiction" Stephen King at his best. He possesses an enviable talent. He can make the potentially deadly-dry recitation of the early years of a writer's career read like an adventure story, complete with drama, excitement, humor, and sage insight.

For King fans who want to get to know King the man a little better, "On Becoming a Brand Name" provides a fascinating glimpse at the man *behind* the brand name.

PUBLISHING HISTORY

1980: *Adelina* (February).
1982: *Fear Itself: The Horror Fiction of Stephen King* (Underwood-Miller hardcover).
1985: *Fear Itself: The Horror Fiction of Stephen King* (Signet paperback).

23

"Remembering John"

*Lennon was a cynic, a poet, a sarcastic son of a bitch, a
public figure, a private man. . . . And he had his fans like
me, who looked at the paper on the morning of Tuesday
the ninth of December and then sat down hard, unable to
believe it at first . . . and then, horribly, all too able to
believe it.*

—from "Remembering John"

What it is: Stephen King's moving eulogy of John Lennon, written
within days after Lennon's assassination on December 8, 1980, and
published five days later.

Chances of finding a copy: extremely difficult if not impossible for
most fans. As with other King writings only published in the *Bangor
Daily News,* you will have to find an online database or a library that
archives back issues of the newspaper. The only other option would be
to use a library in Maine (where the paper is more than likely available)
or write to the *Bangor Daily News* directly (do *not* call) and inquire as
to whether or not specific articles from back issues of the paper are
available for sale to the public.

Like many baby boomers (those born in the post–World War II years,
between 1946 and 1964), Stephen King grew up with the Beatles. The
Fab Four's gestalt permeated the sixties, redefining social mores and
expanding the contemporary global consciousness the way the Renaissance redefined art and culture for mankind from the fourteenth to the

seventeenth centuries. Paul was adorable and clever; George, quiet and shy; Ringo, lovably goofy.

And then there was John.

Lennon was one of those rare characters who dramatically emanated gravitas. His words seem to carry more weight; his art was more serious and less disposable than you would expect from a pop musician; his political and spiritual philosophy grew from the same soil as did that of Ghandi, Martin Luther King, and Christ. John preached love and equality and peace.

Paul and George and Ringo wrote and sang about love, too, but it was often within the context of romantic love and the girl they wanted to hold hands with or dance with.

John, on the other hand, was known to write and sing that love was all you need, and he boldly demanded that the world give peace a chance. Paul was willing to let it be; John wanted a revolution.

No doubt about it, John Lennon was a groundbreaking artistic figure on the landscape of twentieth-century art.

Then, in December 1980, at the age of forty, John Lennon was murdered by a psychopath in New York City, mere steps from the front door of his fortresslike home, the Dakota.

Like many of us, Stephen King was moved to write about Lennon after reading about his untimely death. "Remembering John," King's essay, is the result.

King begins this memorial with a slurry of no-nonsense facts about what John was *not*. He was not the first ex-Beatle to enjoy critical success. (George's *All Things Must Pass* album won that race.) He was also not the *handsome* former Beatle: We all know that award goes to Paul. Nor was John a movie star, as was Ringo.

"But somehow, for me," King writes, "he was the only ex-Beatle who really seemed to matter."

King talks about John's persona and his charm, touching on some of the landmark moments in John's life, including his "We're more popular than Jesus" remark. King also discusses his own initiation into the world of rock and roll. (It was getting a 78-rpm single of Elvis singing "Don't Be Cruel" that did it for King.)

King then astutely coalesces the enormous *difference* the Beatles made and the lines of demarcation that were drawn between parents and kids following the Beatles' arrival on American shores.

King repeats a story told to him by his friend Phil Thompson.

Thompson and his girlfriend were sitting on Phil's living-room floor watching the Beatles' *Ed Sullivan Show* appearance. Phil's parents were sitting on the sofa behind them. Phil remembered that "when the Beatles started to play, I felt something snap between the people that were sitting on the floor and the people who were sitting on the couch."

Ain't it the truth?

About halfway through "Remembering John," King makes some biting remarks about what it feels like to be a celebrity in America:

We make a business here, apparently, of dining upon the bodies of those who have given us the most pleasure and some of our fondest memories; first we lionize them, and then we eat them.

Ironically, though, King then writes about feeling "a little bit like a ghoul" when he went out and spent two hundred dollars on a collection of Beatles records the day after John died—something that millions of other Beatles fans around the world did, too. King can clearly recognize the hunger on the part of fans for more and more of their icons; he, too, cannot help but feed that hunger when it comes to himself.

It's a strange paradigm we're talking about here: If Stephen King were to slip the bonds of this earth someday—for whatever reason—his fans would go out and buy all his books in a vain attempt to be closer to their idol. It happened with Princess Diana, John Denver, and Tupac Shakur, and it happened with John Lennon.

"Remembering John" is a tribute and a tirade and an important essay by one of the world's most important literary figures, but it is also a nostalgic look back by just one more John Lennon fan, except that this fan knows what it is like to be on *both* sides of that strange fan–celebrity coin.

PUBLISHING HISTORY

1980: *Bangor Daily News* (December 13–14).

24

"The Lawnmower Man"

*One trembles to think of that mysterious thing in the soul,
which seems to acknowledge no human jurisdiction, but in
spite of the individual's own innocent self, will still dream
horrid dreams, and mutter unmentionable thoughts.*

—Herman Melville (epigraph of the
December 1981 issue of *Bizarre Adventures*)

The only problem with great days is that they never last. . . .

—from the comic adaptation of "The Lawnmower Man"

What it is: a 21-page, 130-panel, 1,809-word comic-book adaptation
of Stephen King's *Night Shift* short story "The Lawnmower Man."

Chances of finding a copy: good luck. The original-text version of
this story is, of course, readily available. The comic adaptation, though
(with new text written by King based on his original short story), was
published only once in *Bizarre Adventures,* a Marvel comic book, and
never reprinted. Since comics are rarely (if ever) archived in libraries, the
usual book and magazine dealers would be your only sources in scoring an item such as this. There is also a slim chance that Marvel *may*
have back issues of the publication available for sale, but since the magazine was originally published in 1981 and almost twenty years have

passed, the odds are against it. If you're intent on finding this comic, you can try writing to Marvel (*don't* call); you can also try contacting the dealers who specialize in these kinds of items (start with The Overlook Connection and Betts Bookstore). Horror and science-fiction conventions are also a good place to hunt for things like *Bizarre Adventures*. I have seen the magazine occasionally offered for sale in the $15–$25 price range.

Stephen King's short story "The Lawnmower Man" is a quintessential illustration of one of the kernel theses of many of King's tales: an ordinary man is plunged headfirst and without warning into an extraordinary situation.

Harold Parkette is your basic suburbanite, with a beer belly, a fondness for naps and watching baseball on TV, and of course, a *lawn*. The full-page opening panel of this adaptation shows Harold, his wife, and their comely daughter standing in front of a gigantic lawn, the picture of the self-satisfied homeowner and his family.

One day, though, Harold's peaceful life is disrupted when the Castonmeyer's dog chases the Smith's cat, Shasta, under Harold's lawnmower, making the kitty look as if he "spent a hard night in a Mixmaster."

The accident causes Harold to lose his passion for his lawn *and* his Lawnboy, and he ultimately ends up trading the hexed mower for a tank of high-test and a radial tire. When Harold learns that the kid who has been mowing for him (a kid with the last name "Stark," a surname only revealed in the comic version—ring a bell?) has gone off to college, he doesn't hire a replacement. Consequently, Harold's lawn grows and grows and grows.

Harold finally makes a call to Pastoral Greenery. They promise to send out their "best man," a lawnmower man named Karras, and Harold returns to his baseball game and his nap, satisfied.

Harold is awakened by the arrival of Karras, a guy so huge, "Harold half-believed he had swallowed a basketball."

After pointing the way to the backyard, Harold goes back to sleep but is again awakened, this time by a roar from a lawnmower so loud that it sounded to Harold like "the first lap of the Indy 500." When he goes out back to investigate, he encounters a scene he can only describe with horror as a "pure nightmare!"

The lawnmower is mowing the lawn by itself, and following behind it, *stark naked*, is Karras, voraciously eating the lawn clippings. As Harold watches, the lawnmower swerves to chase after a mole; it grinds it up in its blade, and then Karras gleefully eats the remains of the hapless rodent. Harold vomits, faints, and is awakened by Karras, who tells him that his boss—who, it turns out, is Pan, the ancient god of fertility—is always amenable to (and pretty much expects) a sacrifice from his customers after a lawn job well done. Harold tries to humor Karras (he spontaneously tells him, "God bless the grass"), and when Karras heads toward the front of the house to complete his mowing job, Harold runs inside and calls the police.

However, it's too late. Karras's demonic lawnmower bursts into Harold's living room, chews through the coffee table, and then gives Harold what Karras evilly describes as a "whole-body haircut."

The 131 illustrations of this adaptation (the 130 of the story plus the magazine's cover drawing) were rendered by Walter Simonson, the artist who would later draw the final segment of the 1985 *Heroes for Hope Starring the X-Men* comic book that Stephen King would contribute to a few years hence.

Simonson's artwork captured perfectly the odd, mythical feel of King's story. Harold looks precisely as we would expect him to look; his hot-blooded young daughter has a real Demi Moore look; and Simonson does a terrific job depicting Harold's terror through well-drawn panels of overlapping faces and fragments of faces combined with enormous free-floating words.

I especially like the way Simonson draws Karras. The Lawnmower Man devours his prey naked, you will recall, but except for a few modest scenes of Karras's gigantic butt, Simonson keeps this comic-book version determinedly PG—quite an achievement, since there is actually a scene in the story in which the cops ask Harold if he can see Karras's genitals and he replies that he most definitely *can*. King, Simonson, and Marvel all obviously wanted this magazine to be available to teens; the gore was therefore not as graphic as it could have been, and even though Karras may have *hailed* from the nether regions, we were thankfully spared the sight of his own *personal* nether regions.

This Marvel adaptation of King's "The Lawnmower Man" is a truly unique entry in the catalog of King. It is, as far as I know, the only *independently published* comic-book version of one of King's stories. It is also one of only three comic adaptations of King's stories to date, the other two being King's *Creepshow* adaptation of his short story "The Crate" and his adaptation of his story "Weeds," as "The Lonesome Death of Jordy Verrill," also in *Creepshow*.

PUBLISHING HISTORY

1981: *Bizarre Adventures* (no. 29; December).

25

"Between Rock and a Soft Place"

Our writer turned on his radio looking for some hard-driving music, but what he heard was—well, horrifying.

—*Playboy*'s introductory blurb to King's article
"Between Rock and a Soft Place"

What it is: King's lengthy article about the dearth of rock music on AM radio, coupled with an informed and entertaining overview of the history of rock and roll in America in the twentieth century.

Chances of finding a copy: pretty good. Even though *Playboy* is rarely archived in libraries, back issues of the magazine are available from used-magazine dealers all across the country. (Some dealers sell nothing *but* back issues of *Playboy*.) To narrow your search, though, start with the usual King dealers (Betts Bookstore, The Overlook Connection, etc.). *Playboy* itself also sells back issues of the magazine, although their inventory of issues from the sixties through the eighties is incomplete. (*Playboy* says they have a "wide selection of issues from the sixties through the eighties," but certain issues *are* out of print and unavailable.) Call 1-800-345-6066 to search for a particular issue, such as the one in which this King article (January 1982) appears.

It may be a cliché, but many of us really *do* read *Playboy* for the articles. How can we help it when they run important essays like "Between Rock and a Soft Place"—an article about rock music—by America's leading writer of horror fiction? One thing you certainly *cannot* call *Playboy* is *predictable*.

122

In this lengthy article, King talks about renting a car with only an AM radio and not being able to find any kick-ass rock and roll all the way from Boston to Bangor.

It occurs to him that rock and roll is not just *missing in action;* it is, in fact, quite *dead.* He talks about some survivors, like Bruce Springsteen and the Rolling Stones, but there is no doubting that this essay is a eulogy.

"Between Rock and a Soft Place" is undeniably dated; it was written, after all, in 1980, although it wasn't published until 1982. (One wonders about such a lengthy delay.) King's comments about the homogenization of contemporary music and his belief that a type of music is dead when it ceases to influence the culture is as timely as the latest Savage Garden album.

After the death of straight-on rock (thanks, in part, to the disco infection of the seventies), rap was the next musical form that fit King's definition of "living music." Rap influenced the culture of the late eighties and nineties like no other musical form since—well, since rock and roll first reared its hormone-drenched head in the fifties. Rock scared the living bejesus out of an entire population of affluent, postwar parents who thought their kids would grow up to actually *like* crew cuts and wearing ties to dances. Rap manifested the same outlaw sensibility that made adults *nervous.*

With the hindsight of almost twenty years of music and pop culture in our collective consciousness, this article is well worth seeking out and reading. In "Between Rock and a Soft Place," King astutely chronicles the history of contemporary music in America from the fifties on, as he did the entire horror genre in *Danse Macabre.*

King concludes this piece with a sequence that elevates it from just another navel-contemplating baby boomer's look at his past into a wistful and nostalgic memoir about growing up:

Maybe what happened to AM is perfectly simple: It got old. It hung in there through Woodstock, and then it started to run out of gas. Even Dick Clark is starting to show signs of age. It's a sad thought, and it's a little startling, but it fits and it has its own comforting logic. None of us thought we were going to get old when we were 15, and look what happened. If it has to be FM, it has to be—the same way a guy like me says, if it has to be 33

*going on 34, with all-of-a-sudden white in the beard and those
funny little wrinkles around the corners of the eyes, it has to be.*

   *When we were young enough to believe that rock 'n' roll would
live forever, we believed the same of ourselves.*

Amen. Or better . . . rock on.

PUBLISHING HISTORY

1982: *Playboy* (January).

26

"My High School Horrors"

I liked teaching a lot, and most of my high school horrors were small ones. If they were filmed, they'd be grade-B movies.

—from "My High School Horrors"

What it is: a hilarious essay about teaching high school and the "horrors" King experienced during his two years as an English teacher at Hampden Academy.

Chances of finding a copy: almost impossible unless you can find a library somewhere that archives *Sourcebook* or can buy a copy of the 1986 *Castle Rock* reprint appearance of this piece. (Try Betts Bookstore or The Overlook Connection.)

King taught high school English from 1971 through 1973 and for the most part enjoyed the experience. However, there were some unavoidable horrors he had to deal with during this time, and in this essay he discusses six of the more memorable ones.

The Thing That Wouldn't Shut Up

This is the student who, quite simply, *never stops talking*. King notes that teachers always put the Thing That Wouldn't Shut Up at the front of the room, but "it inevitably works its way to the back before long." King also recalls that even if teachers kept all other students away from The Thing, it would then spend the day talking to itself. "Can anything stop The Thing That Wouldn't Shut Up?" King asks. "I don't think so," he concludes. "But teachers can pray for laryngitis."

THE CLASSROOM OF THE LIVING DEAD

This phenomenon, King writes, occurs when the teacher assigns the class something a tad more challenging than they would like, such as a short story by Eudora Welty or even one of James Joyce's brilliant (but difficult) *Dubliners* tales. Even though the class may most assuredly be a discussion period, in the Classroom of the Living Dead, *no one talks*, and the teacher is faced with the horror of *dead air*. King tells the story of his student teaching days and how his supervisor gave him a surefire tactic for resurrecting the Living Dead: She would ask the students a question and give them fifteen seconds to answer. If no one did, she would remove a shoe. She would then remove her other shoe if no one spoke up in the next thirty seconds. "My friends," the supervisor would tell her class, "we are either going to have a classroom discussion or I will be stark naked before 9:15." King does not reveal if he ever tried this version of "strip teaching" on his own classes.

THE SMELL FROM HELL

"Being a teenager is tough on the glands," King writes, and the Smell From Hell is that unique, odiferous emanation—"the horrible smell of sweat, dirt, and various slowly flowing oils"—pouring off those students who deign to shower no more than, say, once a month or so. King concludes this section with the rhetorical question "[S]hould schools issue gas masks to teachers?"

THE INCREDIBLE OSCULATING CREATURE

This creature actually consists of two separate organisms joined at the lips. When a teacher comes across this beast in the hall, an auditorium, or even in class, it is extremely difficult, King reveals, to know what to say. "No matter how the situation is handled, the teacher looks and sounds dumb." King writes that he once stopped a hallway make-out session by asking the male half of the organism, "When you're done, can I try?" He also tells us that this line once almost got him punched out. However, the worst thing about coming upon The Incredible Osculating Creature, King tells us, is coming upon it at 8:15 in the morning. "It makes you feel old."

THE HORROR OF THE UNKNOWN NOISES

There are many sound effects heard in the typical high school class-room, including the "Band Squeak," the "Maxwell House Singing Cof-feepot," and the "Champagne Cork." The Band Squeak is the sweaty palm across the desk sound, the Coffeepot is the cheek-tapping melody sound, and the Champagne Cork is that old pop-the-finger-out-of-the-mouth sound that almost anyone can make. King heard them all when he was teaching and also hilariously notes that there were *other* sounds—"unmentionable sounds" (and we all know what he's talking about)—"and they are most embarrassing when they come from behind the teacher's desk."

THE MONSTER THAT WOULDN'T TURN OFF ITS RADIO

During World Series time, King writes, every student "suddenly sprouts a hearing aid." Then there are those students who carry a radio to class with them every day—"a radio roughly the size of a Samsonite two-suiter suitcase." It's always some other kid who turns it on in a quiet classroom, giving several people—"including the teacher"—heart attacks.

King also writes that there were occasionally more serious problems in his classrooms but that these six are the ones "that regularly put a *gotcha!* into a teacher's day."

"Now," he concludes, "what have I left out?"

PUBLISHING HISTORY

1982: *Sourcebook: The Magazine for Seniors.*
1986: *Castle Rock: The Stephen King Newsletter* (February; as "High School Horrors").

27

Foreword to Harlan Ellison's
Stalking the Nightmare

If I knew I was going to be in a strange city without all the
magical gris-gris *of the late 20th century—Amex Card,*
MasterCard, Visa Card, Blue Cross card, driver's license,
Avis Wizard Number, Social Security number—and if I
further knew I was going to have a severe myocardial
infarction, and if I could pick one person in all the world
to be with me at the moment I felt the hacksaw blade run
down my left arm and the sledgehammer hit me on the left
tit, that person would be Harlan Ellison.

—from King's *Foreword*

What it is: Stephen King's very "Ellisonesque" foreword to the legendary Harlan Ellison's 1982 collection of truly imaginative short stories and nonfiction essays called *Stalking the Nightmare*.

Chances of finding a copy: excellent. *Stalking the Nightmare* is still in
print and is available as a Berkley paperback.

This foreword isn't technically "lost," for it's readily available, but since
it would not have been read by King fans unless they were also big
Harlan Ellison fans (and of course there are many who are), I felt it
warranted inclusion here as a heads-up to King fans who may *not* be
Ellison readers and thus have not seen this terrific piece by King.
   King begins this foreword by telling us, "It drives my wife crazy, and

I'm sorry it does, but I can't really help it." What drives the esteemed Mrs. King—as King so delicately puts it—"absolutely BUGFUCK"? Homilies, little sayings, proverbs, and adages. Things like "There's a heartbeat in every potato." (What?) "You'll never be hung for your beauty." "[F]ools' names, and their faces, are often seen in public places."

Why does King tell us this seemingly irrelevant stuff in a foreword to a book by Harlan Ellison? Because King uses the opportunity of recounting this family anecdote to write it as Harlan Ellison would.

King is—correctly—making the point that Ellison's voice is so singular, so unique, and so individual that after reading him for a while, you cannot avoid writing like him.

King also talks about the art and craft of writing and how important it is for a writer to begin "sounding like himself sooner or later" or risk ending up being nothing more than "a ventriloquist's dummy."

While discussing this "development of a writer" process, King makes a couple of revealing remarks about what it's like to look back and reread stuff written when you were young and inexperienced:

> [T]here comes a day when you look back on the stuff you wrote when you were seventeen ... or twenty-two ... or twenty-eight ... and say to yourself, Good God! If I was this bad, how did I ever get any better?
>
> They don't call that stuff "juvenilia" for nothing, friends and neighbors.

King also lists some of the writers who he believes have influenced his own distinctive narrative voice. They include H. P. Lovecraft, Raymond Chandler, Ross MacDonald, Robert Parker, Dorothy Sayers, Peter Straub, and last but not least, Harlan Ellison.

King then begins his discussion of Harlan Ellison as a writer and man and uses the word "ferocious" several times to describe both Harlan's personality and writing style. He also bluntly admits, "There are folks in the biz who don't like Harlan much."

Those of us who write for a living and who often work in the fields of dark fantasy and science fiction know this to be true, but it is a surprise to read it in a foreword to one of Harlan's own books. However, we *are* talking about Harlan Ellison here, a man who holds the written word in such high regard that there is no chance in hell that he would even *consider* editing out King's comment about his occasionally prickly mien; nor would Harlan likely ever ask King to delete it so that he could look good to his *Stalking the Nightmare* readers.

Harlan Ellison is so ferociously passionate (there's that word again) about writing that he did not even ask King to revise his foreword after King went on at length about a specific short story scheduled to be included in *Stalking the Nightmare* but ultimately cut from the final roster. It is quite something to read a lengthy discourse about the Ellison story "Invulnerable"—complete with a two-paragraph excerpt—and then read Harlan's lengthy footnote explaining why the acclaimed story was *not* in the book.

It's likely that Harlan Ellison is one of the few writers who would have left King's review of "Invulnerable" in his foreword—and probably against the wishes of his editors. This is just a guess, but knowing how this business works, if it was anyone else but Harlan Ellison, King would have received a call or a fax from an editor telling him that one of the stories he talked about was cut and asking, "Could you please revise your foreword accordingly? Thank you very much."

King's foreword to *Stalking the Nightmare* is a literary tour de force and a real display of stylistic virtuosity. In the essay, King notes that milk always takes on the flavor of whatever it stands next to in the refrigerator. (This was another of those sayings—King got it from his mother—that drove his wife Tabitha crazy.)

In the case of Harlan Ellison, he'd probably make everything in the refrigerator taste like him—to expand (badly) a clever and evocative metaphor. King understands this, and in what is probably the surest proof that he did his job with this foreword, I can tell you that you will not finish reading this piece without wanting to *immediately* dive into the collection it introduces.

That's what I did; and you will, too.

PUBLISHING HISTORY

1982: *Stalking the Nightmare* (Phantasia Press hardcover).
1984: *Stalking the Nightmare* (Berkley Books mass-market paperback).

28

The Cannibals

Worst thing I could think of.

—Stephen King, taking about the plot of *The Cannibals*

Cannibal: A human being who eats human flesh.

—*Webster's New Collegiate Dictionary*

What it is: an unpublished 450-page (100,000-word?) novel King wrote in longhand while on the set of *Creepshow.*

Chances of finding a copy: zero. Copies of this manuscript have never surfaced in the collectors' market, and King has not mentioned it since the early eighties.

The Cannibals is a novel King wrote while living in Monroeville, Pennsylvania, in 1982, during the filming of *Creepshow.*

Douglas Winter wrote in *Stephen King: The Art of Darkness* that King came up with the idea for the novel after he was "inspired by his living quarters in Monroeville."

The Cannibals is, from all reports, *dark.* Talking to Winter in 1982 about the novel, King said:

I've got about four-hundred-and-fifty pages done and it is all about these people who are trapped in an apartment building. Worst thing I could think of. And I thought, wouldn't it be funny if they all ended up eating each other? It's very, very bizarre because it's all on one note. And who knows whether it will be published or not?

Fifteen years later, *The Cannibals* has not yet been published, although it is possible that King plundered material from the manuscript for other works that *have* been published in this period.

Nothing of *The Cannibals* has surfaced since 1982 in the collectors' market, either, nor was the manuscript on deposit in the Special Collections archive at the University of Maine library as of 1990.

George Beahm (*The Stephen King Companion*) makes the point in the first edition of *The Stephen King Story* that the plot of *The Cannibals* is similar to that of J. G. Ballard's novel *High-Rise,* in which "the inhabitants of a massive multistory apartment block gradually revert to savagery as the amenities of civilization, which form a restrictive veneer around their lives, break down."

The Cannibals was originally titled *Under the Dome*. The novel may or may not ever be published, but one thing is certain: A Stephen King novel about people resorting to cannibalism to survive is a book *I* sure as hell would want to read.

PUBLISHING HISTORY

1982: never published.

29

"Skybar"

These things happened to me when I was young.

—the Narrator, "Skybar"

What it is: the opening and concluding segments of a horror short story to which the reader contributes the middle section.

Chances of finding a copy: difficult, since the book in which the segment appears (*The Do-It-Yourself Bestseller*) is out of print and was probably not purchased by libraries for circulation. This tome has appeared, however, from time to time in remainder bins, and sometimes rare and used book and magazine dealers come across copies. Start with Betts Bookstore and The Overlook Connection if you're determined to own a copy.

An unnamed sixth-grader and eleven of his friends visit the Skybar Amusement Park one night, and something horrible happens that results in the deaths of ten of the friends. The Narrator recalls: "There were twelve of us went in that night, but only two of us came out—my friend Kirby and me. And Kirby was insane."

What actually happened inside the Skybar—in the adults-only Freak Tent and elsewhere—is up to the reader to imagine, since "Skybar" was a reader-participation story for which King wrote only the first four paragraphs and a final paragraph.

King participated in the book *The Do-It-Yourself Bestseller* by providing the reader/writer with the beginnings of a horror story and the

final line—the first time he had ever contributed something so unusual
to a book.

When King wrote "Skybar," his agent was Kirby McCauley. King's
nod to Kirby in the tale comes in the guise of a character named Kirby
who goes insane after visiting the amusement park.

King authority Michael Collings wrote that "Skybar" "suggests *It*, as
well as demonstrating traditional King stylistics and techniques: brand
names and a painfully precise realism as a backdrop for fear." King
mentions Sunoco and S & H Green Stamps, plus specific amusements
such as Pop Dupree's Dead-Eye Shootin' Gallery, the Mirror Labyrinth,
the SkyCoaster roller coaster, and the aforementioned "adults only"
Freak Tent.

Several other professional writers participated in *The Do-It-Yourself
Bestseller,* including Isaac Asimov, Erskine Caldwell, Robin Cook, Irving
Wallace, Ken Follett, William F. Buckley Jr., Barbara Taylor Bradford,
Steve Allen, John Jakes, Alvin Toffler, and Colin Wilson. All contributed
story fragments which the reader then had to complete.

PUBLISHING HISTORY

1982: *The Do-It-Yourself Bestseller—A Workbook* (Doubleday trade
   paperback).

30

"Peter Straub: An Informal Appreciation"

Peter Straub is a gentle man (as well as a gentleman) with dark hollow spaces inside.

—from "Peter Straub: An Informal Appreciation"

What it is: King's affectionate appreciation for Peter Straub the writer, *and* the man.

Chances of finding a copy: probably impossible. This essay only appeared in the program published for the 1982 World Fantasy Convention in New Haven, Connecticut, and has never been reprinted. Since publications like this program are rarely, if ever, acquired for libraries, the odds on finding an original are in all likelihood slim to none. You might try *writing* to the New Haven Public Library (do *not* call) to find out if they have a copy of the program. You could also try the usual dealers, since oddities like this program do occasionally become available for sale. If an original is found, though, because of its uniqueness and rarity, it will probably be expensive.

This interesting nonfiction essay is ostensibly an appreciation of Stephen King's coauthor Peter Straub. (When King wrote the piece, he and Straub were knee-deep in the writing of *The Talisman.*)

This salute to Straub was written for the 1982 World Fantasy Convention's program (Straub was the guest of honor that year), and as might be expected, King waxes eloquent about Straub, offering insight-

135

ful analysis of several of Straub's novels while also painting a picture of Straub as a man who "always looks out of place at fantasy conventions."

"Peter Straub: An Informal Appreciation," however, is about much more than just Peter Straub and his work. It is also about writing and madness and literary history and the incredibly strange, "have-to-experience-it-to-believe-it" gestalt of science fiction and fantasy conventions, those truly odd, often bizarre amalgams of writers, editors, booksellers, fans, and costumed lunatics.

King begins by describing the style and sensibility of Peter Straub. He tells us that Straub would not wear something "as ordinary as Brooks Brothers." He "is more apt to be clad in a three-piece pinstriped suit from Paul Stuart." His ties are "subdued" but clearly "worn to be seen," and we are told that Straub "does not wear . . . soft lenses. . . . He wears dark plastic-framed spectacles which . . . declare to the world: *No bullshit!*"

King then tells his first Peter Straub story, one that took place at the 1980 World Fantasy Convention. Straub, along with fellow writers Karl Edward Wagner and Dennis Etchison and two fans, were sitting at a table in a hotel bar discussing *The Texas Chainsaw Massacre,* Tobe Hooper's 1974 classic horror flick. The discussion included (necessarily, I suppose) loud chain-saw sound effects that could be heard across the room, where Stephen King was sitting next to two old ladies. One of the women looked over at Straub's table and said to her friend, "Aren't they *awful!*" The other woman replied in the affirmative but said that the "nice bald man" at the table (Straub, of course) was the hotel manager and that he would make them leave soon. At that point, Peter Straub began making his *own* chain-saw noises, and the two ladies fled in what had to be some kind of fear for their lives.

King then discusses his friend's writing, declaring that Straub is the producer of what King calls "the good prose."

"The good prose," King tells us, "is almost always structurally correct . . . [and] "each sentence is as tight as a timelock. . . ." Other progenitors of such handsome writing include Sinclair Lewis, Thomas Hardy, Henry James, and Charles Dickens, whom King describes as "perhaps the greatest practitioner of 'the good prose' to ever work in English."

King writes that the industry in which he works attracts people he describes as "authentic crazy [people]." Peter Straub is one of them, he proclaims. (Interestingly, King also notes that King biographer and genre critic Douglas E. Winter, a man whom I know and admire, "looks almost as straight as Peter, but of course he is utterly mad." King may be right. There *is* something in Doug's eyes that now and then looks a wee bit *askew,* if you know what I mean.)

King writes eloquently about Straub's novels, including *Ghost Story* ("Jamesian diction"), *If You Could See Me Now* ("Chandleresque first-person narrative"), *Julia* (a "classic ghost tale"), and *Shadowland* ("excavating at the very roots of the supernatural tale"), comparing Straub's work to that of Nathaniel Hawthorne, M. R. James, and Henry James.

Straub is a *real writer,* King reminds us, one who takes language to another place; one who manifests "mind-popping" intelligence.

King also speaks about Straub from a personal point of view, stating that his relationship with him has been "complex and enriching." He talks about Straub's love for jazz and children and reveals that Straub's patience and generosity of spirit have occasionally been misinterpreted as *naiveté* but that such a mistake is usually only made *once.*

King concludes this important look at a major writer of dark fantasy and horror by telling one final story. This one took place at the 1981 World Fantasy Convention, in a hotel bedroom populated by naked people fresh out of the hot tub, a costumed Vampira, writers galore, and a drunken Stephen King, who was sitting on the bed watching the flow of strangeness around him. Into the suite marches Peter Straub, impeccably dressed and carrying a Bombay martini. Straub sits down at the end of the bed and asks Stephen King one question, which, to King, apparently defines the essence of this man called Straub: "Stevie," he began, "how bad do you think a house could get? I mean, how really *bad?*"

Good question, wouldn't you say?

PUBLISHING HISTORY

1982: *World Fantasy Convention '82* (program, October 29–31).

31

"*The Evil Dead*: Why You Haven't Seen It Yet . . . and Why You Ought To"

When I met Sam Raimi at the Cannes Film Festival in May of 1982, my first thought was that this fellow was one of three things: a busboy, a runaway American high school student, or a genius.

—from "*The Evil Dead*"

What it is: King's laudatory review of Sam Raimi's gruesome and remarkable *The Evil Dead,* a horror classic which, at the time this piece was written, could not find an American distributor.

Chances of finding a copy: very difficult, but possible with some hunting. *Twilight Zone* ceased publication several years ago, and the odds are almost completely against finding back issues of it in libraries anywhere in the country (a crime, actually); but because it was a genre magazine specializing in horror, fantasy, and science fiction, the usual King dealers (Betts Bookstore, The Overlook Connection, etc.) may be able to scare up (sorry) a copy for you. Expect to pay between ten and twenty-five dollars if you can find one. (This is a terrific issue of *Twilight Zone,* well worth owning even if it did not contain a King piece. It includes fiction by the late and legendary Joseph Payne Brennan, an in-depth interview with that maestro of cinematic mayhem John Carpenter, as well as new reviews of the then-just-released horror and fantasy masterpieces *E.T. The Extra-Terrestrial, Poltergeist,* and *The Thing.*)

King wrote this article for *Twilight Zone* after seeing *The Evil Dead* at Cannes and learning that almost all of the major American distributors had passed on buying the film and that there was a very good chance that American audiences would never get to see this movie, which King describes as a "black rainbow of horror."

The film was ultimately picked up by Image Entertainment and released with an NC-17 rating. Sam Raimi went on to direct two *Evil Dead* sequels as well as write and direct the first film of the *Darkman* series.

In his article, King is passionate about *The Evil Dead,* calling it "the most ferociously original horror film of 1982."

"*The Evil Dead,*" King writes, "has the simple, stupid power of a good campfire story—but its simplicity is not a side effect."

King discusses Raimi's inventiveness with the camera, noting that "the camera has the kind of nightmarish fluidity that we associate with the early John Carpenter; it dips and slides and then zooms in so fast you want to plaster your hands over your eyes."

Raimi and his partners called on a team of investors to get *The Evil Dead* made, and ultimately people did make money on the movie, thanks to some nice foreign-distribution deals. However, the filmmakers' budget was extremely tight, and King quotes Raimi as admitting, "We couldn't afford a Steadicam, so we improvised. We mounted the camera in the middle of a two-by-four about fifteen feet long. A couple of guys grabbed it, one on either end, and they just ran like hell."

These primitive production values gives *The Evil Dead* what King describes as a "grainy . . . weirdly convincing documentary look" that reminds horror-movie aficionados of George Romero's *Night of the Living Dead,* a movie Raimi cites as an important influence on him.

In 1995 I published a book of horror-movie quizzes called *The Gore Galore Video Quiz Book.* I included *The Evil Dead* in the book and wrote:

> The plot of *The Evil Dead* is simple: Five young people in a cabin in the woods awaken demonic forces that want to possess them. They, of course, would prefer that that not happen, and thus the battle begins.
>
> The camera work and effects in this movie are astonishing and daring. We rush through the woods and our wince-inducing point of view is such that we feel as though we are going to certainly

crash into a tree. We see demons that are beyond grotesque and that convince us that if we ever *did* see a real demon, this is what they would look like.

I had it made when I was writing *Gore Galore*: All I had to do was go down to my local video monger, rent *The Evil Dead* (along with six or seven other grisly flicks at the same time—*the looks I got!*), watch it as often as I wanted, and write my chapter.

Back in 1982, however, as King discusses in this article, there was a real likelihood that the movie would never be available to horror fans. Thankfully, that situation was remedied, and *The Evil Dead* is now easily acquired—and often for as little as a buck if you rent it on a Monday, Tuesday, or Wednesday!

"*The Evil Dead*: Why You Haven't Seen It Yet . . . and Why You Ought To" is an attempt by the master of horror to persuade some film distributor to take a chance on an undeniably *extreme* film that King knew could easily have gotten lost in the shuffle if no one singled it out for well-deserved attention. Whether or not the movie was picked up because of King's "call to arms" is debatable and not really important. What *is* important is that *The Evil Dead* is now readily available, and as King tells us, you ought to see it—if you haven't already, that is (and I'll bet a lot of you *have*).

PUBLISHING HISTORY

1982: Rod Serling's *Twilight Zone* magazine (November).

32

"Berni Wrightson:
An Appreciation"

Writing about pictures—from the highest art to the lowliest caricature—makes me uncomfortable.

—from "Berni Wrightson: An Appreciation"

What it is: a two-page appreciation of Berni Wrightson and an introduction of sorts to a limited-edition portfolio of art drawn by Wrightson for King's novella *Cycle of the Werewolf.*

Chances of finding a copy: extremely difficult but possible if you're willing to spend three hundred dollars or more for one of the 350 signed copies of the portfolio in which this "Appreciation" appears. Try the usual sources.

Stephen King begins this brief essay by admitting that he has absolutely no knowledge or expertise in the field of art and then, by way of justifying this love letter to Berni Wrightson's work, quotes a line sung by the Orlons, "I ain't no monkey, but I know what I like."

He explains to his readers that his forte is words: "As a writer," he tells us, "I value exactness of image—as much utter clarity as I can imagine."

King then uses his power with words to communicate to us the excitement he feels when he beholds art by Berni Wrightson, especially Berni's art for King's own *Cycle of the Werewolf.*

King effectively uses the image of the imagination as an engine and the artist the gas station that fuels it. He admits that there are "gas stations" where you can buy the regular 87-octane stuff that many cars use today but that there also used to be places where you could buy the 101-octane, hi-test stuff that used to go into '57 Thunderbirds and the like.

King draws a parallel between the 101-octane gas and Berni Wrightson's art; that is, Wrightson's art does for his imagination what the hi-test used to do for powerful engines.

King also admits that Wrightson successfully created an image *"which existed only in my head."* King is referring specifically to the werewolf fantasy and the little boy in the Yoda (from the *Star Wars* films) mask used for the October illustration in this portfolio. King is effusive in his praise for this work and a little bit in awe of how perfectly Wrightson was able to capture an image King had only held in his mind's eye—and which he described to his readers only in words.

Interestingly, at one point in this essay, King describes his eyesight as "substandard." A dozen or so years later, King would sit for a *60 Minutes* interview and reveal to the world that he suffers from macular degeneration, a progressively worsening eye condition that negatively affects vision. My sources tell me that King now uses very large fonts on his computer screen to make it easier to work without difficulty.

"Berni Wrightson: An Appreciation" is pure Stephen King: It is funny, honest, and astute. It is also replete with King's usual boatload of literary, artistic, and pop-culture references, including the National Endowment for the Arts; *Creepshow*; the World Fantasy Convention; William Faulkner's novel *The Hamlet* (and its main character, the mongoloid idiot Ike Snopes); Winslow Homer; Frederick Remington; Vincent van Gogh; the aforementioned 1957 Thunderbird; 1950s romance magazines; Virgil Finlay; Frank Frazetta; the Metropolitan Museum of Art; Yoda; and the poet Marianne Moore and her memorable image of "real toads in imaginary gardens."

King concludes this ode to Berni by telling us that the "results of this partnership of story and image have been greatly gratifying to me and I hope they have been to you, as well."

He ends the piece with "Thanks, Berni. I ain't no monkey, but I know what I like."

PUBLISHING HISTORY

1983: *Cycle of the Werewolf* portfolio (a signed, 350-copy, limited-edition art portfolio published by Land of Enchantment).

33

"A Novelist's Perspective on Bangor"

Why Bangor specifically? Would not any small American city do? Why, the skeptic might ask, didn't you find a small American city in some state where you don't have to freeze your buns off for three months of the year?

— from "A Novelist's Perspective on Bangor"

What it is: King's nonfiction essay about his hometown (since 1980) of Bangor, Maine, originally delivered as spoken remarks at a 1983 benefit for the Bangor Historical Society during a program called *Black Magic and Music*.

Chances of finding a copy: extremely difficult, if not impossible, for most fans. This type of publication—a program for a charity event—is never archived in public libraries (although you can be certain it will be found in the *Bangor* public libraries); thus, the fan seeking the text has literally no options other than to buy an original copy of the program from the usual sources (The Overlook Connection, Betts Bookstore, etc.). It will be a pricey purchase, though. An original collectible program such as this can sell for $175 and up. If it's signed by King, the price could be substantially higher.

"A Novelist's Perspective on Bangor" is an important and revealing nonfiction statement by Stephen King, but not because it offers insight into why he and his family live in Bangor. That's an interesting element of the essay, of course, but there is a more important reason why this piece is of consequence.

In this essay, King talks about writing *Derry*, a massive novel jam-packed with Bangor myth which he spent years thinking about before its completion. *Derry* was, of course, ultimately published as King's 1986 magnum opus (at least in this writer's opinion), *It*.

At the time of this address (March 1983), King had been sitting with the completed first draft of *Derry* for about a year. He talked about the first draft and discussed the nuts and bolts of putting such a historically evocative novel together:

> *I'm fairly happy with it—as happy as one can be with a first draft, I suppose, because the stories are there. Oh my Lord, my Lord, the stories you hear about this town—the streets fairly clang with them. The problem isn't finding them or ferreting them out, the problem is that old boozer's problem of knowing when to stop. It's entirely possible, I find, to overload completely on Bangor myth (which may be one reason why the novel runs better than 1200 pages in its present form).*

The opening segment of this essay is autobiographical. King speaks openly and honestly about what he and Tabitha wanted for their family by moving to Bangor. He talks about buying the Victorian mansion in Bangor's historic district that was known locally as the William Arnold House. The Kings paid $135,000 for the house in 1980, an Italianate villa that had originally been built in 1856 for $6,000. King jokingly(?) claims that the house did not want them there at first ("I think it *disapproved* of us") but that after about eight months the house began to accept them—toy solders and cats included.

King concludes his affectionate paean to his adopted hometown by telling the story of going to the Bangor Public Library and asking if they had any histories of the town on the shelves. They had twelve of them, and King asked for the best of the bunch. "Isn't one," the librarian replied, and then said no more. King then asked for one with pictures, telling the librarian that he was writing a novel with Bangor as the setting.

The librarian perked up and told King about another writer—Ben Ames Williams—who had written a novel with Bangor as the locale, but then frowned when she told King about the *"awful* things" Mr. Williams had written in his book.

"I'm afraid I've also written some fairly awful things in my book," King told his audience, "but I hope that when local people read it, they will sense those awful things have been informed with a larger love for the place and the people—the love of a resident."

"A Novelist's Perspective on Bangor" is a revealing look at where inspiration comes from and illustrates how the best writers can use a momentary flash of image, a second of impression, as the launching pad for a gargantuan rocket of a book, one that will ultimately explode in the mind of its readers as a million moments of drama, terror, pathos, humor, and above all, *fun.*

The *Black Magic and Music* program concluded with a James Leonard (King's brother-in-law) photo of a bearded King, along with a biographical profile that mishandled *Night Shift* as *Nightshift* and described King's big seminal 1981 nonfiction book *Danse Macabre* as an essay. The profile also revealed that "aside from writing, Steve enjoys playing tennis and softball and has a strong interest in community theater."

PUBLISHING HISTORY

1983: *Black Magic and Music.* (A paperback publication of the Bangor Historical Society published as a program to accompany a benefit for the Historical Society on March 27 at the Bangor House Ballroom. Brad Terry and the Friends of Jazz were the musical entertainment for the evening. The program was later reprinted without advertisements.)

34

"The Leprechaun"

Once upon a time—which is how all the best stories start—
a little boy named Owen was playing outside his big red
house.

—from "The Leprechaun"

What it is: a five-page short story in manuscript form that King wrote
for his son Owen and which he planned on someday expanding into a
novel. It ends with no resolution, so these pages may actually be the
first chapter of the planned novel.

Chances of finding a copy: impossible.

Like "The King Family and the Wicked Witch," the unpublished and
incomplete short story "The Leprechaun" features a King family
member as its main character; in this case, Owen, King's son.

   Written when Owen was five, this charming children's story tells the
story of Owen's attempt to protect a real leprechaun that was living in
their front lawn from the family cat, Springsteen, a sly feline who liked
to eat things (he had had his eye on Owen's guinea pig, Butler, for quite
some time) and who also liked to *play* with things before he ate them.

   Apparently, King had written thirty pages of this story longhand in a
notebook when he lost the precious pages off the back of his motorcycle
somewhere in New Hampshire during a Harley-Davidson trip from
Boston to Bangor.

   King re-created from memory *some* of what he had written, but to
date none of this truncated material has appeared in any of his pub-

lished novels or short stories. The five extant pages are all he had been able to get around to redoing by the summer of 1983, and later episodes of the tale—including one in which Owen makes the injured leprechaun a house from a Band-Aid box—have never surfaced.

"The Leprechaun" is yet another example of King's genius for storytelling: He can just as easily tell an exciting tale to a five-year-old audience as he can to his adult readers.

PUBLISHING HISTORY

1983: unpublished manuscript.

35

"Dear Walden People"

The point is, when you live in your imagination a lot of the time, it may take you anywhere—anywhere at all.

—from "Dear Walden People"

What it is: Stephen King's May 19, 1983 letter to Waldenbooks customers in which he talks about *Different Seasons,* his new book, and in which he also discusses writers known for writing in one specific genre but who, in reality, also write other types of stories.

Chances of finding a copy: difficult but not impossible. This letter was written especially for the Waldenbooks newsletter *Booknotes* and was copyrighted by Waldenbooks, Inc., *not* by Stephen King. Thus, it was fairly easy to acquire reprint rights to the piece, and while the original *Booknotes* appearance is probably impossible to find, there are a couple of other appearances of the letter that might be easier to acquire. George Beahm reprinted King's missive in the *first* edition of his *Stephen King Companion,* but *not* the second edition, so you will have to find a library that has the first edition of the book on its shelves or contact one of the dealers who still may have copies of that edition for sale. The other appearance of the piece was in *Bare Bones: Conversations on Terror with Stephen King,* a terrific collection which was published in both limited and trade editions. Check libraries for the trade edition and the usual dealers for the availability of the limited one.

King begins this letter to customers of Waldenbooks by addressing a question he had apparently been repeatedly asked about *Different Sea-*

sons; namely, Does the publication of this collection mean "that I've reached the end of my interest in such uplifting and edifying subjects as ghouls, ghosts, vampires, and unspeakable things lurking in the closets of little kids"?

The reason King had been asked this question in the first place was because of the nonhorror subject matter of three of the stories in the collection, *Rita Hayworth and Shawshank Redemption, Apt Pupil,* and *The Body* (which was the text source for the movie *Stand by Me.*)

Rita Hayworth and Shawshank Redemption is about a prison escape; *Apt Pupil* is about a twisted, oddly symbiotic relationship between a teenage boy and a Nazi war criminal; and *The Body* is a coming-of-age story about the journey of four young boys to see a dead body.

King responds by reminding his readers of the subject matter of the *fourth* story in the collection, *The Breathing Method,* a "pretty gruesome" tale which can be summed up in a couple of well-chosen words: "headless Lamaze." (Interestingly, one of the *Inside View* cover headlines visible in Mark Pavia's 1997 film adaptation of *The Night Flier* is about *The Breathing Method*'s very determined mother-to-be.)

King describes himself as ultimately "one of the Halloween people" and cites the old chestnut by Robert Bloch in which Bloch told an interviewer that he had the heart of a small boy; he kept it in a jar on his desk.

King then discusses other writers who were known for writing in one particular genre but who veered off now and then to write material completely different from what they were known for.

He talks about epic novelist Herman Wouk, who wrote a comic novel of childhood called *The City Boy*; "Fletch" creator Gregory McDonald, who also wrote *Love Among the Mashed Potatoes,* a novel about a lonelyhearts columnist; "Travis McGee" creator John D. MacDonald, who also wrote science fiction ("damn fine" science fiction, King tells us); and "87th Precinct" crime novelist Ed McBain (Evan Hunter), who also wrote science fiction and westerns.

King also mentions the writer who was a major influence on his own work, Richard "I Am Legend" Matheson, noting that Matheson also detoured from his signature genre of horror and science fiction to write a war novel called *The Beardless Warriors.*

This letter from Stephen King is a warm and informative introduction to *Different Seasons,* but it is much more than that. It is a piece of valuable advice from a man who has read widely in many genres and who has also *written* in more genres than just horror, no matter what the unwashed masses who only know King from "his" movies may think.

King concludes with a typically Stephen King warning: He reminds us that when you turn out the lights and get into bed each night, "*anything* could be under it; anything at all."

Publishing History

1983: *Waldenbooks Booknotes* (August).

1988: *Bare Bones: Conversations on Terror with Stephen King* (Underwood-Miller limited edition; McGraw-Hill trade hardcover).

1989: *The Stephen King Companion* (Andrews and McMeel trade paperback).

36

The Plant

What's happening with The Plant? *The Plant's a little book that I gave up—"gave up"—that's a Freudian slip—it's a little book that I gave out to friends as a Christmas card, and what happened was, I went to see* The Little Shop of Horrors *between the second and third installment and realized that's what I was writing and decided I better stop right away. So that's what I did.*

> —Stephen King, speaking about *The Plant* during a lecture at the Pasadena (California) Library on April 26, 1989.

What it is: the first three chapters of an aborted novel that Stephen King self-published through his company, Philtrum Press, and sent out to friends and family members for three years as a signed and numbered, limited-edition Christmas gift before abandoning the project in 1985.

Chances of finding a copy: good (I'm being sarcastic) if you are willing to spend between $4,500 and $6,000 for a complete set of the three chapters. (Individual installments routinely sell for well over $1,000 each.) If you will not (or cannot) indulge in such expenditures, then the chances of finding a less expensive version are nonexistent, since *The Plant* has never been reprinted in a trade edition. Sets of *The Plant* often become available in the secondary market, but they are very rare (most recipients never choose to give theirs up) and thus are extremely pricey. The sets signed to the same person are the most expensive. Because of *The Plant*'s uniqueness and the fact that only 226 copies of each install-

ment exist, the genuine limited editions occasionally offered for sale on
the secondary market are the only ones currently legally available.

> Gentlemen:
> I have written a book you might want to publish. It is very
> good. It is all scary and all true. It is called True Tales of
> Demon Infestation.
>
> —the opening passage of part 1 of The Plant.

Stephen King has often admitted that he was bothered by the imper-
sonal nature of Christmas cards, so he decided to go Hallmark one
better and create his *own* Christmas greeting, something that the people
on his mailing list could also read and enjoy instead of just hanging up
and then throwing out the first week of January.

The Plant is an abandoned epistolary novel-in-progress. This means
that the story is told entirely through letters, interoffice memos, journal
entries, newspaper articles, and the like. This literary form originated in
1740 with Samuel Richardson's *Pamela,* which is the story of a young
servant girl's triumph over her lecherous master's attempts to seduce
her. Other notable examples of this type of novel are Samuel Richardson's *Clarissa* (1747–48), Tobias Smollett's *Humphrey Clinker* (1771),
and Fanny Burney's *Evelina* (1778). A more recent twentieth-century
example of the novel in letter form is Ring Lardner's *You Know Me Al*
(1916). (King's only published epistolary works include the short story
"Jerusalem's Lot" in *Night Shift* and the short story "The End of the
Whole Mess.")

King was obviously familiar with the form and decided to experiment with it for this privately published, very unique work.

The Plant begins when John Kenton, an overworked and underpaid
editor with the failing Zenith House publishing company, receives a
query letter from a Rhode Island nurseryman named Carlos Detweiller.
Carlos has written a book called *True Tales of Demon Infestations* that
he would like Zenith House to publish because they are "the publishers of *Bloody Houses,* which was quite good."

To continue the story of this truly unique King creation, I am happy
and proud to relinquish the stage to my friend, the inestimable Tyson
Blue, the writer who can legitimately lay claim to an astonishing fact:

Tyson has written more articles, reviews, interviews, and essays about Stephen King and his work than anyone else on the planet.

Tyson is also the author of two terrific books, *The Unseen King* and *Observations From the Terminator,* and was contributing editor of *Castle Rock: The Stephen King Newsletter.* Since *Castle Rock*'s demise in 1989, Tyson's columns of Stephen King news have appeared in *Midnight Graffiti* and *Twilight Zone* magazines.

His ongoing column, "Needful Kings & Other Things," appears monthly in *Cemetery Dance,* and the worldwide version of the column, "Needful Kings International," appears in Canada, France, Germany, Italy, Scandinavia, and the United Kingdom in several languages.

Ladies and gentlemen, Tyson Blue . . .

THE PLANT

Stephen King's Private, Unfinished, Unseen, Unconventional, Un-Christmas Un-Card

by Tyson Blue

(*Note:* The following is an edited, slightly revised version of the longer fifth chapter of my 1989 book, *The Unseen King,* available from Borgo Press.—TB)

While most of the material discussed in this book could be called rare, there is one seldom-seen Stephen King work which is truly in short supply—226 copies and a handful of printer's overruns, to be exact. I am referring, of course, to *The Plant.*

Of *The Plant,* writer and essayist Harlan Ellison, in his collection, *Harlan Ellison's Watching,* said, "Those of us who have been privileged to read the first couple of sections of *The Plant,* King's work-in-progress privately printed as an annual holiday greeting card, perceive a talent of uncommon dimensions."

When King began publishing *The Plant* through his Philtrum Press back in 1982, he did not intend to create an item which would become a near-legendary collectible.

"The idea was to substitute *The Plant* for Christmas cards, which I find pretty useless," King explains. "People buy them in job lots and they don't mean much in most cases, do they, because no work went into them, just the five or ten bucks you paid the Girl Scouts (or fifteen if you wanted THE HENDERSONS printed at the bottom in red)."

As a Christmas card, *The Plant* is more than impressive—it's a knockout! All three parts are packaged identically—each book is the size of a small hardcover, covered in dark olive wrappers with the title, author's name, part number and a floral design in black. The interior pages are printed on a cream (or buff) colored paper made in Italy by Cartiere Miliani Fabriano, and it is a heavy, textured stock which is a joy to touch, let alone to read. It bears the imprint of King's Philtrum Press, which also printed the limited editions of *The Eyes of the Dragon* and *Six Stories,* also famous for their gorgeous presentation.

The Plant appeared only three times, in 1982, 1983, and 1985. In 1984, the people on King's Christmas card list received the Philtrum Press limited edition of *The Eyes of the Dragon* instead—which should have been ample consolation for anyone!

But there is more than a pretty package to *The Plant.* There is also a light-hearted tale of the supernatural. If anything, it echoes the hit films (and play) *Little Shop of Horrors,* although they share few if any plot elements in common. King himself noted the similarity upon viewing the musical film version, saying "Now I can never finish that story!" And, for whatever reason, he did, in fact, abandon the story at that point, which is a shame.

The hero of *The Plant,* John Kenton, is an editor at Zenith House, a seedy paperback publisher which has fought its way to fifteenth place in a market of fifteen companies, specializing in formula horror and men's adventure novels. The story is told in epistolary form, by means of letters, interoffice memos, diary entries and other communications between Kenton, his editor-in-chief, Roger Wade, and others at Zenith House and elsewhere.

Kenton is queried by Carlos Detweiller, a man who, like *Little Shop*'s Seymour, works in a flower shop in Central Falls, Rhode Island. Detweiller wants to sell Zenith House a book he has written entitled *True Tales of Demon Infestations.* It is, he maintains, "all scary and all true." Kenton figures that the book might have something in it which could be ghost-written and sold to the *Amityville Horror* market. He agrees to look at a chapter or two and a synopsis.

What he gets is the completed manuscript and a series of obviously posed photographs, purportedly portraying an authentic black mass.

However, four of them appear to show a genuine human sacrifice. After consulting Wade, Kenton calls the police, who in turn contact the authorities in Central Falls.

An investigation in Rhode Island reveals that the victim in the pictures is alive and well, watching television in the flower shop. Detweiller quits his job and vanishes. He sends Kenton an irate letter, addressed to "Mr. John 'Judas Priest' Kenton, Zenith Asshole-House, Publishers of Kaka, 490 Avenue of Dog-Shit, New York, NY 10017." The letter, weighted down with exclamation points and capital letters, promises revenge in terms which indicate unequivocally that Detweiller is insane.

Two weeks later, Kenton receives a letter from a "Roberta Solrac," claiming that she will be sending him a plant to thank him for editing a Zenith horror series of which she is a fan. Realizing that "Solrac" is "Carlos" spelled backward, Kenton orders Riddley Walker, Zenith's janitor, to incinerate the plant if and when it arrives.

Riddley, a young black man who affects a jiveass personality on the job, is, we know from reading his diary entries, a very erudite person who is gathering material for his novel and helping one of Zenith's female editors act out her bizarre sex fantasies. When the plant—an ivy plant named Zenith—arrives, Riddley does not get rid of it, but rather places it on a high shelf in his office. The plant is unlike anything Riddley has seen in any botany book, and it continues to flourish—even though it is never watered.

Meanwhile, Kenton, who has been dumped by his girlfriend, is thinking of quitting Zenith House. Herb Porter, a colleague, knows something of what Kenton is going through, since a few years back he had incurred the wrath of General Anthony "Iron Guts" Hecksler, a retired military man who had written a book called *Twenty Psychic Garden Flowers*, which Porter had rejected for Zenith House. Hecksler had gone crazy on learning of this and went out and stabbed an Albany bus driver. Hecksler has been confined in an asylum ever since.

In Part Three, Hecksler escapes and begins making his way to New York, noting in his diary, which he keeps in black Green Stamp books: "Have had a dream. Prophecy. Ally. Must link up. In my dreams he says his name is CARLOS. Can a man with a spic name be an ally? His voice seems a true voice. Talks about plants."

Is there a connection between Carlos and the general? What of both men's ties with plants?

"*The Plant* is like all my other novels in one respect," King says. "I thought I knew where it was going when I started. Now certain characters—like the mad general—have suddenly stepped forward.

"It's unlike the others in another," he goes on. "I pick it up in June, work on it for a month or so, and put it down for a year. There seems to be no problem with this, as there usually is with a novel where I feel under pressure to finish. Another thing: I write *The Plant* longhand in first draft. I haven't done that since I was a kid. It's extremely trying but rewarding as well—that's hard to explain, but it seems more intimate that way."

One benefit to this episodic format is that it gave King the chance to go back and make adjustments to the story. The sole example of this takes place in Part Two, where a large portion of the book is a simple reworking of the end of Part One.

"It was to make it flow better," King admits, "but it was also a case of what I'd call pilot error. I ended Part One in the middle of a segment—a longish one—and went back to the start of that segment for the sake of continuity."

King had projected the length of the finished novel at 400 pages, and projected that it would take another seven years to finish.

There seems to be no historic precedent for a writer giving out segments of a work-in-progress as a Christmas card. "I think M. R. James used to write his horror stories annually, to be read aloud on Christmas Eve (a time for spooky stories in England as All Hallows' Eve is a time for them here)," King has commented.

Perhaps the most famous of all Christmas ghost stories is Charles Dickens' *A Christmas Carol*. Dickens is also important in considering another aspect of *The Plant*, to wit, its appearance in serial form. During the latter half of the Nineteenth Century, the novels of Dickens and others were serialized in magazines and newspapers. This figured even more prominently in King's decision in 1996 to publish *The Green Mile* in serial form.

Thus, while there is a precedent for the telling of spooky tales at Christmastime, as well as a precedent for the serial release of novels by popular writers, the use of *The Plant* as a Christmas card is apparently unique with, and original to, Stephen King.

Because of its extreme rarity, feedback on the story has been scarce. "Most people like it," says King. "Like *The Eyes of the Dragon*, it's a fantasy, but of a different sort; *Eyes* was a grown-up's novel masquerading as a children's story (to be fair, I think novels are only novels and the distinctions are artificial; a good children's book like *Treasure Island* or the *Oz* books or the *Narnia* books can be read by adults, and good adult novels, like *The Lord of the Flies* or *A Separate Peace* can be read by children), while *The Plant* is social satire."

Perhaps the single unpleasant side-effect of *The Plant*'s rarity is that it has become a collector's item of very high value on the speculative market. Asked if he is bothered by having something he had produced as a gift being bartered for four figures on the collector's market, King is self-deprecatingly sanguine.

"*The Plant* is a present," he explains. "If I gave someone a coffee maker and they sold it at a yard sale, it wouldn't bother me. If they want to sell *The Plant,* fine. It's theirs. They can tear out the pages and use 'em for toilet paper, if that's what they feel like doing. For the record, I've never seen an inscribed copy for sale. Some that are sold may be printer's overruns."

Since this interview was conducted in 1986, at least two inscribed sets have been offered for sale, but the majority of those who received them have known them for what they are—gifts not just from King but *of* him as well, and have kept them. It is interesting to see how King modernizes the epistolary format in this story. In older novels and stories using the form, the tale is mostly moved forward by letters and diary entries. And although he uses these as well, much of the early story is told by way of interoffice memos and other official communications, as well as newspaper accounts, each distinguished by its own unique typeface. Had he continued to write the novel, it might well have consisted of e-mail messages and faxes as well, and had it been collected for publication as a novel after its projected 1992 completion, these advances in epistolary communication would almost definitely have made their way into the tale.

A seeming restriction of the form, the filtering of the story through the perceptions of the characters from whose viewpoint it is being told actually serves a number of purposes, providing the humor and keeping the story moving and heightening reader interest, even though the story was still being set up at the point where it stopped.

The format also provides an insight into King's characterization skills, since much of what we learn about these characters comes from what they write in their memos. For example, Roger Wade picks on Kenton in his memos by calling him a college boy—a motif which has appeared in King's film *Maximum Overdrive* and in the short-story "Graveyard Shift." From this, we can infer that Roger Wade, like other Stephen King bosses, did not go to college. The sarcasm in these memos also tells us that Roger has little sympathy for his subordinates.

And it is from reading Riddley's journal entries that we learn that he is not the shuffling stereotype he pretends to be. His contempt for the people for whom he works is also evident between the lines. A surprising amount of information is conveyed about these characters beyond what they actually set down. I have always regarded King's gift for filling in his characters without impeding the flow of his narrative as one of his greatest assets, and it is seldom used to greater effect than here.

Nothing is quite what it seems in *The Plant*. Kenton thinks his girl loves him even as she composes her (literal) Dear John letter; Riddley is not the jive-talking dummy he pretends to be; Detweiller's sacrificial victim is not dead, as he appears in the photograph he sends Kenton— at least, the police saw him sitting and watching television; and General Hecksler appears at one point to have committed suicide by crawling into a crematorium and flicking his Bic, but that is not the case either. Even the name of Kenton publisher, Zenith House, is an ironic comment on its position, at the nadir of its field.

The humor in *The Plant* is more important than in King's more traditional horror tales. This has surfaced only rarely in his work, in "The Body," "The Wedding Gig," and in portions of *Christine*, for example. But generally, the very nature of horror fiction tends to discourage humor.

For those lucky enough to have read it, the first quarter or so of *The Plant* provided moments of uproarious satiric humor side-by-side with creeping dread and suspense, albeit with tongue "plant"-ed firmly in cheek. It is a highlight of King's work, one which deserves to be re-examined by the author and eventually completed.

PUBLISHING HISTORY

1982: Philtrum Press ([Part 1, 32 pages] December: 226 copies, all signed by King; 26 lettered from A–Z; 200 numbered from 1–200).

1983: Philtrum Press ([Part 2, 36 pages] December: 226 copies, all signed by King; 26 lettered from A–Z; 200 numbered from 1–200).

1985: Philtrum Press ([Part 3, 56 pages] December: 226 copies, all signed by King; 26 lettered from A–Z; 200 numbered from 1–200).

37

"On *The Shining* and Other Perpetrations"

The job of the writer is to impose order on chaos, to create the necklace we call "story" from the various unstrung beads of ideas, images, character, tone, mood.

—from "On *The Shining* and Other Perpetrations"

What it is: Stephen King's lengthy biographical essay in which he discusses his early years as a struggling writer; the genesis and writing of what many consider to be one of his finest novels, *The Shining*; the necessity in his mind for a prologue to the novel (see the chapter on "Before the Play"); and how writers really feel about that odious and inevitable question: "Where do you get your ideas?"

Chances of finding a copy: extremely difficult but not impossible if you have deep pockets. This essay has only appeared in print once, in Stuart Schiff's wonderful magazine *Whispers*. Copies of the August 1982 issue—the special "Stephen King" issue containing this essay, "Before the Play," and a revised (for the third of *four* times) version of "It Grows on You"—are occasionally offered for sale by dealers who specialize in horror and science fiction, but at a price. I recently saw a signed copy of the magazine listed at $250. The price will probably be higher now. Nonetheless, copies do circulate in the collectors' market, and acquiring an original is probably the only way you'll be able to read the piece in its entirety, since the odds are against *Whispers* being found in many (if any) libraries.

People are always asking Stephen King where he gets his ideas. Usually, if he can, King will take the time to explain the birth of an idea and the development of it into a story, but every now and then he just doesn't have the energy to be that forthcoming. One memorable time, King recounts in this article, he was asked "the Question" and just blurted out, "I get them at 239 Center Street in Bangor, just around the corner from the Frati Brothers Pawnshop."

King begins this entertaining essay by discussing the difference between being asked, "Where do you get your ideas?" and being asked, "Where did you get the idea for 'Salem's Lot?" The latter question is the one that is answerable because, as King writes, "a story or a novel is, after all, only a chain of coherent imaginative thoughts tied together with occasional bursts of that mysterious nerve-lightning we call creativity."

The far more general question about where a writer gets his or her ideas is a much more difficult one to answer coherently. King makes the metaphorical point that many different sexual encounters can produce a gaggle of different—yet related—children, just as many different ideas can produce a veritable library of books, related in that they are by the same author, yet each standing alone as an individual creative product.

When it comes to a single story or novel, though—well, that's a whole other story.

King talks about how obsessive a person can be about what he or she is *really into* and cites a telling example from his college years. The night the *Eagle* landed on the Moon, one of King's classmates insisted on showing King his fishing scrapbook, "totally oblivious" of what was probably the most significant exploratory event by human beings in the history of mankind. (King also admits that, in his opinion, this "fishing" story had no place in the essay but that he couldn't resist telling it. Contrary to King's self-effacing editorial flagellation, I think his fishing story perfectly illustrates the point he was making about the difference between the general "ideas" question and the *specific* "ideas" question.)

King then moves into a discussion of the birth of *The Shining*, revealing that it was a ten-year pregnancy. He writes that the keynote idea of Ray Bradbury's classic short story "The Veldt" (the notion that a person's dreams could become real) was his initial jumping-off point for *The Shining* but that "the idea sat there in limbo for ten years." Finally, in the shower one day, the idea bloomed into something tangible, and the next day King began a novel called *Darkshine,* a tale he wanted to set in an amusement park. The amusement-park setting didn't work, however, and the idea went back into that subconscious filing cabinet where creative thoughts are puréed and ingredients are added until they're ready to be put back into the oven.

The catalyst that transformed King's vague and unformed idea into a full-blown contemporary literary classic was his and his wife Tabitha's 1976 trip to Estes Park, Colorado, where they spent a weekend at the Stanley Hotel. During their stay, King had a dream in which one of the hotel's fire hoses chased his three-year-old son Joe through the halls. King writes that he woke up from this nightmare and sat by a window for a while, and within the time it took to smoke *one* cigarette, he had "the bones of the book firmly set in my mind."

King then discusses the autobiographical elements in *The Shining.* He candidly reveals that the early years of his marriage were difficult. He was teaching high school (a job he says here that he hated); he and his wife had two kids, which prevented Tabitha from working full-time; money was terribly tight (King told the phone company to remove his phone just so he and Tabitha did not have to endure the indignity of having them pull it out for lack of payment); and King was terrified that he would never make it as a writer and be allowed to do the one thing he knew was his true calling—to write stories. He was drinking too much, gambling away huge chunks of his paycheck, and he notes that he "felt like a man caught in a malign funhouse."

By the time King decided to write *The Shining,* all of his circumstances had changed for the better, thanks to an ill-fated teenaged girl named Carrie White, but as King admits, "the scar was there." He still had vivid memories of the tough times he and his family endured as he struggled to make a career as a writer, and he poured all of the attendant feelings into the character of Jack Torrance and the story of *The Shining.* King describes *The Shining* as "a ritual burning of hate and pain" and acknowledges what many suspected after reading *The Shining:* that it came about almost through "automatic writing"; the words flowed straight out of King's subconscious. This is an experience an artist can only hope and pray for and, as King also admits, "must count himself blessed" if it does happen. Writers in particular have a phrase to describe this transcendental, almost mystical experience: We say a piece "wrote itself."

King then reveals that his original plan for *The Shining* was that it would follow "a five-act Shakespearean tragedy, with scenes instead of chapters." This kind of rigid, highly structured narrative form gave King "an incredibly strong sense of visualization" when it came to writing the story. He ultimately added a prologue, "Before the Play" (see the chapter on "Before the Play") and an epilogue, "After the Play." The prologue was scrapped (it would have made the book just long enough to add a dollar to the price—a no-no this early in King's career), and the epilogue was absorbed into the novel's ending. (Unlike *The Stand*, which was originally published with even harsher editorial cuts for length,) King has not indicated any interest in publishing the "complete and uncut" version of *The Shining*. An abridged version of "Before the Play" was eventually published in *TV Guide*, and King has said that "After the Play" is lost for all time.

King concludes "On *The Shining* and Other Perpetrations" with a few paragraphs about his other story in this issue, "It Grows on You."

He writes that the original tale was greatly influenced by both Sherwood Anderson's *Winesburg, Ohio* stories and Thornton Wilder's classic play *Our Town*. "It Grows on You" was originally written in 1973 (this version was apparently never published), rewritten in 1975 for publication in a literary journal called *Marshroots*, and then rewritten yet again for publication in 1982 in *Whispers*. Apparently even this third version of the story did not satisfy King. In 1993 a *fourth* revision of the tale was published in King's short-story collection *Nightmares & Dreamscapes*. If you can get your hands on a copy of the *Whispers* appearance, it is very interesting to compare the two latest versions.

PUBLISHING HISTORY

1982: *Whispers* (no. 17/18; August).

38

"Before the Play"

The Overlook was at home with the dead.

> —from scene v of "Before the Play"

What it is: Stephen King's unused five-scene Prologue to his 1977 novel *The Shining* in which he tells the sordid "pre–Jack Torrance" history of the Overlook Hotel.

Chances of finding a copy: "Before the Play" has appeared in print twice; once in an unabridged version and once in an abridged form. The complete version appeared in a limited edition of *Whispers* in August 1982 (along with "On *The Shining* and Other Perpetrations"; see the chapter on that essay). The abridged version appeared in *TV Guide* prior to the 1997 airing of *Stephen King's The Shining* on ABC with scenes i and iii deleted. The *TV Guide* issue should be relatively easy to come by from any of the usual sources and also from used-magazine dealers throughout the country. The *Whispers* appearance is much more difficult to find, and if you do, it will be expensive—at least $250 and possibly much higher. (Stephen King originally gave me permission to reprint "Before the Play" in my 1990 book *The Shape Under the Sheet: The Complete Stephen King Encyclopedia* but decided against it at the last minute, telling me that he felt it needed work and he did not have the time to handle the revisions. I have a sense that he was referring to scenes i and iii, since these were the two chapters he deleted from the *TV Guide* appearance of the piece in 1997. In his brief introduction to this appearance, King wrote of the prologue, "I'm glad to see *the best of it* restored to print here."

163

[emphasis added] He obviously felt that scenes ii, iv, and v were the best of "Before the Play")

"Before the Play" was King's way of setting the stage for the terrible events that would take place in *The Shining*; it was a *beginning* that he wrote *after* completing the novel proper.

King wanted to tell (know?) more about the Overlook's history, and so he wrote this five-part prologue as a way of seeing more fully in his own mind the history that imbued the hotel and that changed all who set foot in it.

Here is a brief synopsis of what goes on in each of the five dramatic "scenes" of "Before the Play."

SCENE I: THE THIRD FLOOR OF A RESORT HOTEL FALLEN UPON HARD TIMES

The 1907 construction of The Overlook by Bob T. Watson; the tragic death of his son from a riding accident on the grounds; the hotel's premier season ("a nightmare"); the first hints that something unseen might be living in the Overlook; the choking death of a congressman in front of Bob T.'s inaugural guests ("It was as if . . . Poe's story about the Red Death had come to life in front of all of them"); Bob's refusal to admit defeat when the place starts hemorrhaging money (*"I'll still be running this hotel in 1940!"*); his eventual sale of the hotel and new career as the Overlook's maintenance man; the unexplained screams and sobbing he and his son begin to hear; the beginning of the nightmare of the hedge topiary.

SCENE II: A BEDROOM IN THE WEE HOURS OF THE MORNING

Lottie Kilgallon and her husband of ten days, publishing heir William Pillsbury, are spending their honeymoon at the Overlook. Lottie has been having nightmares ever since she arrived: A corpse takes her on an elevator ride to hell; she is attacked by the topiary animals; a fire hose comes alive and wraps itself around her while the hotel is on fire. Lottie begins sensing that there is something wrong with the boiler and that the whole hotel "creeps." She tries to cope with all this until one night when "a hand reached out from under the bed and gripped her wrist." She becomes almost catatonic and insists that they leave immediately.

Lottie ultimately commits suicide twenty years later, leaving a note that said, *"I wish we had gone to Rome."* It was as if the hand that had grabbed Lottie's wrist at the Overlook had never let go.

Scene III: On the Night of the Grand Masquerade

Lewis Toner, the discarded homosexual boy toy of the new owner of the Overlook, Horace Derwent, is found dead in the bathtub in his room on the night of a big masquerade party at the hotel. There is no sign of drugs in his body or foul play, and yet we readers had watched as Lewis swallowed three strange-looking pills from a bottle labeled "Seconal" that he had found in the medicine cabinet of the room. Derwent bought off the coroner and the town, and the story never made more than page 2 of the papers.

Scene IV: And Now This Word From New Hampshire

This scene tells the story of how Jack Torrance's father broke Jack's arm in 1953 when he came home drunk after wrecking the family car, foreshadowing the day when Jack Torrance himself would break his son Danny's arm years later when *he* came home drunk and found that Danny had made a mess of his papers. The scene ends with Jacky Torrance thinking, *"What you see is what you'll be,"* over and over.

Scene V: The Overlook Hotel, Third Floor, 1958

This final scene of the prologue tells the story of a brutal and violent mob hit on an organized-crime figure in the Presidential Suite of the Overlook ("a wet fan of blood, brains, and bits of flesh splashed across the cherry striped wallpaper"), concluding with the line, "The Overlook was at home with the dead."

Publishing History

1982: *Whispers* (August).
1997: *TV Guide* (abridged; April 26–May 2).

39

"Horrors!"

(CROSSWORD PUZZLE)

59 ACROSS: *fictional town where the natives get up late.*

—from "Horrors!" (The answer—for those who want [or need] it—is at the end of this chapter.)

What it is: a horror-themed crossword puzzle for which Stephen King wrote the 118 clues. (The grid was created by Mike Shenk.)

Chances of finding a copy: probably pretty good. Until the fall of 1997, this puzzle had only appeared in print twice, once in *Games* magazine in 1983 and once in *Castle Rock* in 1985. If it had never been reprinted after those two appearances, your chances of finding a copy would have been ranked as "extremely difficult but possible." In the fall of 1997, however, *Games* published a special twenty-year "Anniversary Issue" and included King's puzzle in the issue. This issue was pulled off the newsstands on December 9, 1997, but there *is* the possibility that back issues may still be available directly from *Games* magazine (see Sources and Resources section). I am not telling you that back issues of this "Anniversary Issue" *are* available; I'm just suggesting that it is worth writing to *Games* to see if they have them in stock. (Do *not* call.) Magazines do run out of copies of some of their issues, but anniversary issues are often kept in print because of their importance. Buy a recent issue of *Games* for an address to which to write for back-issue availability. Of course, if you are interested in the 1985 *Castle Rock* appearance of this puzzle, then you will have to try the usual rare book and magazine dealers, but the price (if you can even find one) will be significantly higher than a back issue of *Games* is likely to cost.

Games introduced "Horrors!" with the following:

> When he's not plotting his blood-curdling stories or sitting in on the filming of his latest bestseller, Stephen King likes curling up with a good crossword. For this collaborative effort, King put aside the convoluted world of the horror novel for the equally convoluted world of puzzledom.

"Horrors!" was graded three stars, which was *Games*'s code for "proceed at your own risk."

Stephen King must have had fun coming up with the clues for this nineteen-by-nineteen square-grid crossword puzzle. He used the opportunity to include some clever clues, such as names of horror novels and movies; historical references; and, of course, several of his ubiquitous pop-culture references.

Since this is a puzzle to be solved, I will only discuss the *clues* King wrote, leaving the answers to be determined by you, King's constant readers (and puzzlers!).

A good clue is 19 ACROSS: "Mia Farrow had a devilishly hard time in this fright film (1968)"; as is 48 ACROSS: "Streiber novel, Bowie movie"; 2 DOWN is clever: "Max Schreck in the classic 1922 film (he's a sucker for a pretty face!)"; as is 14 DOWN, "Maxwell's Silver Hammer, maybe?"; and 87 DOWN: "What Janet Leigh got at the Bates Motel" (and it's not what you think!).

King refers to several horror notables in this puzzle, including Ira Levin, Peter Straub, George Romero, Val Lewton, Vincent Price, John Carpenter, and Alfred Hitchcock; also, "nonhorror" artists such as William Shakespeare, Stanley Kubrick, Henrik Ibsen, Paul Schrader, Hammer films, Led Zeppelin, and Attila the Hun. King also refers to himself in the puzzle, using his body of work as a source of some of the clues and answers.

"Horrors!" is a very unique Stephen King creation, the kind of odd little project that he does not seem to have the time to do anymore.

Pity.

PUBLISHING HISTORY

1983: *Games* (October).
1985: *Castle Rock: The Stephen King Newsletter* (May).
1997: *Games* (fall; "Anniversary Issue").

The answer to **59** ACROSS is:

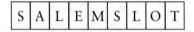

40

Silver Bullet

I think we should go against expectation and show the WEREWOLF—this first murder should be bloody and explicit—R-rated.

—from the "January" section of Stephen King's
1984 *Silver Bullet* script revision

What it is: Stephen King's handwritten (but unused) revision of the *Silver Bullet* screenplay, the film adaptation of his novel *Cycle of the Werewolf*.

Chances of finding a copy: impossible. These eight handwritten pages appear only in *The Stephen King Notebook*, a spiral-bound notebook King donated to a charity auction in 1988. It has traded hands a couple of times among collectors but is not available to the public in any form.

This outline by King for *Silver Bullet* is organized by month and stops (at least it does in *The Stephen King Notebook*) at August.

King's text flows naturally as the story progresses, and it is a testament to his narrative genius that you do not need to have read *Cycle of the Werewolf* to appreciate and enjoy these few pages of script outline (but it would undoubtedly help).

This chapter provides an abridged rundown of King's eight-month look at the events in Tarker's Mills. (King's final *Silver Bullet* screenplay was published in a trade paperback edition that also included the complete *Cycle of the Werewolf* novella and a new foreword by King.

Comparing the published screenplay with this handwritten outline will also be enlightening, since there are many changes from one to the other.)

(*Note:* The first time a character is mentioned in King's outline, his name appears in all caps.)

CAST OF CHARACTERS

(in order of appearance)

Arnie Westrum	The Pretty Girl
Marty Coslaw	The Pretty Girl's Father
Mr. Coslaw, Marty's father	Arnie Knopfler
Mrs. Coslaw, Marty's mother	Randall the Deputy
Uncle Al, Marty's mother's brother	Milt Sturmfuller
Stella Randolph	Andy Kincaid, Brady's father
Reverend Lester Lowe	Mrs. Kincaid, Brady's mother
Brady Kincaid	Mrs. Sturmfuller
The Drug Store Clerk	The Church Custodian
Sheriff Roy Neary	

JANUARY (3 SCENES) Arnie Westrum is murdered; Marty and his parents make their first appearance; "Uncle Al" becomes "Uncle Red" in the film; Reverened Lester Loew berates the pregnant Stella Randolph for being a sinner.

FEBRUARY (3 SCENES) We get our first glimpse of Tarker's Mills; we still don't know Marty is crippled; there are no leads in the Westrum murder case; Stella attempts suicide but is killed by the werewolf instead.

MARCH (6 SCENES) There's a full moon; we see Marty in his Silver Bullet wheelchair for the first time; a pretty girl Marty likes tells him about hearing noises in the shed behind her house; we first meet Uncle Al and learn he's a boozehound; the werewolf kills the pretty girl's father when he goes out to investigate the shed noises; the following morning the father's body is collected in three different plastic bags.

APRIL (7 SCENES) Marty and Brady fly kites; town vigilantes start to get riled up; the werewolf attacks Brady in the park and rips him to pieces; Brady's funeral; Brady's mother accidentally pours a vase of water on Marty's head.

(*Clockwise from top*) King's Victorian mansion, a popular tourist site in Bangor, Maine (GB Photos). A look at the first page of "Jhonathan and the Witchs," one of King's earliest short stories, written when he was nine (Author's Collection). Part of the contents page of *People, Places, and Things.* Note that "Steve King" had not yet become "Stephen King" (Author's Collection). The cover of the 1983 Bangor Historical Society's *Black Magic and Music* program containing King's appreciation for his hometown (The CF Collection).

The Glass Floor

by Stephen King

WHARTON MOVED slowly up the wide steps, hat in hand, craning his neck to get a better look at the Victorian monstrosity that his sister had died in. It wasn't a house at all, he reflected, but a mausoleum — a huge, sprawling mausoleum. It seemed to grow out of the top of the hill like an outsized, perverted toadstool, all gambrels and gables and jutting, blank-windowed cupolas. A brass weathervane surmounted the eighty-degree slant of shaky shingled roof, the tarnished effigy of a leering little boy with one hand shading eyes Wharton was just as glad he could not see.

Why was the old man so reluctant to let him see the room in which his sister had died?

Part

Chapter 1

The engine of the old Ford died, for the third time that morning. It died in the town square of a little South Carolina hamlet that, from the signs on the buildings, had been Graybill,

Will Be Necessary To Stop The Weeds

A chilling new story
by the author of "Carrie"
and "Salem's Lot."

BY STEPHEN KING

● Jordy Verrill's place was out on Bluebird Creek, and he was alone when the meteor traced low fire across the sky and hit on the creek's east bank. It was twilight, the sky still light in the west, purple overhead, and dark in the east where Venus glowed in the sky like a two-penny sparkler. It was the Fourth of July, and Jordy had been planning to go into town for the real fireworks show when he finished splitting and banding this last smidge of sugar maple.

SPECIAL CHET WILLIAMSON ISSUE!

Weird Tales

Fall 1990

US $4.95

STEPHEN KING
•
IAN WATSON
•
R. BRETNOR
•
FRED CHAPPELL
•
DARRELL SCHWEITZER

(*Clockwise from top left*) The real-world Bangor Standpipe, a landmark that figures prominently in King's novel *It* (Author's Collection). The opening page of King's first professional sale "The Glass Floor" (Author's Collection). A peek at the opening page of King's first novel, *The Aftermath*, which remains unpublished (Author's Collection). The cover of *Weird Tales* containing the rare reprint of "The Glass Floor" (Author's Collection). The rare *Cavalier* publication of "Weeds," the text version of the *Creepshow* segment, "The Lonesome Death of Jordy Verril" (Author's Collection).

(*Clockwise from top right*) The cover of the November 1982 *Twilight Zone* magazine containing King's appreciation of the horror movie classic *The Evil Dead* (Author's Collection). The manuscript of "The Killer" (Author's Collection). The first issue of the now-defunct Stephen King newsletter, *Castle Rock* (Author's Collection). The Bangor little league field, built by Stephen and Tabitha King for the local team (GB Photos). The *Whispers* title page of King's rare essay about writing *The Shining* (Author's Collection).

On The Shining and Other Perpetrations

by
Stephen King

MOST WRITERS will agree—with an almo[...]
bane of their existence is that question, "Where[...]
the fact is, they are a lot more ambivalent about[...]

The Killer
By Steve King

Suddenly he snapped awake, and relized he didn't know who he was, or what he was doing here, in a munitions factory. He couldn't remember his name, or what he had been doing. He couldn't remember anything.

For FJA —
with all best
wishes, Stephen
King

CASTLE ROCK

JANUARY 1985   **The Stephen King Newsletter**   ISSUE #1
****

This is the premiere issue of CASTLE ROCK, the Stephen King Newsletter. Our goal is to keep you up-to-date on the work of this prolific writer. CASTLE ROCK will be a monthly newsletter and we will have, along with all the news, trivia, puzzles, reviews, classifieds, contests, and, we hope, reader contributions.

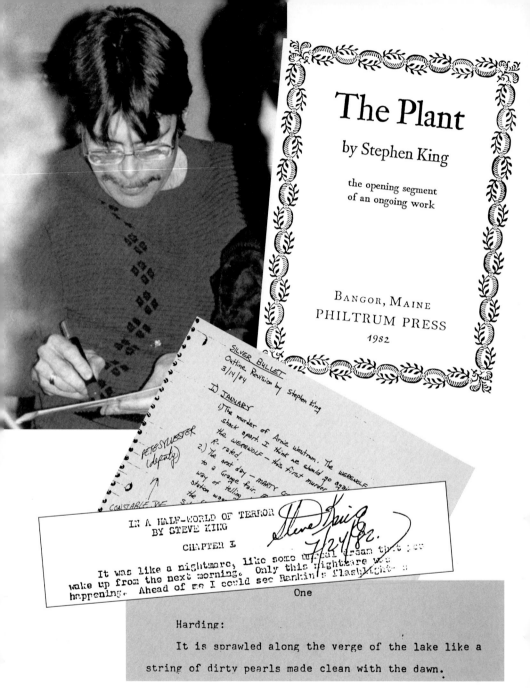

The Plant

by Stephen King

the opening segment
of an ongoing work

BANGOR, MAINE
PHILTRUM PRESS
1982

SILVER BULLET
Outline Revision by Stephen King
3/14/84

1) JANUARY
1) The murder of Arnie Westrum. The WEREWOLF
shook apart. I think we should go again
the WEREWOLF - this first murder
R- rated.
2) The next day - MARTY C
to a Grange fair. P
way of telling
the

PETE SYLVESTER
(deputy)

CONSTABLE

IN A HALF-WORLD OF TERROR
BY STEVE KING

CHAPTER I

It was like a nightmare, like some unreal dream that you
wake up from the next morning. Only this nightmare was
happening. Ahead of me I could see Rankin's flashlight a

One

Harding:

It is sprawled along the verge of the lake like a
string of dirty pearls made clean with the dawn.

(*Clockwise from top left*) King signing autographs at the *Graveyard Shift* press conference
(GB Photos). The title page of the first segment of King's abandoned serial novel, *The Plant*
(Author's Collection). King's handwritten revision of the *Silver Bullet* screenplay as it
appeared in what has come to be known as *The Stephen King Notebook* (The CF
Collection). The opening segment of "In a Half-World of Terror" (Author's Collection).
The first page of a very early King novel, *Sword in the Darkness*, still unpublished
(Author's Collection).

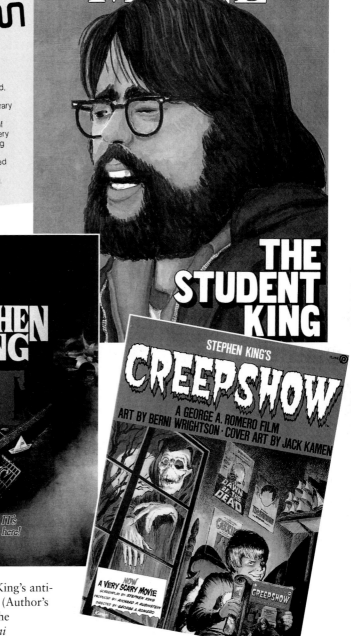

Every book that I've ever had published, with the exception of two, has been banned from one public-high-school library or another. *Cujo* has been banned so often now that it is on the ACLU's list of the top ten banned books. And I'm very proud of that, because I'm never going to win a Nobel prize or a National Book Award. But being on that list of banned books, I'm in the company of greats: Flannery O'Connor, Harper Lee, J. D. Salinger, and John Updike.

(*Clockwise from top left*) King's anti-censorship essay for *Omni* (Author's Collection). The cover of the *University of Maine Alumni Association* 1989 magazine featuring a cover story on King (Author's Collection). The cover of the comic book version of *Creepshow* (Author's Collection). The cover of the *Book-of-the-Month Club News* containing King's essay "How *IT* Happened" (Author's Collection).

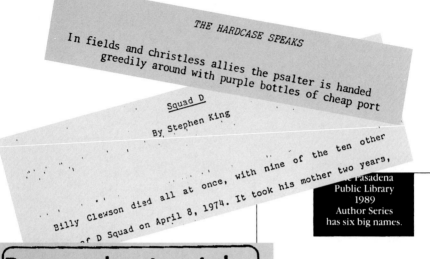

THE HARDCASE SPEAKS

In fields and christless allies the psalter is handed
greedily around with purple bottles of cheap port

Squad D

By Stephen King

Billy Clewson died all at once, with nine of the ten other
f D Squad on April 8, 1974. It took his mother two years,

e Pasadena
Public Library
1989
Author Series
has six big names.

Remembering John

By Stephen King
(Copyright 1980 Stephen King)

*"I read the news today oh boy/About the lucky man
who made the grade..."*

Following the breakup in 1971, he was not the first ex-
Beatle to have a critical success on his own; that was

Marjorie Hansen Shaevitz

Larry McMurtry

Sue Grafton

Barbara Wood

Stephen King

Nikki Giovanni

| Central Library |
| Donald R. Wright Auditorium |
| 285 E. Walnut St. |
| 7:30 - 9 p.m. |

(Clockwise from top) One of the rarest of King's works, his poem "The Hardcase speaks" (Author's Collection). The opening lines of King's unpublished short story, "Squad D" (Author's Collection). The ticket to King's Pasadena Library lecture, during which he talked about Almost Stories (Author's Collection). King lecturing at one of his infrequent public appearances (Author's Collection). King's eulogy for John Lennon (*Bangor Daily News*).

(*Clockwise from top left*) The July 1986 issue of *The Writer,* to which King contributed a how-to article (Author's Collection). King at the *Graveyard Shift* press conference (GB Photos). The reprint of King's "Horrors!" crossword puzzle as it appeared in *Games* magazine (Author's Collection). The first page of a very early King novel *Blaze,* which remains unpublished (Author's Collection). The cover of the rare *X-Men* comic to which King contributed a story segment (Author's Collection).

Turning the thumbscrews on the reader

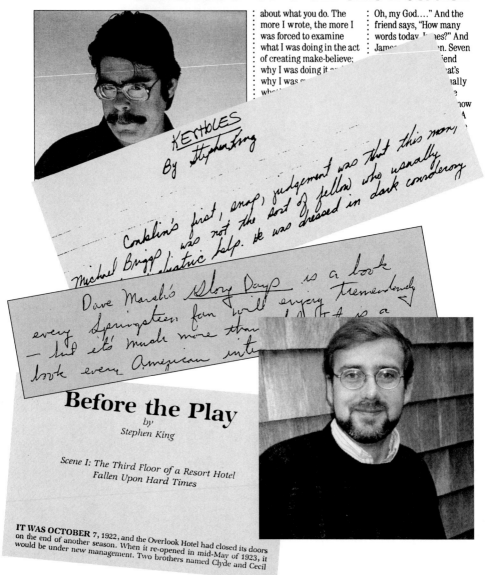

about what you do. The more I wrote, the more I was forced to examine what I was doing in the act of creating make-believe; why I was doing it ... why I was ...

Oh, my God...." And the friend says, "How many words today ... es?" And Jam... n. Seven ... end ... at's ... ally ... ow

KEYHOLES

By Stephen King

Conklin's first, snap, judgement was that this man was not the sort of fellow who usually ... Michael Briggs ... iatric help. He was dressed in dark corduroy ...

Dave Marsh's *Glory Days* is a book every Springsteen fan will enjoy tremendously — but it's much more than ... it 4 is a book every American int...

Before the Play
by
Stephen King

Scene I: The Third Floor of a Resort Hotel
Fallen Upon Hard Times

IT WAS OCTOBER 7, 1922, and the Overlook Hotel had closed its doors on the end of another season. When it re-opened in mid-May of 1923, it would be under new management. Two brothers named Clyde and Cecil

(*From top to bottom*) King's discussion of writing *Misery*, which appeared in the *Book-of-the-Month Club News* (Author's Collection). The handwritten manuscript for "Keyholes," a heretofore unpublished work, as it appears in *The Stephen King Notebook* (The CF Collection). King's handwritten appreciation of Bruce Springsteen written for Dave Marsh's book *Glory Days* but never used (The CC Collection). James Cole, director and screenwriter of the short film adaptation of King's short story "Last Rung on the Ladder" (Author's Collection). King's prologue to *The Shining*, "Before the Play" (Author's Collection).

MAY (4 SCENES)   There's another full moon; a drunken vigilante mob has been formed; they head out of town to look for the killer; in the woods the werewolf attacks the vigilantes and kills four of them, including Milt Sturmfuller.

JUNE (4 SCENES)   Tarker's Mills is in a panic; talk of a werewolf is rampant; Reverend Lowe has a "werewolf dream"; the Church Custodian is found "horribly massacred."

JULY (6 SCENES)   Fourth of July; a TV crew ("professional ghouls") arrives in town; Marty injures the werewolf's eye with fireworks he got from Uncle Al; we later see Reverend Lowe with a bloody eye socket.

AUGUST (3 SCENES)   Marty is sent to a camp for crippled children; Marty learns that Reverend Lowe is now wearing an eye patch; Marty writes to Reverend Lowe. The final scene of King's revision describes "dialogue at Knopfler's bar (or maybe at the barber shop?), in which Sheriff Neary assures Alfie . . ."; and that is where the revision ends.

Reading through King's revision of the screenplay and then comparing it to first the published novel, then the published screenplay, and finally the completed film provides an invaluable education for budding screenwriters.

Because of the many existing versions of this story, a student of film (or just a serious fan of Stephen King's) can watch the evolution of a movie and see how characters and scenes change and how compromises are made in order to translate a novel to the screen.

PUBLISHING HISTORY

1984: *The Stephen King Notebook.* (The *Silver Bullet* text is dated March 14; nothing in the *Notebook* has ever been published.)

SEE ALSO:

1985: *Silver Bullet* (October; New American Library trade paperback).

41

"1984: A Bad Year If You Fear Friday the 13th"

I try to stay at home cowering under the covers on Friday the 13th. God, I once had to fly on Friday the 13th—I had no choice—and while the ground crew didn't exactly have to carry me onto the plane kicking and screaming, it was still no picnic. It didn't help that I'm afraid of flying, either. I guess I hate surrendering control over my life to some faceless pilot who could have been secretly boozing it up all afternoon or who has an embolism in his cranium, like an invisible time bomb. But I have a thing about the number 13 in general; it never fails to trace that old icy finger up and down my spine. When I'm writing, I'll never stop work if the page number is 13 or a multiple of 13; I'll just keep on typing until I get to a safe number.

—from "The *Playboy* Interview: Stephen King" (June 1983)

[T]he year I'm really dreading is 1996. In that triple-whammy year I'll be 49. Can you add 4 and 9? As Mr. Rogers says, "I knew you could."

—from "1984: A Bad Year if You Fear Friday the 13th"

What it is: a nonfiction essay of about a thousand words about triskaidekaphobia—the irrational(?) fear of the number 13.

Chances of finding a copy: not too difficult if you have access to a good library (i.e., one that archives years of back issues of the *New York Times*) and you know how to work a microfiche reader. A more difficult source for the piece would be the *Castle Rock* issue in which this article was reprinted in 1987.

I have always preached (usually to the converted, I'll admit) that Stephen King has one of the most engaging nonfiction writing voices in print today, and this informative and entertaining article for the *New York Times* once again proves my point.

King begins with a discussion of the historical origins of the fear of the number 13, citing the story of the twelve Norse gods invited to party at Valhalla. The uninvited Loki—the thirteenth god—crashed the fete, got into a beef, and Balder, "the most popular god in the pantheon" was killed. King also mentions that Jesus was the unlucky "thirteenth" member of his band of disciples and that he was crucified on a Friday.

King talks about the "three on a match" superstition and admits that he still refuses to light three cigarettes on one match.

The thesis of this essay, though, is that there are dreadful consequences that can befall us all in what King calls a "triple whammy" year—a year in which there are not one or two but *three* Friday the thirteenths in the span of twelve short months.

King then looks at some of the events that took place in triple-whammy years, including the terrible flooding in Indiana in 1959, a deadly military plane crash in 1956, and the fact that Jack the Ripper claimed his final victim in 1888—a three Friday the thirteenth year. "My rational mind," King admits, "just loves information of this sort."

(At the time that I was working on this chapter, in September 1997, Princess Diana was killed in a tragic car accident in Paris. As you'll recall, this was probably the single biggest news story of the year, and the media all reported the same details, one of which gave me the feeling of a cold finger scraping up my spine: Diane's car crashed when her driver lost control and slammed into the *thirteenth* support pillar of the tunnel they were driving through. Maybe King's got a point?)

For the Stephen King fan, though, all this fascinating historical info pales when compared with the personal details King reveals in the essay. When talking about his own secret fears of the number 13 (with, as he describes it, "shamefaced honesty"), he tells us how he manages to cope with this "neurosis" (his word):

> *I always take the last two steps on my back stairs as one (making 13 into 12). . . . When I am reading, I will not stop on page 94, page 193, page 382, et al.—the digits of these numbers add up to 13.*

This behavior, he rationally acknowledges, is "neurotic" (again, his word), but it is also, he believes, "safer."

King obviously did his research prior to writing this article. He cites historical events with surety and notes that even though it might just be coincidence that bad things happen in history's triple-whammy years, "veteran triskies such as myself are not convinced."

King then concludes his essay with a revealing look at Stephen King in the year 1984, a guy he describes as "doing the best he can under circumstances that would give even the hardest triskie fits." King notes that in addition to 1984 being a triple whammy year and that this year he had been married thirteen years—he had a daughter who was thirteen years old and had thus far published thirteen books. Interestingly, King chose to ignore the fact that he had actually published *nineteen* books by 1984, but he could not, of course, reveal the Richard Bachman titles he had also authored—*Rage, The Long Walk, Roadwork,* and *The Running Man.* (King also seems not to have included his only nonfiction book, *Danse Macabre,* and the comic collection *Creepshow* in his rendering.)

"1984: A Bad Year if You Fear Friday the 13th" is yet another example of Stephen King's talents and enviable ability to both entertain *and* educate at the same time—and all within the confines of a brief, 1,000-word essay taking up only about four short columns of a much bigger newspaper.

PUBLISHING HISTORY

1984: *New York Times* (April 12).
1987: *Castle Rock: The Stephen King Newsletter* (November).

42

"My First Car"

*It was a 1964 Galaxie. Sharp. I was about 17. I bought it
from my brother for $250; he had gotten it as junk.*

—from "My First Car"

What it is: King's nostalgic remembrance about the first car he ever
owned.

Chances of finding a copy: extremely difficult, although if you do
find one, it will probably not be too expensive, perhaps in the $7–$20
range. *GQ* (*Gentlemen's* Quarterly) is infrequently archived in libraries,
although it should be. Try your local library and ask them to do a
search for libraries in your state that have back issues of the magazine.
They may come up with one near enough to make a trip for a photo-
copy. Another choice is to write to *GQ* (don't call) and inquire about
the availability of back issues, although the chances of their having an
issue from almost fifteen years ago are slim. Your last shot at acquiring
an original of this piece is to try the usual dealers. If they don't have
one, they may be able to keep a watchful eye out for one that does
become available on the secondary market.

This brief article by King was one of several that appeared under the
umbrella title "My First Car." (Contributors included Johnny Carson,
Roy Blount Jr., and many others.)

King's piece was accompanied by a photo of him standing beside his
second car, a 1956 Plymouth named Christine.

In his article, King remembers his first car fondly and talks about growing up in Durham, Maine, and living seven miles from his school and seven miles from the place he worked after school and summers— a textiles mill he would hitch a ride home from, often all alone at midnight.

King then relates what he describes as a "very memorable, very embarrassing, experience." His Galaxie's needle valve froze, and he and his girlfriend got stuck in the middle of a bridge (he later used this method to break down a car in *Cujo*), blocking traffic to and from the mill in both directions. "Sell it for parts!" he remembers hearing shouted at him as he waited to be extricated from this humiliating ordeal.

King concludes this affectionate memoir by admitting that "it was a beautiful car" with a "bright red vinyl interior" but that now "this car would probably look like shit to me. It's just in my memory that it seems great."

Ain't that always the case?

And not just with cars?

PUBLISHING HISTORY

1984: *Gentlemen's Quarterly* (July).

43

"Keyholes"

Conklin's first, snap judgment was that this man, Michael Briggs, was not the sort of fellow who usually sought psychiatric help.

—from "Keyholes"

What it is: an unfinished short story (or possibly the opening scenes of a novel?) consisting of two-and-one-half handwritten pages from a loose-leaf notebook. The text comprises twenty-six paragraphs and 768 words.

Chances of finding a copy: zero.

"Keyholes" is one element of a collection of oddities found in a spiral-bound notebook that King initially donated to a charity auction back in the eighties (the American Repertory Theater Benefit Auction, May 1, 1988) and which has since traded hands several times on the secondary collector's market (each time for a *lot* of money).

The Stephen King Notebook, as the aforementioned notebook has come to be known to fans, contains the unfinished "Keyholes"; several notes from King to himself and his wife, Tabitha; King's handwritten revision of the screenplay for his film *Silver Bullet* (based on his novel *Cycle of the Werewolf*—see the chapter on this revision); and page after page of King's solving algebraic equations by hand. What there is of "Keyholes" is brief.

 The entire segment appearing in the *Notebook* takes place in the office of a psychiatrist named Dr. Conklin. Dr. Conklin is preparing for a session with a construction worker named Michael Briggs, a troubled man who wants to talk to the good doctor about his son, Jeremy.

There is something going on with Jeremy, and Briggs isn't sure exactly what is happening. He tells Dr. Conklin, "I just want to know what's going on with my kid—if it's me or what."

The characters in "Keyholes" immediately spring to life: We can see Dr. Conklin, probably an older, dignified gentleman living a very nice life, thanks to his obviously thriving practice. His nurse describes him as an "expensive New York psychiatrist," with the emphasis on "expensive." We are also told that Dr. Conklin is trying to quit smoking by limiting himself to half a pack of smokes a day. Every morning he fills his cigarette case (probably sterling silver, or at the very least, pewter or silverplate?) with exactly ten Winston 100's—no more, no less—and when the cigarettes are gone, he is through smoking for the day.

Nancy Adrian is a strong character in "Keyholes"; in fact, she's the one who convinces Dr. Conklin to see Briggs.

King also intimates that Dr. Conklin and Nancy Adrian might have been an item once: "[O]nce over drinks, he had called her the Della Street of psychiatry, and she had almost hit him."

Michael Briggs is very reminiscent of another Stephen King troubled father character: Lester Billings, from King's seminal *Night Shift* short story "The Boogeyman." As in that story, Briggs is a single parent in "Keyholes," except that Briggs is a widower, while Billings was divorced.

As to what is going on with Jeremy, we're never told.

In this brief opening segment, King sets the stage, introduces the characters, and then simply stops writing (in the *Notebook*, that is, he could very well have much more of "Keyholes" written and has just never published it). At one point, though, Nurse Adrian remarks that "[Briggs] sounded like a man who thinks there's something *physical* wrong with his son." [emphasis added]. Except that he's telling his story to a psychiatrist.

After the expositional opening paragraphs that set the stage, we're back in the present time (*story* time, that is), and the piece ends with: "And here it was, Wednesday afternoon . . . and here was Mr. Briggs sitting opposite him with his work-reddened hands folded in his lap and looking warily at Conklin."

There is one clue early on in "Keyholes" when King describes the wary look Briggs gives the psychiatrist's couch in Dr. Conklin's office.

Whether or not that look actually means anything is never confirmed. All we're told is that Jeremy is seven, something is going on with him, and Briggs is very distraught about it. We can wonder if the title "Keyholes" would have ultimately revealed something about the situation, but unless King completes and publishes the story, we can only speculate.

It is fascinating to see how King works when he writes by hand.

For this story, he apparently just sat down and began writing. This story segment reads remarkably "finished" for a first draft. There are only eight or nine cross-outs, and the dialogue reads like a final draft. There are only a couple of errors in the story, and both involve the names of characters: Twice King refers to Nurse Adrian as "Nurse Abrams," confusing the name of the doctor he referred to early in the story with the name of Conklin's nurse. (There is also one—and only one—spelling error: King misspells corduroy as "courderoy." Overall, this handwritten first draft is remarkably clean.)

The partial manuscript of "Keyholes" offers a revealing glimpse at the working habits of one of the world's most popular writers and provides a rarely (if ever) seen insight into the actual creation of a story.

PUBLISHING HISTORY

Mid-1980s: never published.

44

"The Politics of Limited Editions"

*A real limited edition, far from being an expensive
autograph stapled to a novel, is a treasure. And like all
treasures do, it transforms the responsible owner into a
caretaker, and being a caretaker of something as fragile and
easily destroyed as ideas and images is not a bad thing but
a good one . . . and so is the re-evaluation of what books
are and what they do that necessarily follows.*

—from "The Politics of Limited Editions"

What it is: essentially a justification of limited editions of his books,
this two-part essay is King's response to readers who had been very
vocal about their dislike for limited printings of *The Dark Tower: The
Gunslinger; The Eyes of the Dragon;* and *Cycle of the Werewolf.*

Chances of finding a copy: extremely difficult if not impossible. "The
Politics of Limited Editions" has only appeared in *Castle Rock* and has
never been reprinted. Try the usual dealers if you're considering pur-
chasing the two original issues of the newsletter containing the piece. Be
forewarned, though. They will probably be pricey.

Back in the mid-eighties, when Stephen King published three books in
extremely small (for him) printings, booksellers all over the country
became extremely upset with him. King was, after all, a "Bestsel-
lasaurus" a writer people came into the store and actually *asked* for; a
writer whose books kept people working, children fed, and stores in
business.

Stephen King is prolific. Like Michael Noonan, the bestselling mystery writer in *Bag of Bones* who built up his own "literary savings account" by publishing one book a year but writing *one-and-a-half* books a year, King admits to having written two books a year for the decade spanning 1975 through the year of the publication of this article, 1985.

Such an output presents a problem for the publishing industry, since it directly contravenes the industry rule of thumb that a novelist should publish no more than one book a year. King had previously gotten around this arbitrary rule by creating *another* Stephen King—the now-"deceased" Richard Bachman—and using the Bachman pseudonym to publish five novels before the ruse was discovered.

King's motivating ideology regarding the art of writing is that publication of a work is the final step of the creative process. King fervently believes that "a novel in manuscript is like a man with one leg; a novel which has been printed and bound is like a man with two." Therefore, to *not* publish what he has written feels to King as though a "creation has been willfully crippled."

King makes the point in this long essay that he did not deliberately publish *The Dark Tower: The Gunslinger; The Eyes of the Dragon;* and *Cycle of the Werewolf* in small print runs initially to antagonize booksellers and frustrate his fans. He honestly believed that his mainstream "constant readers" would perhaps not be as interested in these odd works, but *he still wanted them published.*

The Dark Tower: The Gunslinger was a series of five connected stories that were originally published in five issues of the *Magazine of Fantasy & Science Fiction* and which were so much different from the novels for which he had become known that King did not think anyone would mind (or perhaps even notice) if he did a Donald Grant limited edition of the five stories in a small, attractively designed print run.

The Eyes of the Dragon was a fantasy fable written especially for his daughter Naomi and which likewise did not fit neatly into the Stephen King oeuvre. Again, King *wanted it published,* and since his usual publishers were glutted with King novels for the foreseeable future, he went ahead and did it on his own.

Cycle of the Werewolf specifically came into being as a calendar for a small press publisher, ended up evolving into a novel, and again was published because King wanted to see it in book form and his publishers simply did not have room for another King book at the time he wanted to see it released.

All of these works were, of course, eventually released in hardcover trade editions in enormous printings and are now also available in inexpensive paperback editions. However, when they were first published, King did not think they would go beyond the small audience that had bought the limiteds.

King's fans went rabid when King naively included *The Gunslinger* in the list of "Other Works" in the trade edition of *Pet Sematary*. Doubleday, Don Grant, King's office, and even Viking were immediately and relentlessly "deluged" with inquiries about the book. King eventually allowed Donald Grant to do another ten thousand copies of the book, an edition which King now wearily refers to as the "pissing on a forest fire" edition. (I have a copy of this second printing of the limited. I paid $45 for it in 1988. It is now estimated to be worth around $350 or more.)

As partial justification for his desire to publish his books in limited editions, King recounts an almost certainly apocryphal tale about J. D. Salinger. In this story, Salinger is seen by a fan depositing manuscripts in a bank. When he is confronted and asked why he doesn't publish these precious creations, Salinger reportedly replies, "Publish them? What for?"

King has his own answer to Salinger's question: "Publish them? What else?"

"The Politics of Limited Editions" is Stephen King's attempt to explain to his fans his belief that writing is more than just making toasters, even though bookstores treat books (rightly, I suppose) as nothing more than merchandise—commercial goods that must be replaced each year with the latest model. Writing is the *creation of art,* and King makes the point, firmly and with complete confidence, that the *artist* is the final arbiter of how, when, and *whether or not* his or her work should be made available to the people who want to experience it. The fact that I am successful, King seems to be saying, and my books support a great many people does not give my fans the right to tell me how to publish or when to publish. (In this essay, King also tells for the first time the story about James Joyce being upset because he had written seven words one day—a very good output for Joyce—but was troubled because he did not know in what order the words belonged! (See the feature on "Turning the Thumbscrews on the Reader" for more on King's use of this anecdote.)

In this essay, King is passionate about being able to publish his work in limited editions, but one cannot help but feel that King is ultimately a softie when it comes to his fans: After all, all of the limited-edition books he felt obligated to defend for their rarity are now available everywhere. I think that says more about King the man than King the writer. Deep down he is a fan; as such, he knows what getting his hands on the latest offering of a favorite writer means and how exciting such an experience is. Which assures the poorest of King's readers that no matter how expensive a limited edition of one of his books may be, there will undoubtedly be an inexpensive paperback edition of the book available at the grocery store, the drugstore, and the library.

Stephen King once gave Douglas E. Winter a signed first edition of *The Shining,* and his inscription in that rare and valuable book seems to sum up his feelings about assigning too much importance to limited editions. "Here's a True Fact collectors don't seem to know," King wrote. "It's the same story even if you print it on shopping bags,"

PUBLISHING HISTORY

1985: *Castle Rock: The Stephen King Newsletter* (part 1; June).
1985: *Castle Rock: The Stephen King Newsletter* (part 2; July).

45

Heroes for Hope Starring the X-Men

. . . the food melts into a sickening slush of putridity . . .
maggots squirm in the rotted remains of the sirloin . . .

—from Stephen King's segment of *Heroes*
for Hope Starring the X-Men

What it is: a special-edition *X-Men* comic book with story and art contributions from renowned writers and artists. All proceeds from sales of this comic went to famine relief in Africa.

Chances of finding a copy: difficult but not impossible. You certainly will not find a comic book in too many libraries (if any!), so you'll have to track down an original copy. The usual sources may have copies, or you can keep an eye open for a comics convention in your area. That's where I got my two copies—at the ridiculously low price of around three dollars each. As King fans, we are, of course, mostly interested in King's section, but the whole issue is terrific and boasts exciting writing by a legion of legends and wonderful drawings by an array of artists.

In 1984, 300,000 Ethiopians died from famine caused by devastating droughts in sub-Saharan Africa. Through 1985, more than 1 million people died from starvation and epidemic disease caused by the droughts. Worldwide relief efforts were hampered by warring factions engaged in a bloody civil war that refused to allow aid shipments free passage to the desperately needy.

Nevertheless, the world did respond to this terrible tragedy, and ultimately foreign grain did reach those in need. *Heroes for Hope Starring the X-Men* was one of the charitable projects undertaken to help those in need on the African continent.

Marvel Comics' editor in chief, Jim Shooter, wrote in an afterword to this special issue, "One night, a few months ago, artist Jim Starlin called me at home to propose an idea that his friend and fellow artist Berni Wrightson had suggested to him—that Marvel Comics publish a special issue of *The X-Men,* a benefit book for famine relief in Africa."

Thus, *Heroes for Hope Starring the X-Men* was born. On its cover we were told, "ALL PROCEEDS FROM THIS COMIC BOOK ARE BEING DONATED TO FAMINE RELIEF AND RECOVERY IN AFRICA." The issue sold for $1.50.

Shooter and his team recruited a truly stellar group of writers for this issue, including Stan Lee, Ed Bryant, Alan Moore, Harlan Ellison, and Stephen King.

Stephen King wrote the text for pages 10–12 of the issue. His colorist was Christie Steel; his penciler, Berni Wrightson; his inker, Jeff Jones; and his letterer, Tom Orzechowski.

Heroes for Hope Starring the X-Men reunited King with his *Cycle of the Werewolf* artist Berni Wrightson, and King's pages were the only ones in which Wrightson participated.

King's segment consisted of three pages, with a total of seventeen panels of art. His text ran 320 words.

The story grabbed the reader from the very first page.

One day, the mutant X-Men are confronted by a brutal physical *and* psychic onslaught by a powerful and horrifying enemy able to mentally break through the superheroes' defenses and force each of them to experience their own worst fears.

The enemy is actually a living manifestation of world hunger, a demon come to life as a dark force determined to destroy mankind and the world with its merciless horrors.

After they realize who is attacking them, the X-Men fight back with all their powers and travel to Africa to unload planes, feed the hungry, and bury the dead.

The story ends as it does in the real world: There is no real end to hunger and famine, but there is always hope and the promise of a better future:

And in the chill darkness of the African desert, they wait. For morning. For the next flight of relief planes, for the arrival of others as qualified for this struggle as the X-men are for those they must face back home. Together, human and mutant wait . . . and hope.

Stephen King's segment of this story is typically Kingish, and it is a testament to his talent that he can create a frightening and meaningful scene in the brief space of just three pages and 320 words.

In his segment, King adds depth to the malefic character of Hungry—the manifestation of world hunger—by having him torture X-Man Kitty Pryde. Hungry makes Kitty experience deadly starvation ("she has never been so hungry") and then torments her by offering her steak and buttered corn that transforms into a putrescent mush rampant with maggots when Kitty reaches for the food "with shaking hands which have become little more than bones wrapped in skin."

Hungry is uniquely eloquent for a Homo sapiens–hating, world-devouring, eternal and omnipotent revenant. He describes himself to Kitty as "Misery's Maître d'," "the Chef of Starvation," "Waiter to the Waifs of the World," and "Hash-Slinger to the Homeless."

While cruelly tempting Kitty with the rotten food, Hungry perverts the recitation of grace by chanting at the dying X-Man, "Good food, good meat, good God, let's eat!" This echoes King's *Skeleton Crew* short story "Cain Rose Up" in which King has Curt Garrish, the psychotic main character in that tale, chant, "Good drink, good meat, good God, let's eat!" as he begins shooting people from his college dorm window.

Heroes for Hope Starring the X-Men was a philanthropic attempt by creative artists to help put an end to the starvation and dying in Africa. All the artists and production people involved donated their efforts to the project, and by the end of 1985, the famine in Africa had abated, thanks to the countless humanitarian shipments of supplies and food, some of which were paid for by the money raised from sales of this comic book.

Publishing History

1985: *Heroes for Hope Starring the X-Men* (December 1; Marvel Comics Group special *X-Men* issue).

46

"My Say"

This 1985 "My Say" article was written by Stephen King in response to an earlier *Publishers Weekly* interview with Ron Busch, a publishing-industry veteran who headed Ballantine Books for four years and Pocket Books for six.

The Busch interview was titled "People Are Not Waiting Around for the Paperback," and in it Busch offered his thoughts as to why the mass-market paperback market was in what he saw as a precipitous decline.

Busch believed that several factors were contributing to this drop in sales, which he said was 50 million fewer copies in the first seven months of 1985 compared to the same period a year earlier.

Busch believed that sales were in the doldrums for several reasons, including paperback prices in excess of $3.95(!); "the mass marketing of hardcovers; the paucity of money-saving innovations; the lack of unique product; the discounting of hardcover books; the inflexible high overheads."

Busch asserted that paperback publishers were not thinking aggressively, nor were they keeping up with the changing times.

"The industry is not doing anything to find out what's wrong with it," he states. "If I were in paperback publishing today, I would want to do market research and find out those things about my customers that other mass merchandisers find out about theirs."

Busch believed that crossing the $3.95 price threshold was a mistake and also suggested in-book advertising as a possible cure for this ailing segment of the market. He also felt that book companies should follow the example of movie companies and seek out and work with "independent producers."

Busch's ideas and suggestions were somewhat radical and obviously did not sit too well with Stephen King, a writer who knows a little something about selling paperbacks. He found Busch's interpretation of the market flawed and did not like his suggestions for fixing it. Less than one month after Busch's interview appeared in *Publishers Weekly*, Stephen King's response was published in its "My Say" column.

Here is Stephen King's essay in its entirety.

(The author and publisher would like to express special thanks to *Publishers Weekly* librarian Gary Ink for his assistance in the reprinting of this piece.)

MY SAY

by Stephen King

It's wonderful that Ron Busch has had some time to think about the problems in paperback publishing. . . . He has pinpointed the problem, but has missed the clearest cause.

Why aren't people waiting around for the paperback? I offer my own experience as an answer. During the first 24 years of my life I bought only one hardcover book—William Manchester's Death of a President—*to give as a gift. Although I was (and am) a book-junkie, the idea of buying hardcovers never crossed my mind. I used to look into the windows of bookstores with the idle curiosity of, say, a construction worker looking at the necklaces in the display windows of Tiffany's. I grew up in lower middle-class circumstances, married early, became a father early. My first job as a breadwinner was pumping gas and some time after, I became a schoolteacher with a yearly income of $6,400. The hardcovers in our house always went back to the library in two weeks. What books we bought were paperbacks. I was not the exception but the rule. My good wife and I, along with those in our age group, were the paperback market in its golden age of sales. We were Baby Boomers, members of a generation with the widest reading ability and the greatest income expectation in history.*

I started buying hardcovers after Doubleday sold the paperback rights of my first novel, Carrie, *to New American Library for $400,000. All of a sudden I could afford to buy hardcovers. Maybe I beat some of my fellow Baby Boomers by a couple of years, and maybe I'm making more dough than most of them now, but my experience still parallels* *theirs. We came of age in an economy depressed by war, a glutted job market, and financial recession. We, the media's Flower Children of '72, became the media's Yuppies of '84—making not just a living wage but a relaxing one.*

What have we done with our discretionary income? Among other things, we have become bookbuyers. And what Ron Busch doesn't mention is this: we stopped waiting for the reprint because we could afford to buy at the source. I can trace that crucial market transition in my own career. Although Busch mentions me as one of today's bestselling authors who started in paperbacks, that is not the case; Doubleday was my original publisher. I don't think I got radically better between The Stand *(which topped out at #12 hardcover and at #1 in paperback) and* The Dead Zone *(which was #1 on both lists); I think that many of the readers in my age-group had, like myself, finally reached a financial point in their lives where they no longer* had *to wait for the paperback.*

Busch points to the fairly recent practice of discounting hardcovers as one of the reasons why paperback sales have lagged, and he's right, but he fails to put it in context. You can't discount an item unless it sells. If you try it, you take a beating. Discounting could not happen until volume sales made it possible. So my idea is simply this: paperback sales have not slumped because paperbacks finally broke the $3.95 threshold; similar fears about the $2.95 threshold proved unfounded. They slumped because paperbacks have become steadily less necessary to those in the mood to buy. Ironically, paperback prices have probably been pushed up for the same reasons that hardcover prices escalated so rapidly in the '60s and '70s: when your volume is off, you gotta raise your unit price and hope for a hit.

What can paperback publishers do? The obvious answer is not in-book advertising or independent production (which, in the movie business, has led not to the encouragement of creativity, but to a repetitive series of sexy teenpix, slasher films, and neo-war movies) but a mind change. This is very traumatic for book people; they think well, but are innovative as a last resort.

Part of the problem is simply self-image. Since 1945 or so, paperback publishers have seen themselves simultaneously as the only game in town and the junkyard dogs of the book business. Now, suddenly neither is true. That there is still an audience for paperbacks can be shown by a curious negative—the dog that didn't *bark, as Holmes might have said. When John Saul and V. C. Andrews—both extremely popular writers of paperback originals—were published in hardcover, the results were disappointing, yet the sales of these writers in softcovers have been and continue to be phenomenal.*

Sales potential exists now. Realization of that potential depends upon the willingness of paperback publishers to develop their own stable of reliable, salable writers (and this, as Busch indicates, depends to a large degree on the willingness of houses who sell both hard and soft to separate their trade and to drum into the heads of all concerned an 11th commandment: They Shalt Not Covet Thy Neighbor's Scribbler) and to widen their commitment to sell books not already pre-sold, either by the name of the writer or by their own megabuck investments.

Paperback publishers need to go back to the beginning and start looking not just for bucks but for good writers; to form a supportive bond with these writers. In the past, paperback publishers have been reapers. Now they must begin to plant and cultivate as well. *

Publishing History

1985: *Publishers Weekly* (December 20).
1989: *The Stephen King Companion* (George Beahm; Andrews and McMeel hardcover).
1998: *The Lost Work of Stephen King* (Stephen J. Spignesi; Birch Lane Press hardcover).

47

"Hello Mary Lou, Goodbye Rick"

[Rick Nelson], his fiancée, and his band were flying in a DC-3 that crashed and burned following a fire that may have been caused by a torch used to smoke freebase cocaine.

—from "Hello Mary Lou, Goodbye Rick"

What it is: a eulogy of sorts for someone *Spin* magazine hailed as "the whitest rock singer of them all," Rick Nelson, who had died at the age of forty-five several months earlier on New Year's Eve in a plane crash on his way to a gig.

Chances of finding a copy: very difficult. I know of no libraries or online magazine databases that archive *Spin* magazine. Back issues may be available from *Spin* itself, although the odds are that they will not have copies of an issue published a dozen or more years ago. The usual sources for King collectibles may be able to help (at a dear price probably if they even *have* an original copy of the issue), but this is one of those onetime King appearances that essentially vanishes into the ether if you do not buy it when it is first published.

Stephen King has been a rock-and-roll fan since way back (see the feature on his experiences with his band the Rock Bottom Remainders in the chapter "The Neighborhood of the Beast"), and in this essay he chronicles Rick Nelson's career and also provides an insightful look at the early years of rock's "golden age."

King was a Ricky Nelson fan, and he describes his output as "honest work by an honest worker."

He acknowledges that Nelson "had no soul in the Otis Redding/Sam Cooke/Jackie Wilson sense, or even in the Elvis/Jerry Lee/Buddy Holly sense." There was, however, something about Rick Nelson that was enormously appealing, and as King convinces us in this entertaining article, he also possessed a woefully underrated talent:

> *I think Nelson* did *discover soul somewhere along the way—he worked steadily to make himself better at his craft, and did so. In the mid-'70s he recorded a wonderful live album with the Stone Canyon Band, and one of those cuts is Nelson's version of Bob Dylan's "She Belongs To Me." Nelson's studio version was a modest country hit, peaking at number 32 or so. The live version is maybe the best cover of a Dylan song ever recorded, and what makes it so eerie is that Rick Nelson actually* sounds *like Dylan did on his* John Wesley Harding *and* Nashville Skyline *albums.*

King astutely discusses Ricky Nelson's experience with both unimaginable success and unexpected failure. (Like "Little" Stevie Wonder, who dropped the "Little" when he grew up, and "Ronny" Howard, who became "Ron," Ricky Nelson became "Rick" on his twenty-first birthday.)

From 1952 through 1966, Ricky costarred with his parents and brother, David (and later their real-live wives), in ABC's enormously popular show *The Adventures of Ozzie & Harriet.* (He and David had begun playing themselves in 1949 on the radio version of the show.)

From around 1957 through the end of the series, Ricky would often perform one of his songs during the show ("I'm Walkin' " was his first million-selling hit) either as part of the plotline of that week's episode or in an unconnected clip (I guess you could call them one of the first incarnations of the music video) that were unapologetically tacked on to the end of the episode.

Nelson's star faded in the mid-1960s after a string of singles that went nowhere, and his career was in the doldrums until his 1972 musical tirade against his detractors, the hit single "Garden Party," which he wrote after being booed off the stage during a concert at Madison Square Garden.

Stephen King apparently saw Nelson's response to his failing fortune as a sign of a greater artistic impetus, an inner strength and confidence that motivated him to just keep on rockin' no matter how small his fan base became. Nelson, King reminds us, was not on his way to a giant stadium show or an MTV concert when he died in a Texas field. He was heading for a party at a Dallas hotel where he and his band would play for the revelers just like any of a million local bands who play gigs at nightclubs and weddings on weekends all over the country.

As King puts it, Ricky did not whine or self-destruct when his TV show was canceled: "He simply went on rocking the best way he knew how."

"You were one of the good guys," King concludes, and he is, of course, right.

"Hello Mary Lou, Goodbye Rick" is just one more example of King's keen insight into the vagaries of pop culture and fame and another superb expression of a nonfiction sensibility that is sometimes eclipsed by his gargantuan presence in the world of fiction.

PUBLISHING HISTORY

1986: *Spin* (April).

48

"Everything You Need to Know About Writing Successfully— in Ten Minutes"

I know it sounds like an ad for some sleazy writers' school, but I really am going to tell you everything you need to pursue a successful and financially rewarding career writing fiction, and I really am going to do it in ten minutes, which is exactly how long it took me to learn.

—from "Everything You Need to Know . . ."

What it is: an entertaining "how-to" article in which King fulfills the promise of the title and teaches budding writers essentially all there is to know about writing successfully through a series of twelve to-the-point instructions that apply to the formation of just about every piece of successful fiction (and nonfiction as well, even though King is specifically discussing fiction writing) ever published.

Chances of finding a copy: shouldn't be too difficult, although you will have to find either a library that archives back issues of the magazine the *Writer* or one that has the out-of-print book *The Writer's Handbook* on its shelves. (Even though *The Writer's Handbook* is updated annually, new editions do not contain the same articles as previous editions, so you will have to find the 1989 edition in order to get your mitts on the King piece.)

By 1986, the year in which this article was first published, Stephen King had achieved such monumental success as a writer that he could write an instructional essay purporting to teach the reader everything there was to know about successful writing. There would be absolutely no doubt that he was telling the truth and that he knew what he was talking about.

King had published a couple of dozen bestsellers by 1986 (the year of this piece's first appearance), and the previous fall he had had *four* books—*Skeleton Crew, The Talisman, Thinner,* and *The Bachman Books*—on bestseller lists at the same time, a truly extraordinary event in the history of the written word.

When reading this article, one gets the sense that deep down King will always be a teacher at heart. "Everything You Need to Know . . ." is Stephen King at his most "teacherly."

King begins the essay by telling the story of "How Stephen King Learned to Write." He learned to write, it turns out, from John Gould, the editor of a small-town newspaper whom King ended up stringing for as a pseudopunishment for scatologically ridiculing some of his teachers in his own personal homegrown newspaper the *Village Vomit.*

King remembers turning in a piece about a basketball game and being incredibly enlightened after watching Gould go at his writing with the merciless blue pencil (Gould actually used a black pen) of a seasoned editor.

Here is what King remembers originally turning in:

Last night, in the well-loved gymnasium of Lisbon High School, partisans and Jay Hills fans alike were stunned by an athletic performance unequalled in school history: Bob Ransom, known as "Bullet" Bob for both his size and accuracy, scored thirty-seven points. He did it with grace and speed . . . and he did it with an odd courtesy as well, committing only two personal fouls in his knight-like quest for a record which has eluded Lisbon thinclads since 1953. . . .

Here is the revised version after Gould had edited it:

Last night, in the Lisbon High School gymnasium, partisans and Jay Hills fans alike were stunned by an athletic performance

unequalled in school history: Bob Ransom scored thirty-seven
points. He did it with grace and speed . . . and he did it with an
odd courtesy as well, committing only two personal fouls in his
quest for a record which has eluded Lisbon's basketball team since
1953. . . .

This experience placed some basic rules of writing on the creative
floor of King's multilevel brain.

For this *Writer* article, King thoughtfully listed each of his carefully
honed twelve cardinal rules and then explained in detail how precisely
to implement these decrees and turn out the kind of writing that people
will consistently pay for.

I will not delineate King's specific advice about each rule (track down
the article to read them for yourself), but it is of interest to at least
review the twelve commandments that King considers to be the essence
of everything you need to know to write successfully.

They are:

1. Be talented.
2. Be neat.
3. Be self-critical.
4. Remove every extraneous word.
5. Never look at a reference book while doing a first draft.
6. Know the markets.
7. Write to entertain.
8. Ask yourself frequently, "Am I having fun?"
9. Know how to evaluate criticism.
10. Observe all rules for proper submission.
11. An agent? Forget it. For now.
12. If it's bad, kill it.

"Everything You Need to Know About Writing Successfully—in Ten
Minutes" is an important and valuable essay. It neatly coalesces the
tenets of consistently effective commercial writing. King makes some
excellent points in the piece, one of the most relevant being: "The
biggest part of writing successfully is being talented, and in the context
of marketing, the only bad writer is one who doesn't get paid."

"The only bad writer is the one who doesn't get paid." That dictum

should be laminated and hung over the desk of every writer who aspires to greatness but who still has a mortgage to pay and kids to feed.

King's point is that if people are buying your work, then you are a successful writer, even if you're writing melodramatic science-fiction novels at the rate of two a year to pay the bills when what you really want to write is your own *War and Peace,* or even your own *Gone With the Wind,* for that matter.

As in King's own fiction writing, his voice in this article reeks with realism: Here is the situation, he tells the aspiring Stephen King (or Dean Koontz or Danielle Steel); deal with it or find another line of work.

One truly important rule (number 6), "Know the markets," is especially important. I personally have known writers who have sent cookbook proposals to military-book publishers. Talk about shooting yourself in the foot, eh?

Another important rule that many novice writers overlook is number 2, "Be neat." My editors (and I have had many over the past decade of writing professionally) have shared some amazing stories with me regarding inappropriate submissions. I personally have seen full-blown book proposals written *in longhand.* I felt like asking the writer, Would you show up for a job interview at a Fortune 500 company wearing shorts and a Hawaiian shirt? A book proposal written by hand is metaphorically the same thing.

A great many avid readers are also writers. Some get published; most do not. (The rule in the arts is, after all, failure. The successes are the exception, whether we're talking about TV, movies, acting, or books.)

With this fascinating and instructive article, Stephen King attempts to improve the odds for the determined yet unpublished writer, and he does it all—quite effectively, too—in just ten short minutes.

Publishing History

1986: *Writer* (July).
1989: *The Writer's Handbook* (The Writer Inc. trade paperback, 1989).

49

"For the Birds"

"It's a pun!" the King added in an offended tone, and
everybody laughed, "Let the jury consider their verdict,"
the King said, for about the twentieth time that day.

—from *Alice's Adventures in Wonderland*
by Lewis Carroll

What it is: a comedic short-short King wrote for a pun-laden anthology.

Chances of finding a copy: probably not too difficult. The anthology *Bred Any Good Rooks Lately?* is available in many libraries, and though out of print, copies of the book for purchase may often be found through rare- and used-book dealers.

☠ By 1995 the air in London has gotten so bad that the rooks (an Old World bird related to the American crow and similar in size and color) are dying off and jeopardizing London's tourist trade (especially the money generated by "Yanks with their Kodaks"). The London City Council hires a guy to breed rooks in Bangor, Maine, a city with a climate similar to London's but without the pollution. The start-up materials for the Bangor-based North American Rook Farms was two cases of rook eggs. The rook raiser was paid $50,000 a year by the London City Council to raise rooks so that London would not become "a rookless city." Since the Brits are especially eager to bring new life to their tourism business, they send the Downeaster a telegram every day which reads, "Bred any good rooks lately?"

"For the Birds" is a very short (and very funny) piece. King describes it as "a science fiction joke."

He wrote it for a collection titled *Bred Any Good Rooks Lately?* in which well-known writers (Annie Dillard, Roy M. Blount Jr., John D. MacDonald, Lawrence Block, Peter Straub, Robert Bloch, and others) all wrote short stories that ended with an absolutely horrendous pun. Editor James Charlton liked King's so much that he used it for the title of the book.

PUBLISHING HISTORY

1986: *Bred any Good Rooks Lately?* (Doubleday trade paperback).

50

"Pinfall"

Why is it that lazy, illiterate, slovenly, good-for-nothing imbeciles are always so righteously proud of their stations in life?

—Reggie Rambeaux, in "Pinfall"

What it is: an unfilmed segment of the *Creepshow 2* screenplay.

Chances of finding a copy: essentially impossible unless a copy of the *Creepshow 2* script is found in a script store.

☠ Two bowling teams, the Yuppified Regi-Men and the Archie Bunkerish Bad News Boors, end up going head-to-head in a play-off for a million dollars, which has been willed to the bowling team that ends up in first place at the end of the season. The money was left by an elderly millionaire who had a massive heart attack and died while bowling.

The insufferably arrogant Regi-Men decide to tilt the odds in their favor by killing off the Boors. They loosen the bolts on the right front wheel of the Boors' Econoline van, and the vehicle ends up flying off a cliff and exploding ("KA-BLOOOOOOOOOOOOOOOOOOEY!"), gruesomely killing all the Boors.

Late one night, after all the other teams have gone home, the Regi-Men stay at the lanes to practice and are visited by the "living dead" Boors, who kill off the Regi-Men one by one. One they kill by impaling on the hot-dog rotisserie and then microwaving his face. One they kill by drilling holes in his head with the ball drill. Another they dispatch by ripping his head off at the neck.

Sweet (and bloody) revenge ultimately belongs to the Bad News Boors.

"Pinfall" was reportedly dropped from the final *Creepshow 2* script because the special effects necessary to depict the gruesome deaths of the Regi-Men would have pushed the film considerably over budget.

"Pinfall" was clearly influenced by the classic *E.C. Comics* and has the same kind of dark sense of humor that many of the old "E.C." tales did.

Even though "Pinfall" was written as part of a screenplay (based on an unpublished King short story), King's special touch is clearly evident in the stage directions in the script. In the following excerpt, King, in his inimitable way, describes what the dead Chooch Mandolino (one of the Boors) looks like:

> [He] *looks more like an overcooked roast with nothing but black sockets running dark-colored fluids where its eyes and nose should be. The teeth make us realize it is a face. The grinning teeth that seem to be trying to shape the rotting flesh around them, trying to speak, but just rasping, gurgling.*

As the epigraph to this chapter reveals, King used "Pinfall" to make some trenchant comments about the kind of pompous arrogance so common in people who consider people from small towns "hicks," a title King feels no compunction about wearing with pride. When asked in a 1986 interview he did with *Inside,* the Orono High School student newspaper, "Why do you stay in Maine?" King replied, "I'm a hick. I grew up here. I went to one-room schoolhouses. There were outhouses. I am a hick and this is where I feel at home."

PUBLISHING HISTORY

1986: *Creepshow 2* screenplay (unpublished, unfilmed).

51

"Banned Books and Other Concerns: The Virginia Beach Lecture"

My idea about what a really good book is, is when the writer—whether he's alive or dead—suddenly reaches out of the page and grabs you by the throat and says: You're mine, baby! You belong to me! Try to get away! You want to cook some dinner for your husband? Too bad! You want to go to bed? Tough shit! You're mine! You belong to me!

—from the Virginia Beach Lecture

What it is: a lengthy "Banned Books Week" lecture and question-and-answer session delivered by King at the Virginia Beach Public Library on September 22, 1986.

Chances of finding a copy: excellent. Even though King's public lectures are extremely difficult to find in print, this particular talk—an important one—is available as a verbatim transcript in the revised edition of George Beahm's the *Stephen King Companion,* still in print in trade-paperback format.

King starts off this lecture by talking about banned books and what it feels like and means to him to be banned.

During her introduction of King, library volunteer Kelly Powell ticked off several recent incidents of King's books being yanked from school or public libraries for reasons that included foul language, graphic violence, explicit sex, and in one case, for being "garbage."

King good-naturedly (and a little sarcastically) acknowledged these attempts at censoring him by beginning his talk with: "That's the most uplifting introduction I've ever had. Think of all those places I've been banned."

This talk (given while King was battling strep throat) is less polished and more informal than his writings because, according to King, it is mostly unrehearsed. "I don't lecture because I don't really know how," he told his audience, "and I don't make speeches because I don't know how to do that. What I do is let my jaw fall open and let it run by itself."

King peppers his talk with anecdotes about his life and career. One particularly astute (and funny) story King tells is about a little old lady who came to hear King speak after 'Salem's Lot was published. She later told him that she liked the story but that she "didn't like all that foul language."

She then went on to tell King that she saw no need for a story to have all that foul language in it, to which King replied that he was writing "the way guys talk in the barbershop on Saturday morning."

The woman then told him that she herself had been in a barbershop on a Saturday morning and that the men she met there certainly did not speak like the characters in King's books.

"Madam," King patiently said, "I am writing about the Saturday mornings you *didn't* come."

King then talks about fiction and truth, once again making the point that he has made so many times before that "the real truth of fiction is that fiction is the truth; moral fiction is the truth inside the lie."

King speaks passionately during this talk about First Amendment rights and accurately reminds his listeners that "some of our most famous leaders have been book-banners, like Hitler, Stalin, Idi Amin."

The second half of this program consisted of King answering questions written out by audience members before the lecture and also taking some "live" questions from the congregation.

The written questions were typical, the first being, of course, "Where do you get your ideas?" Instead of jokingly replying "Utica," as he did in " 'Ever Et Raw Meat?' " King answered simply, "I don't really know; they come."

When asked what it felt like to be famous, King told the story of giving an autograph while sitting on a toilet in a hotel public bathroom during a book tour.

King also talked about the scenes that actually scared him as he was writing them (the ax and blowtorch scene in *Misery*, the dead woman in the bathtub scene in *The Shining*, and the entire final sequence of *Christine*); and he also discussed pending film adaptations of some of his books.

Other topics touched on by King during this entertaining talk were: collaborating on *The Talisman* with Peter Straub (he enjoyed it but would not do it again); whether or not any of his stories are truly auto-biographical (they often start out that way, but then he changes everything around to fit the story); and whether or nor he was a Boston Red Sox fan. ("Do ursine mammals excrete in high foliage inside the woods?")

The lecture and question-and-answer period lasted about ninety minutes, and then King left, with two security guards, to return home in his private chartered jet.

The following day, the Virginia Beach mayor's office and the library each received complaints about King's drinking beer during his talk (he was using it to soothe his irritated throat) and his use of foul language in public. (He had used the word "bullshit.")

These petty gripes were the only backlash of King's successful appearance, one which raised quite a bit of money for the library. According to George Beahm, who covered the appearance and transcribed the lecture for his book *The Stephen King Companion*, when King returned home, he sent the library his personal check reimbursing them for any royalties he would have earned on King books sold prior to the lecture.

PUBLISHING HISTORY

1989: *The Stephen King Companion* by George Beahm (verbatim transcript; Andrews and McMeel trade paperback).

1996: *The Stephen King Companion: Revised Edition* by George Beahm (verbatim transcript; Andrews and McMeel trade paperback).

52

"How *It* Happened"

*I'm not a bright novelist, no Graham Greene or Paul
Bowles. If I wrote a book with a conscious theme I would
end with a bunch of sound and fury.*

—from "How *It* Happened"

What it is: a short nonfiction essay in which King talks about how he
came up with the idea for his massive novel *It.*

Chances of finding a copy: difficult. I know of no libraries that
archive the *Book-of-the-Month Club News,* the journal in which this
piece originally appeared in its entirety. The abridged version in the
Writer is available in some libraries but will be a tough find.

King originally wrote this "behind-the-scenes" essay on his magnum
opus, *It,* to accompany the novel's offering as the main selection by the
Book-of-the-Month Club in October 1986.
   "When an idea comes," King wrote, "it comes all at once. It's so
bright it blinds you like a flashbulb in a darkroom."
   King then talks about the moment when he thought about the fairy
tale "The Three Billy-Goats Gruff" and how the image of a bridge and
the trolls who lived beneath it evolved into the town of Derry and the
monster that lived beneath it in its sewers.
   King also evocatively uses the image of a yo-yo as a metaphor for an
idea: "[I]t may go to the end of its string, but it doesn't die there; it only
sleeps. Eventually, it rolls back into your palm."
   King also reminisces about his childhood in Stratford, Connecticut,

and the public library there, which was divided into adult and children's sections by a short corridor. The corridor became yet another symbol for the bridge. "Sometime in the summer of 1981," King wrote, "I realized that I had to write about the troll under the bridge or leave him—*It*—forever."

King concludes his discussion of the process of writing *It* (the book this writer considers King's finest work) with an image (appropriately, I think) from J.R.R. Tolkien's *Hobbit*; specifically Bilbo Baggin's notion that the road leads ever on and that "way may lead on to way."

THE *BOOK-OF-THE-MONTH CLUB NEWS* VERSION

The *Book-of-the-Month Club News* published the complete essay. It included the complete story of the "troll under the bridge," with details on precisely what King was doing when the image "blinded" him.

King and his family were living in Boulder, Colorado, in 1978. One day, on their way back from lunch at a pizza place, the transmission in their brand-new AMC Matador fell out, leaving them stranded in a busy thoroughfare in the middle of Boulder.

According to King, "two guys from the local dealership eventually came, smoked Camels, and finally hooked the car to a tow truck." (Call me odd, but I consider that to be one of the funniest lines King has written.)

Two days later, the car was fixed, and King decided to walk the three miles to the dealership to pick it up. It was nearing twilight when he finally got to the road connecting the industrial park, where the dealership was, to the city of Boulder. A quarter of a mile along this road was a wooden bridge spanning a stream. King was wearing his cowboy boots at the time (he was in Colorado, after all), and his heels made a clicking sound on the wood as he crossed the bridge. It was then that the image of the trolls under the bridge came to him and *It* was born.

THE *WRITER* VERSION

The version of "How *It* Happened" that was reprinted in the *Writer* eight months after its original appearance completely deleted the whole opening "dropped transmission" story.

Other than that cut (which was definitely an edit for space, not for content), the remainder of the essay was printed as it appeared in the *Book-of-the-Month Club News*.

In the Beginning . . .

Along with "How *It* Happened," the *Writer* also reprinted an excerpt of a 1975 essay by King called "Writing a First Novel" in which he talked about the day he learned that he had sold his first novel, *Carrie*. It is notable for the inclusion of the complete text of the telegram King's first editor, Bill Thompson, sent to King after he had secured the novice writer a book deal:

CARRIE OFFICIALLY A DOUBLEDAY BOOK. $2500 ADVANCE AGAINST ROYALTIES. CONGRATS, KID—THE FUTURE LIES AHEAD. BILL.

This brief excerpt begins with King's on-the-money remembrance of what it felt like to sell your first book:

Remembering where you were and what you were doing when you found out your first novel had been accepted for publication is as easy as remembering where you were on Pearl Harbor Day or on November 22, 1963—although the circumstances are much more pleasant.

King was preparing for an American literature class at Hampden Academy, the school where he was teaching at the time, when his wife, Tabitha, called, breathless with the good news.

After admitting that he had just sold the paperback rights to *Carrie* for "a goodly sum" and that the movie rights to the book had been optioned, King offered some advice to the beginning novelist: "*Don't* write your novel with the best-seller lists or movie companies or rich paperback houses in mind." [emphasis added].

King was still a novice in terms of a publishing track record when he wrote "Writing a First Novel," but he had had years of experience just *writing,* and he made the concluding point that even if a writer decided his or her first novel was dead, the experience of writing it was valuable: "If nothing else, he's not a beginner anymore when he sits down to write that second book."

Publishing History

1986: *Book-of-the-Month Club News* (October).
1987: *Writer* (April; abridged version).

53

"The Dreaded X"

[T]he Brits don't rate movies the same way we do. They rate according to quality and effect.

We Americans, on the other hand, count.

What do we count? Heads (if they roll, that is); breasts; nipples; pubic thatches; blood-bags; profanity; mutilations; acts of violence.

—from "The Dreaded X"

What it is: King's lengthy discussion of the movie-ratings system and how his movie *Maximum Overdrive* almost received an "X" rating (this was written in the pre "NC-17" era) because of several graphic scenes of violence.

Chances of finding a copy: difficult. The *Castle Rock* appearance and the original *Gauntlet* magazine appearance are likely now only available through the collectors' market. The Borderlands Press anthology, which collected several articles from *Gauntlet* magazine, may be available in some libraries, although many school and public libraries would not buy the book because of several pieces in it that had explicitly sexual themes or which discussed graphic violence.

"The Dreaded X" is an important and reasoned look at what can only be described as America's schizophrenic movie-ratings system, one that classifies Steven Spielberg films as "PG" movies no matter what kind of violent scenes they contain (remember the bloody-face and corpses-in-the-swimming-pool scenes in *Poltergeist?*) but considers breasts and the word "fuck" "R" ratings criteria.

King talks about the "Dreaded X," and looks at the transformation of that rating from something that serious filmmakers could use to tackle blatantly adult topics (*Midnight Cowboy* and *Last Tango in Paris* were both originally released as X-rated movies) to a rating appropriated by the porno world as their own. Since this essay was written over ten years ago, King was amazingly precognitive. The corruption of the "X" rating and its appropriation by the "adult" filmmakers was precisely the reason the ratings system was revamped in the nineties and the films that would have previously been rated "X" are now rated "NC-17" (*no one* under seventeen admitted, period).

Back in 1986, "X" ratings were still being doled out, and extreme violence was one of the elements in a movie that would assure its makers of a "dreaded X" rating. Brian De Palma's *Scarface* received three "X" ratings (for extreme violence, including the arm-dismemberment-with-a-chainsaw scene and 123 1/2 uses of the word "fuck") before finally receiving an "R" after several return trips to the editing room. (The "half a fuck" comes when Al Pacino is interrupted as he is saying, "What the fu—")

King does not like the "count the titties and count the fucks" philosophy of the American ratings system. He believes that the scenes (both sexual and violent) and language of a film should be considered within the context of its entirety—as is the practice in England.

After discussing how the ratings system affects the horror-movie genre, King makes the point that "if it has a place in life . . . it has a place in art." He is saying that art that lies is fraudulent and artists that lie are frauds.

King clearly has a point, which he effectively illustrates with the following "down and dirty" hypothetical passage:

> *Our Hero is a guy who's been tied up and left in the empty cellar of a deserted house. The villain could have killed him outright but instead decided to leave him there so he—Our Hero, that is— would starve by slow degrees. . . . Hours pass. Days, perhaps. . . . There's some give in the ropes holding him but not quite enough to allow him to slip free. Looks like it's all over.*

> *Then, inspiration!*
> *Our Hero shits his pants!*
> *He shoves one hand into the mess, smears his wrists with excrement, and, with the aid of this organic lubricant, is able to slip free of his bonds.*

King makes the point that such a scene will never be filmed because it is *too* real and society is not ready for *that* much "real life" in a movie. Yet scenes showing more gore and blood than the average person will ever see in ten lifetimes are routinely accepted and rated. Silver screen schizophrenia abounds and reigns!

King concludes the essay with the detailing of his own new movie-ratings system. He begins by suggesting that a rating should be mandatory for every feature film released in the United States. (Rating is most certainly *not* mandatory—it's purely voluntary—and today many studios will opt for releasing a film unrated if they are certain it will get a box-office-crippling NC-17 rating and they absolutely do not want to cut a single frame from the movie.)

King also thinks that we should shift to a ratings system that looks at a film's gestalt rather than isolated scenes and words—again, in the manner of the Brits. He then suggests a new "AV" rating—no one under eighteen admitted due to scenes of explicit violence—and a new "AS" rating—no one under eighteen admitted due to scenes of explicit sexual content. King also wants to impose stepped rating fees: "G" movies would cost the least to rate; "AV," "AS," or "X" films would cost the most.

Today we are seeing a move toward more informative ratings, but, ironically, this is happening in TV, not movies. TV shows routinely carry ratings now, and many networks now also add an "L" for language, "V" for violence, "D" for explicit dialogue, or "S" for sexual content to their ratings.

"The Dreaded X" was obviously inspired by King's frustration with the ratings system while shooting *Maximum Overdrive*. He wanted to show a little kid getting splattered by a steamroller and having the kid's head explode. Dino de Laurentiis, the film's producer, shook his head and told King, "It will never get by the ratings board. This is X, Stephen." As King learned more, he realized that he *had* to say something about this bizarre system. In so doing, he ended up making a larger statement about America's national "immaturity," for want of a better word, when it comes to matters of sex, especially the kind you pay seven dollars to go see on a giant screen in a building that shows nine movies at once.

Publishing History

1986/1987: *Castle Rock: The Stephen King Newsletter* (December/January).
1991: *Gauntlet: Exploring the Limits of Free Expression* (April).
1991: *Gauntlet 2* (Borderlands Press anthology; May).

54

"My Ten Favorite Fantasy-Horror Novels"

AND

"My Ten Favorite Fantasy-Horror Short Stories or Novellas"

I'll stand by these . . . and probably hang by them.

—from King's afternote

What it is: King's two contributions to *How to Write Tales of Horror, Fantasy & Science Fiction,* J. N. Williamson's 1987 Writer's Digest Books nonfiction anthology.

Chances of finding a copy: good. Even though Williamson's book is ten years old, a trade paperback edition is still in print but may not be in stock in that many bookstores. You might have to special-order a copy, but the book should still be available.

Stephen King was asked to contribute his Top Ten lists to a lengthy section at the conclusion of Williamson's *How To* book, and he provided an interesting and eclectic list of horror-fantasy novels and short stories.

In 1987, at the time he wrote this piece, King's ten favorite horror-fantasy novels were:

Something Wicked This Way Comes by Ray Bradbury
The Doll Who Ate His Mother by Ramsey Campbell
The Body Snatchers by Jack Finney
The Haunting of Hill House by Shirley Jackson
The Ceremonies by T.E.D. Klein
Burnt Offerings by Robert Marasco
I Am Legend by Richard Matheson
Interview With the Vampire by Anne Rice
Donovan's Brain by Curt Siodmak
Ghost Story by Peter Straub

King's ten favorite horror-fantasy short stories or novellas were:

"In the Hills, the Cities" by Clive Barker
"Sweets to the Sweet" by Robert Bloch
"Small Assassin" by Ray Bradbury
"Slime" by Joseph Payne Brennan
"The Companion" by Ramsey Campbell
"The Lottery" by Shirley Jackson
"Children of the Kingdom" by T.E.D. Klein
"The Pale Brown Thing" by Fritz Leiber
"Prey" by Richard Matheson
"Nightcrawlers" by Robert R. McCammon

King makes the point in an afternote that he listed these works in alphabetical order and did not include anything by H. P. Lovecraft because of editor Williamson's cutoff date.

King also provides a list of also-rans that he wishes he could have included; this addendum alone is worth the price of admission. (King's runners-up included more stories by Fritz Lieber, Ray Bradbury, and Clive Barker, as well as Richard Matheson's novel *The Shrinking Man*, William Sloane's novel *The Edge of Running Water*, and Anne Rivers Siddon's classic novel *The House Next Door*.)

In the novel category, several titles stand out as being significant. King wrote a screenplay of *Something Wicked This Way Comes* that was never produced. *I Am Legend* was a clear and obvious influence on King's *'Salem's Lot*. (For that matter, Richard Matheson has been an important influence on *all* of King's writing.) In 1970, King wrote a poem called "Donovan's Brain," which was inspired by both Siodmak's novel and its subsequent film adaptation, and of course King coauthored *The Talisman* with Peter Straub, author of *Ghost Story.*

Interestingly, many of Stephen King's *own* works were mentioned in the other contributors' Top Ten lists. (Other participants in this horror-fantasy roundtable included Orson Scott Card, Harlan Ellison, Ramsey Campbell, Ardath Mayar, Jane Yolen, Douglas E. Winter, Joe R. Lansdale, Richard Christian Matheson, Stanley Wiater, F. Paul Wilson, Chet Williamson, Roger Zelazny, and many others.

Here is a listing of the Stephen King works cited as "Favorites" by this august conclave of writers:

Carrie	*The Breathing Method*
'Salem's Lot	"Crouch End"
The Shining	"The Reach"
The Stand	"Gramma"
The Dead Zone	"The Gunslinger"
The Talisman	"I Am the Doorway"
Pet Sematary	"The Monkey"
It	"Night Surf"
The Body	"Nona"
The Mist	"Quitters, Inc."
"Children of the Corn"	"The Raft"
"The Mangler"	"Sometimes They Come Back"
"Popsy"	"Strawberry Spring"
Apt Pupil	"Survivor Type"
"The Boogeyman"	"Word Processor of the Gods"

How to Write Tales of Horror, Fantasy & Science Fiction is much more, however, than just a listing of Top Ten reading suggestions. It is a literal gold mine of advice and inspiration for budding genre writers, and even though you may buy it just for King's contributions, you will find a great deal more of value in the book, whether you're a writer or just a reader.

PUBLISHING HISTORY

1987: *How to Write Tales of Horror, Fantasy & Science Fiction* (Writer's Digest Books hardcover).
1996: *How to Write Tales of Horror, Fantasy & Science Fiction* (Writer's Digest Books trade paperback).

55

"A Postscript to *Overdrive*"

"I thought the scene where the steamroller ran over the kid was particularly good," Angus Young [guitarist of AC/DC] said. . . . "Not because it was bloody and gory . . . but because it's something one doesn't expect to see."

—from "A Postscript to *Overdrive*"

What it is: Stephen King's final thoughts on directing *Maximum Overdrive* and his feelings about the three cuts they had to make in the movie in order to score an "R" rating.

Chances of finding a copy: essentially impossible unless you can find a dealer who has an original February 1987 issue of *Castle Rock* and is willing to sell it. This essay appeared in *Castle Rock* around the time *Maximum Overdrive* was released on video and has never been reprinted.

In this brief essay, King talks about what he and his fellow *Maximum Overdrive* filmmakers had to go through in order to get their movie rated "R." As a follow-up to "The Dreaded X," King once again discusses the sometimes ludicrous American film-rating system.

King and company screened the original, uncut version of *Maximum Overdrive* three times prior to its national release, once in New York, once in Las Vegas, and once in King's hometown of Bangor, Maine. King recalls (somewhat gleefully) that at one of the screenings none other than George *"Night of the Living Dead"* Romero gasped and turned away at the steamroller scene.

Ultimately, the Movie Ratings Board decided that the uncut version of the movie contained thirty-one "areas of concern." The board told King and his colleagues that these "areas of concern" might have "possible deleterious effects on children."

King's reaction? "I don't blow my top easily," King wrote, "but I blew it then. In fact, I think it went into orbit."

Why? Because King and his producers were *deliberately* going for an "R" rating for *Maximum Overdrive,* one that would prohibit children from being admitted to the theater without a parent or guardian. This rating forces parents to take responsibility for what their kids will see, and for the ratings board to worry about children possibly being damaged by scenes in a movie they *were not even supposed to see* unless their parents said they could struck King as the epitome of absurdity.

After receiving their findings, King made a suggestion to the ratings board: "Take your list and cram it up Jack Valenti's old tan track."

Finally, the thirty-one pernicious-scenes list was reduced to a mere three. By making this trinity of edits, King and Dino de Laurentiis would avoid the "dreaded X" rating that would have not just killed the movie at the box office but actually delivered it stillborn.

The three cuts King and company agreed to make were the following:

1. Six seconds of the Dixie Boy shoot-out. Reason? Too many blood bags.
2. Six seconds of a close-up in which a traveling salesman's face falls off into his lap.
3. The last three seconds of the steamroller-running-over-the-kid scene.

"A Postscript to *Overdrive*" finds King looking back with sage perspective on an experience that excited him, frustrated him, and also taught him how the Hollywood machine—*and* Jack Valenti's ratings board—works.

Reading this essay in conjunction with "The Dreaded X" makes it easy to believe the rumor that, after directing *Maximum Overdrive,* Stephen King is reported to have said he would never direct another movie again. And who could blame him?

The world of movies is, after all, one in which a Steven Spielberg can show a guy pulling his face off in bloody chunks in *Poltergeist* and get a "PG" rating, and yet when a Stephen *King* shoots a similar scene, he is threatened with an "X."

Doesn't hardly seem fair, now, does it?

PUBLISHING HISTORY

1987: *Castle Rock: The Stephen King Newsletter* (February).

56

"Why I Wrote *The Eyes of the Dragon*"

Writing The Eyes of the Dragon *was a satisfying and exciting act; like Naomi, I was a little sorry to see it end.*

—from "Why I Wrote *The Eyes of the Dragon*"

What it is: King's personal essay about writing his fantasy *The Eyes of the Dragon* specifically for his daughter, Naomi, who, by the age of thirteen, had never read one of his books.

Chances of finding a copy: the only way to read the entire essay would be to buy an original copy of the ten-year-old issue of *Castle Rock* in which it was published in its only unabridged appearance. An abridged version of this piece (*very* abridged—only four paragraphs) was used for the back flap copy of the Viking hardcover edition of *The Eyes of the Dragon*. *None* of this essay was used for the Signet paperback edition of the novel. (Go figure.)

What I like the most about this essay is King's recounting of the moment he sat down to begin writing his fantasy novel *The Eyes of the Dragon* (which, at the time, he was calling *The Napkins*).

He was alone in his western Maine house, and a "screaming northeaster was blowing snow across the frozen lake outside." Now picture Stephen King inside this house, sitting in front of a roaring woodstove with a yellow legal pad in his lap and a beer on the table next to him.

Now watch as Stephen King writes on the top line of the pad, "Once, in a kingdom called Delain, there was a King with two sons."

King may have smiled after writing those words and then taken a sip of his beer before continuing on to tell the story—sorry, the *tale*—of Peter and Thomas and King Roland and the sinister Flagg in one of his most enchanting narratives to date.

In "Why I Wrote *The Eyes of the Dragon*," King reveals that his teenaged daughter, Naomi, had never read one of his books and that she did not count him as one of her favorite writers. "She's made it clear that she loves *me*," King writes, "but has very little interest in my vampires, ghoulies, and slushy crawling things."

Thus, he decided to write something that would specifically appeal to his daughter, a "gentle soul" whose tastes leaned more towards Piers Anthony, John Steinbeck, Tanith Lee, and Shakespeare.

He tells us that when he finished the book, he turned the manuscript over to Naomi. She took it from him "with a marked lack of enthusiasm."

As she began to read the story, however, she got so caught up in it that she *retreated* with it, "the way you're supposed to with a story you like." When she finished it, she hugged her father and told him she didn't want the story to end.

"That, my friends," King tells us, "is a writer's favorite song, I think."

"Why I Wrote *The Eyes of the Dragon*" is an intimate look at the creative process as well as an intriguing glimpse of King's personal life and his obviously close relationship with his children. King wrote *The Eyes of the Dragon* to order, so to speak, and with a specific audience in mind—an audience of one. Well, actually, an audience of *two*: Naomi and himself. As King puts it at the close of this essay, "I did her the courtesy of writing for myself as well as for her. I think to have done otherwise would have been to falsify the act."

PUBLISHING HISTORY

1987: *The Eyes of the Dragon* (February; Viking hardcover; excerpts used for back flap copy).

1987: *Castle Rock: The Stephen King Newsletter* (February; unabridged version).

57

"What's Scaring Stephen King"

Nobody tells me what to read; nobody tells me what I can look at.

—from "What's Scaring Stephen King"

What it is: a passionate anticensorship essay in which Stephen King compares censorship to fascism.

Chances of finding a copy: difficult but not impossible. In your favor is the fact that *Omni*—an important and influential science and science-fiction magazine—*is* often archived in libraries and thus may be available in a public institution near you. Also, back issues of the magazine may be available from the publisher (*Omni* is one of Bob "*Penthouse*" Guccione's periodicals, and his company is still in business and approachable), and the usual book and magazine dealers may also have copies available. With a little digging, you will probably be able to unearth a copy of this issue.

When this essay first appeared in 1987, Stephen King had published around two dozen books. He notes in the opening of this powerful piece: "Every book . . . with the exception of two, has been banned from one public-high-school library or another." (I will hazard a guess that the two that skated through were *The Eyes of the Dragon* and *Stephen King's Danse Macabre*—nope, nothing wrong there!)

King writes that he is proud of *Cujo* being on the ACLU's list of the Top Ten banned books of all time because it put him in the company of Flannery O'Connor, Harper Lee, J. D. Salinger, and John Updike.

King then discusses *in loco parentis,* the legal mandate that schools must act in the role of a parent to protect minor children, a power often misused by some school districts to justify book banning. King makes it clear that this kind of censorship, when confined to grammar and high schools, does not bother him in the least. "When it comes to anything else," he asserts, "I draw the line: I'm not going to let them take my books out of public libraries or bookstores."

Even though King deliberately refuses to defend his books to school boards who want to ostracize his work from their shelves, he does make a pointed argument against the blatant and unconscionable hypocrisy on the part of the book banners. *The Shining,* he writes, cannot be read by children because it's "bad for children to read a story about how a father ends up hunting down his own son." However, the story "Hansel and Gretel," he notes, is a standard in schools, even though it's about a stepmother who orders her husband to disembowel his kids and bring her their hearts. Dad decides to "mercifully" leave them in the woods to starve to death instead, and when the two kids show up at a witch's house, she informs them that they are going to be her next meal.

There are some things, King admits, that simply are *not* suitable for kids. He cites the example of four-year-olds seeing George Romero's horror classic *The Night of the Living Dead.* However, it's their *parents'* obligation—not society's, he insists—to see to it that these tykes *don't* see a little girl eat her mother's intestines with a gardening trowel.

King concludes this important homily by telling the story of *Kristallnacht*—Crystal Night—that horrible night in 1939 when the Germans decided to get rid of all "decadent" literature. They started by burning philosophy books, and they then moved on to burn to the ground bookstores and music stores owned by Jews.

"That's what's always down the road when you begin to censor," King warns. "Crystal Night."

PUBLISHING HISTORY

1987: *Omni* (February).

58

Foreword to Dave Marsh's
Glory Days

I love Bruce Springsteen . . .

—Stephen King, from the June 1983 *Playboy* interview

*Cultural phenomena are common; good current biographies
are a good deal more difficult to find; real artists are the
most difficult of all. For these three elements to combine is
as rare and wonderful as Halley's Comet . . . and occurs
with roughly the same frequency.*

—from King's unused foreword to *Glory Days*

What it is: Stephen King's brief, unused foreword to *Glory Days*,
Dave Marsh's acclaimed biography of Bruce Springsteen.

Chances of finding a copy: impossible.

Stephen King has often been described as the "Bruce Springsteen of
American popular literature." In his unpublished notes on several of
King's unpublished novels, King biographer George Beahm writes that
King displays the same blue-collar sensibility in his writing that Spring-
steen manifests in his music.

   Also, Bruce Springsteen is mentioned in Stephen King's writings,
including *Cujo,* in which a Springsteen tune plays on Donna Trenton's
Pinto radio, and in *It,* in which the character of John "Webby" Garton

dresses like the Boss. It makes sense, then, that King would agree to write a foreword to Dave Marsh's biography of Springsteen. Unfortunately, King's foreword was not used in the book, reportedly because it was submitted too late to be included.

In the piece, King praises Marsh's book, calling him "Springsteen's Boswell," and also throws a little dig at Frank Zappa, who, in 1978, said, "Rock journalism is people who can't write interviewing people who can't talk for people who can't read." King calls Dave Marsh "rock's best writer" and proclaims that *Glory Days* not only brilliantly chronicles the life and times of Springsteen but that the book also shows us what America can be, and is a tome that Americans "will find valuable and thought-provoking . . . and, I think, tremendously hopeful."

King makes the point that Springsteen is one of many phenomena of the eighties—he mentions Vanna White and Trivial Pursuit—but with one *enormous* difference: "Springsteen is a genuine artist, one who has kept rock and roll alive . . . and who may be its last great voice as the generation that created it moves inexorably toward Social Security."

Stephen King has always been one of our keenest social observers, and he possesses the enviable ability to see the big picture, describe it evocatively, and put the whole shebang in context. In a few short paragraphs, King places Bruce Springsteen in an artistic and sociocultural context; in so doing, he does more than just introduce a biography. He paints an evocative picture of America and places the Boss in the forefront of the scene.

King really liked *Glory Days*. Dave Marsh traveled with Springsteen during his Born in the USA tour and was with him in the studio as he recorded his *Darkness at the Edge of Town* and *Nebraska* albums. This level of access makes *Glory Days* a revealing book, and King, a Springsteen fan from way back, was obviously enthralled by it.

King concludes his foreword by bestowing upon *Glory Days* a huge compliment: His last line is: "Good golly, Miss Molly, what a book!"

Note: King and Dave Marsh would join forces again in 1994 as members of the literary rock-and-roll band the Rock Bottom Remainders, a glorified garage band in which Stephen King played rhythm guitar and Dave Marsh was part of the "Critic's Chorus." (See the chapter "The Neighborhood of the Beast.")

PUBLISHING HISTORY

1987: Never published (handwritten manuscript dated April 14, 1987).

59

"Turning the Thumbscrews on the Reader"

Writing books is the only thing I know how to do. I'm like Paul, the hero in Misery, *in that way. I lead a fairly boring life, except when I write. And when I write, man, I have wonderful adventures.*

> —from "Turning the Thumbscrews on the Reader"

"Indeed, sister," said Dunyazad, "this is a wonderful story."

"The rest is still more wonderful," replied Scheherazade, "and you would say so, if the Sultan would allow me to live another day, and would give me leave to tell it to you the next night."

King Shahryar, who had been listening to Scheherazade with pleasure, said to himself, "I will wait till to-morrow; I can always have her killed when I have heard the end of her story."

> —from "The Story of the Merchant and the Genius"
> in *The Thousand and One Nights* (One
> of King's inspirations for *Misery*)

What it is: a one-page essay by King (originally given as an interview) in which he discusses writing *Misery.*

Chances of finding a copy: virtually impossible, since *Book-of-the-Month Club News* is not archived in libraries and I've never seen back issues of this newsletter offered for sale by any of the usual King memorabilia dealers. You might try contacting the Book-of-the-Month Club directly, but the odds are against their having a system in place with which to provide back issues of their monthly newsletter, especially one more than ten years old.

A thumbscrew is an instrument of torture in which the thumb is compressed—*crushed* is closer to the truth—more and more with each slow turn of a screw.

The excruciating pain this device causes is relentless, and it gets progressively worse with each turn of the screw. Thus, "Turning the Thumbscrews on the Reader" is a very apt metaphor for what Stephen King did to us all with his brilliant 1987 novel *Misery*. This brief rumination (it's less than six hundred words all told) is a rare glimpse into the psyche of a writer.

King admits right up front that he could "hardly believe" what he had done when he finished writing *Misery*, asserting (correctly) that it was unlike anything he had ever written before. King writes that about three-quarters or so of the way through the book, he realized that he was "talking about something as opposed to just telling a story." It occurred to him that he was discussing *The Thousand and One Nights* as well as what he did for a living.

In *The Thousand and One Nights,* King Shahryar, upon discovering that his wife has been unfaithful to him, has her and her lovers killed. Because of this betrayal, Shahryar now hates all women, and so he concocts a truly grim and merciless punishment that is to be applied to any women unfortunate enough to be chosen to be his wife: King Shahryar begins marrying and killing a new wife every single day.

Shahryar's vizier (a high officer in the Moslem government, especially in the old Turkish Empire) has a daughter named Scheherazade, who devises a clever plan to keep herself and the other women in the kingdom alive. Scheherazade demands that her father give her in marriage to King Shahryar. Her father agrees, and after the two are wed, Scheherazade tells the king a new story every night but refuses to finish each one, instead promising to reveal the ending the following night. Scheherazade tells such wonderful and exciting stories that the king cannot bear to be deprived of their endings. Thus, Scheherazade, through the *telling of stories,* guarantees the safety of her own life as well as the lives of the women the king *would* marry if he had killed Scheherazade.

In *Misery,* the only way writer Paul Sheldon can stay alive is by writing a new *Misery* novel and letting Annie Wilkes read the pages as he finishes them. Like Scheherazade, Paul must tell the most wonderful tale he can and leave Annie wanting more in order to assure that he will live to see tomorrow. King does a very effective job of communicating Paul's terror at realizing that his very life depends on his ability to put words—and the *right* words, of course—on paper.

In "Turning the Thumbscrews," King also talks about how much fun it is to write. Describing writing as a "twitch" ("You do it because you have to"), King says that writers tell others ("civilians," I guess) that writing is such torture "because they're having such a good time and if they told people they'd get lynched."

King then relates the classic story about the author of *Ulysses*, James Joyce, who was tormented because he had only written seven words in an entire day. When a visiting friend reminded Joyce that he usually only wrote three or four words a day and should therefore be pleased with his output, Joyce exasperatedly replied. "Yes, but I don't know what order they go in!" King grants that "a writer like that, I can see being tortured."

King then self-effacingly discusses himself as a writer, telling us that he is most definitely not a "big-deal fancy writer." He then says, "I don't have the ability to write the dazzling prose line." I *completely* disagree with King's overly harsh self-assessment and have written often in the past of King's ability to write lyrical and, yes, *dazzling* prose.

Most recently I was blown away by one small but lovely image that was part of the virtuoso, lengthy opening paragraph of King's most recent Bachman novel, *The Regulators*. After beautifully capturing the sense, the smell, and the *heat* of a mid-July day in central Ohio, King concludes the paragraph with ". . . and surrounding everything like an auditory edging of lace, the soothing, silky hiss of lawn sprinklers."

"Don't have the ability to write the dazzling prose line"? That, my friends, is, as Robin Williams has so eloquently said, "bovine residue."

King concludes the piece by noting that he knows about what most Americans know about—TV dinners and housing developments, as compared to knowing the head waiter at the Four Seasons.

It's been more than ten years since "Turning the Thumbscrews on the Reader" was published. Considering King's successes in this period, I would say that it's a pretty fair bet that at one time or another Stephen King has indeed enjoyed some acquaintance with the head waiter at the Four Seasons. However, that still does not change the fact that thumbscrews hurt like a sumbitch, and Stephen King still knows how to turn them.

PUBLISHING HISTORY

1987: *Book-of-the-Month Club News* (June).

60

"Entering the Rock Zone, or How I Happened to Marry a Rock Station From Outer Space"

I ended up owning a small AM rock and roll station in my home town about the same way most people get married: one happy accident followed by a chain of circumstances, followed by the preacher and the vows.

—from "Entering the Rock Zone"

What it is: an essay in which King discusses buying the Bangor AM radio station WZON as well as his passion for kick-ass rock and roll.

Chances of finding a copy: virtually impossible, since this essay only appeared in *Castle Rock,* the now-defunct King newsletter. Back issues of the newsletter are occasionally available from the usual sources, but the odds on finding this one are slim.

Stephen King bought himself an AM radio station because he was one day given a rental car that only had an AM radio and during a four-hour drive from Boston to Bangor he was mortified by the dearth of decent rock and roll on the AM band.

The outlaw-renegade sensibility of rock and roll has always permeated King's writing. One of the most on the money descriptions of King's writing style I've ever read was the comment by writer Richard Christian Matheson (Richard Matheson's son) during an interview for my *Complete Stephen King Encyclopedia* (all of which is included in the *Encyclopedia*):

> Stephen King should have a shoulder strap holding that word processor. It's like he's picking off these strange sort of Fahrenheit solos and just zapping, and it's very rock—it's very rock-oriented. I got a lot of my playfulness with language from King. He convinced me that you could do it . . . can we call it "heavy-metal language?"

King was frustrated by the tolling of the death knell for AM rock and roll and decided to do something about it. He understood that FM was the more appealing format: It reached more people, plus it was in stereo.

However, back in 1987, most of FM radio sucked. (Frankly, it still does.) Why? Because, as King acknowledges in the essay, all the jocks sound as if they're on 'ludes, and all the music sounds like Madonna or Michael Jackson or Lionel Ritchie or Whitney Houston or (lately—God help us) Kenny G. Even when an FM station does venture into the Land of Zeppelin, all they ever play is "Stairway to Heaven," for mercy's sake.

King decided to remedy this by buying WZON in Bangor and programming music he—and many others, it was apparent—wanted to hear. Stuff like the BoDeans, the Rainmakers, John Eddy, Mason Ruffin, Robert Cray, the Georgia Satellites, the Beat Farmers, Patti Smyth, Hank Williams Jr., Omar and the Howlers, and the Del Lords.

King honestly admits that he did not buy the station to make money. In an accompanying article in this issue of *Castle Rock*, station manager Christopher Spruce, King's brother-in-law, said, "It's not that Steve doesn't care about making money or paying the bills. It's just that his priorities are more with the music, the personalities and the image of WZON than with the bottom line. He truly believes there is an audience for the true Rock 'n' Roll music we play on the Z and one of the things I've come to learn about Steve over the years I've known him is that he has very good instincts about things like that."

King concludes his article by telling of an encounter with a listener shortly after he bought the station. A fortyish guy walked up to him and told him he liked the station and particularly liked the "song about the outlaw" (which King deduced was "Gunslinger Man" by the Long Ryders). The guy told King it reminded him of Credence and also reminisced that when Credence was playing he had a lot more hair.

King then asked him if he was still rockin', to which the guy replied that he was.

"Then I guess it doesn't matter," King told him. "So's Fogarty. So am I. *You* keep rockin' and *I'll* keep rockin'."

"Good deal," the guy replied, and King ends this nostalgic and entertaining article with: "And for me, that's just what the Rock Zone has been: a good deal."

Publishing History

1987: *Castle Rock: The Stephen King Newsletter* (October).

61

Nightmares in the Sky: Gargoyles and Grotesques

I am suggesting that the gargoyles you will come upon in this book may continue to perform their original function: to drain away that which might otherwise cause rot and erosion. Their horrible, stony faces offer a unique catharsis; when we look upon them and shudder, we create the exact reversal of the Medusa myth: we are not flesh turned to stone, but flesh proving it is flesh still, if only by the bumps that cool flush of fear always produces.

—from *Nightmares in the Sky*

What it is: a lengthy essay written to accompany a collection of photos of architectural gargoyles taken by f-stop Fitzgerald.

Chances of finding a copy: excellent. *Nightmares in the Sky* is still in print, and the latest edition is a trade paperback. Even better, however, is that the beautiful Viking Studio hardcover edition of the book has been remaindered for several years now and can be found at many book warehouses and on the remainder tables of bookstores. A few years back I bought a first edition of the hardcover for $4.98, but as recently as fall of 1997, the hardcover was still available at that price as a remainder in department stores and the book department of some grocery stores. (For all you "completists" out there, an excerpt from the essay appeared in the September 1988 issue of *Penthouse*.)

It is easy to understand why Stephen King chose to write the text to accompany f-stop Fitzgerald's compelling photographs of stone monsters: *Nightmares in the Sky* is a magnificent book, an artistic artifact that is at once both beautiful and thought provoking, powerful and intimate, exhilarating and frightening. Stephen King's essay does these photos justice.

King's piece consists of eight sections, and each one has a different focus and tone. He begins by admitting his reluctance to tackle such an imposing project, even though he was approached because he was thought to be the "ideal person" to write the essay.

I will not attempt to rewrite King's piece by recounting and discussing every subject he tackles in the composition. Suffice it to say that if you like Stephen King's nonfiction writing—prose that is often as entertaining and appealing as his fiction—then *Nightmares in the Sky* is, unquestionably a must-read for you. King's essay contains autobiographical musings, thoughts on writing and fear, reflections on TV and movies, and some genuinely intuitive ideas about morality and mythology.

Nightmares in the Sky is more evidence that Stephen King may justifiably be considered a thinker first and a writer second. King may not like such a distinction, but this essay is proof of a powerful mind, one that is constantly deliberating, analyzing, *thinking,* and that such reflection persists whether he chooses to write his thoughts down or not.

Publishing History

1988: *Nightmares in the Sky: Gargoyles and Grotesques* (Viking Studio Books hardcover).

1989: *Nightmares in the Sky: Gargoyles and Grotesques* (Viking Studio Books paperback).

62

" 'Ever Et Raw Meat?' and Other Weird Questions"

[N]ow and then someone will ask a really interesting
question, like, Do you write in the nude? The answer . . . is:
I don't think I ever have, but if it works, I'm willing to try it.

—from " 'Ever Et Raw Meat?' and Other Weird Questions"

What it is: a *very* entertaining nonfiction essay in which King reveals some of the questions he is asked on a regular basis and discusses how he responds to them.

Chances of finding a copy: no problem, assuming that all you're interested in is the text. King's *words* for " 'Ever Et Raw Meat?' " are easily accessible: Just go to your local university or public library and ask for the December 6, 1987, *New York Times Book Review* (it'll probably be on either microfilm or microfiche); fumble with the film or fiche reader until you give up and ask the librarian to load it for you; find the " 'Ever Et Raw Meat?' " essay, hit PRINT, pay your ten or fifteen cents, and voilà, you own it. If, however, just the words themselves do not satisfy you, then the *Letters From Hell* limited-edition broadsheet is the item you want. This five-hundred-copy edition is now selling for $350 and up and is only available through the secondary collectors' market. Start with The Overlook Connection or Betts Bookstore to track down this extremely rare King publication.

Stephen King gets a lot of fan mail. When I interviewed his sister-in-law Stephanie Leonard (then the editor of *Castle Rock*) for my *Complete*

Stephen King Encyclopedia back in the late eighties, King was receiving at least five hundred pieces of mail a week. It is probably much higher than that today.

Some of these letters to King contain some very odd questions.

Stephen King is one of the more recognizable writers working today, and thus he is often approached by fans while out in public. Some of them ask him very odd questions. After a decade or so of dealing with this strange by-product of his fame, King decided to write about it, and " 'Ever Et Raw Meat?' " was born. King discusses twenty-three questions in this very funny essay.

One habitual book stealer (she admitted to having stolen every one of King's books and was writing to King from prison) asked King if it was possible that *Different Seasons* was one of his best books, because she actually considered returning it to the library she stole it from after she had read it. (It wasn't revealed whether or not she followed through on her magnanimous impulse and actually returned the book.)

As might be expected, many of the questions King is repeatedly asked are about the specifics of writing. Some of them include queries about where he gets his ideas (he usually replies, "Utica"); where he gets his inspiration (this question was once accompanied by an ounce of marijuana); how to get an agent; how to get published; how to start a novel; how to sell your book to the movies; how to write bestsellers, etc.

King also discusses a common question he is asked at book signings. Fans will invariably come up to him as he is signing away and ask, "Don't you wish you had a rubber stamp?"

It has been my honor on a few occasions to contribute an article or an essay to a limited-edition book. These books are usually signed by the contributors, and many of my friends and members of my family have seen me sit with a stack of several hundred limitation sheets and sign my name over and over and over.

The people who have seen me do this will—without fail—ask me why I don't have a rubber stamp made.

I understand the question; it's just that the onlookers don't understand the *point* of a signed limited edition: The purchaser wants to know (and is willing to pay for this knowledge) that the writers actually signed with their own hand the book he or she now owns.

King knows why people want books signed and so has come up with a simple but honest answer to this rather uninformed question: He tells them he really doesn't mind.

King has also been asked some genuinely strange questions during his career, including:

- "I see you have a beard. Are you morbid of razors?"
- "Will you soon write of pimples or some other facial blemish?"
- "Why do you keep up this disgusting mother worship when anyone with any sense knows a *man* has no use to his mother once he is weened?"
- "How could you write such a why?"

He has also been asked the title question about eating raw meat and about writing in the nude and whether or not he beats his wife and/or children.

" 'Ever Et Raw Meat?' " is a rare glimpse into the life of an enormously popular writer whose fans feel close enough to him to approach him and ask him some genuinely ridiculous questions (although we still don't know if that's something he ever "et").

It is a sign of King's high regard for these fans that even though he has written an article about just how ludicrous some of these questions are, he never ridicules the askers. He just tells us about them and lets us all marvel at some of the situations the world's most successful writer has to deal with while drinking coffee in a diner or walking through a mall.

Publishing History

1987: *New York Times Book Review* (December 6).
1988: *Twilight Zone Magazine* (June; as "Who Ever Et Raw Meat").
1988: *Writer* (July).
1988: As *Letters From Hell* (September; a Lord John Press five-hundred-copy, limited-edition broadsheet signed by King; this broadsheet was also reproduced in reduced format in an advertisement in *Castle Rock: The Stephen King Newsletter* in December 1988).
1989: *Book Talk* (winter).

63

"Stephen King on Censorship"

The issue behind censorship is always somebody saying,
"My point of view is more valid than your point of view."
If the censorship initiative succeeds, then the answer is,
"Yes, my views are more valid than your views; my views
are more moral than your views."

—from "Stephen King on Censorship"

What it is: a brief videotaped interview King gave to New American Library's sales force in 1989 in which he spoke about censorship.

Chances of finding a copy: difficult but not impossible. The only published transcript of this interview appears in *War of Words,* a 1993 Andrews & McMeel trade paperback, edited by George Beahm. The book may still be found in many bookstores and is certain to be available in libraries across the country. The videotaped interview that was the source of this transcript has never been released commercially.

This "oral essay" by King (for lack of a better term) is worth seeking out because even though the entire interview is only three paragraphs long, King essentially coalesces his entire philosophy on censorship in a few carefully chosen words.

King has been banned in junior high and high school libraries almost since he began publishing. This does not bother King; in fact, he has stated that it makes him very proud: "I'm in the company of greats." Indeed he is. The list of books banned in schools over the past couple of centuries includes such works as George Orwell's *1984,* Ernest Hemingway's *Farewell to Arms*, J. D. Salinger's *Catcher in the Rye*, Alice Walker's *Color Purple*, Margaret Mitchell's *Gone With the Wind*, John Steinbeck's *Of Mice and Men*, Ken Kesey's *One Flew Over the Cuckoo's Nest*, Mark Twain's *Adventures of Huckleberry Finn*, Anne Frank's *Diary of Anne Frank*, F. Scott Fitzgerald's *Great Gatsby*, Ray Bradbury's *Martian Chronicles*, Harper Lee's *To Kill a Mockingbird*, and Harriet Beecher Stowe's *Uncle Tom's Cabin*.

Unbelievable, eh?

Glib deflection aside, though, King takes the banning of books very seriously, and in this interview he makes the point yet again that censorship is nothing more than a "power trip" and that "as far as censorship in public institutions and libraries, censorship has no place."

King willingly allows that schools have the right of "parental initiative" (as they act *in loco parentis*) to remove books from their libraries, but this is far from condoning such actions or admitting that what a small group of parents do not want kids to read should *not* be read by *all* kids. King is blunt about this:

> My advice to kids would be: "Whatever it is that your parents and teachers don't want you to read is probably the thing that you need the most to find out."

He then recommends that kids run to the nearest public library or bookstore and seek out the banned books—whether it is his own *Cujo* or works like *Lord of the Flies* or *Lady Chatterly's Lover*.

"Stephen King on Censorship" is the essence of Stephen King's very astute and absolutely correct views on the unceasing effort by *some* people to tell *other* people what they can or cannot read.

PUBLISHING HISTORY

1989: New American Library videotaped interview (never commercially released).

1993: *War of Words* (George Beahm, editor; Andrews & McMeel trade paperback).

64

"What Stephen King Does for Love"

*The heart has its own mind, and its business is joy. For me,
those two things—joy and reading—have always gone
together, and another of my life's pleasures was discovering
that sometimes they mature together.*

> —from "What Stephen King Does for Love"

What it is: a lengthy article for the young female readers of *Seventeen* magazine about books and reading.

Chances of finding a copy: very difficult. Many U.S. libraries do not archive *Seventeen* magazine, and since *Seventeen* was the only place this article ever appeared, the fan interested in acquiring a copy will have to find a used- and rare-book and magazine dealer who has one of the original 1990 issues of the magazine.

This is one of the most important nonfiction articles Stephen King has ever written. Why? Because in this revealing essay King discusses at length the influences on his writing; his resistance to reading what was assigned him in school; and the differences between reading for love and reading because you're *told to*—a paradigm he describes as consisting of two continents called "Wanna Read" and "Gotta Read."

As is common for many high schoolers, King hated many of the classics he was assigned to read. King has a sharp recollection of the reading he had to swallow like bitter medicine. He singles out Herman

Melville's *Moby Dick;* Shakespeare's *Hamlet;* George Eliot's *Silas Marner;* the poems of Emily Dickinson and Robert Frost; Charles Dickens's *Pickwick Papers;* Mark Twain's *Adventures of Huckleberry Finn;* John Updike's *Pigeon Feathers;* James Fenimore Cooper's *Deerslayer;* all of Ernest Hemingway; and, most surprisingly, the works of Edgar Allan Poe.

King takes no prisoners in his "review" of these writers and their works:

> *As a high school student I found Edgar Allen Poe a prolix, leather-lunged bore who was about as scary as the prize in a box of Cracker Jacks; I condemned Robert Frost as a pedestrian hick; considered Hemingway a macho jerk with an elephant gun where his heart should be.*

What's especially fascinating (and revealing) about this essay is that King the man realizes that much of his resistance to these works and his animosity toward their authors was based on the immaturity of King *the high schooler.* He frankly admits that he was wrong about several of the texts assigned to him in high school and that when he reread them as adults, he saw new beauty, talent, and yes, even felt excitement and got goose bumps from specific moments in the works.

King still hates *Moby Dick* and *Pigeon Feathers,* but his sensibility has matured to the point where he now finds *Hamlet* "tremendously exciting." *Huckleberry Finn* gave him the aforementioned goose bumps when his kids *insisted* that he read it to them after he finished reading them *Tom Sawyer*: They absolutely *demanded,* he tells us, "to know the rest of the story."

The writing legend and icon that is "Stephen King" (separate from Stephen King the *guy*) exists as a manifestation of countless influences, not the least of which is a massive and ceaseless exposure to the popular culture of the twentieth century.

In "What Stephen King Does for Love," King talks about the voracious reading he did when he was a kid, noting that if he had a dime for every book he read on his own, he could buy a car with the money.

He specifically cites as favorites John D. MacDonald's "Travis McGee" novels; Ed McBain's "87th Precinct" stories; the work of Shirley Jackson, especially *We Have Always Lived in the Castle* and

The Haunting of Hill House; Tolkien's "Middle Earth" tales; the tele-
plays of Reginald Rose, Tad Mossel, and Rod Serling; the dark horror
novels of Dickens's contemporary Wilkie Collins; Ken Kesey's *One Flew
Over The Cuckoo's Nest;* early essays by Tom Wolfe; "about a trillion
comic books"; plus the works of Robert Howard, Andre Norton, Jack
London, and others. He also admits to having read three sex manuals
in one week when he was a curious young lad, moving straight from *A
Sex Guide for Troubled Teenagers* to the far more mature *Kinsey
Report.*

For King fans interested in who King himself believes to have influenced his writing, there is a very interesting section on the writer
Thomas Hardy. King writes in the school of naturalism, a literary philosophy that revolves around the belief that fate rules man but through
free will we have the ultimate power to make moral—or immoral—
choices. King's introduction to naturalism came when he was assigned
Hardy's classic *Tess of the D'Ubervilles.* He admits that he didn't care
about the underlying literary foundations that propelled *Tess* forward;
he was only interested in Tess's *story* and describes her as a character
"so naive that she was raped without knowing it."

King tells us that *Tess* so impressed him that he went on to read
other Hardy works and was also extremely moved by Hardy's final
novel, the gloomy *Jude the Obscure.* (Interestingly, both *Tess of the
D'Ubervilles* and *Jude the Obscure* were originally published in magazines in serial form. In 1996, King published his own novel *The Green
Mile* in six separate monthly paperback installments, a groundbreaking publishing event that prompted the release of several serialized
novels in the months to follow.)

"What Stephen King Does for Love" is Stephen King at his most
engaging; it is Stephen King as teacher. Reading this essay brought to
mind something that Clive Barker, King's contemporary and fellow
horror writer, once said about reading: "I forbid my mind nothing" (or
something along those lines), making the point that King has often
made about censorship and forbidding kids to read certain works. In an
essay covered in this volume, "The Book-Banners: Adventure in Censorship Is Stranger Than Fiction," King advises kids to go to the public
library or bookstore and read what their parents and teachers most definitely do not want them to read (including some of his own books).

"You can't legislate . . . Steinbeck in place of Steel," King writes.
"[K]ids are going to go right on reading for love, and God love them

for it." The whole point of "What Stephen King Does for Love," then, is not simply to dump on the classics or relate the story of how one man grew to appreciate the stuff he loathed as a kid. That's there, of course, but I think the underlying point King is making is that kids should read *everything and anything* that they want to—even comic books, sex manuals, and science fiction. It is the *reading* that counts, not necessarily *what* is being read. He is telling us that even though high school English teachers seem to sometimes deliberately assign stuff guaranteed to bore their students to tears, this should *not* sour young people on reading (as it so often does). They should just go out and get their hands on what they *want* to read, even if it's something as "unliterary" (for lack of a better word) as Jack London's thrilling Alaska story *White Fang*.

Seek literary adventure, King exhorts in this essay. "Do more than enjoy it; swim in that heady brew, fly in that intoxicating ether. Why not?"

Why not, indeed.

PUBLISHING HISTORY

1990: *Seventeen* (April).

65

An Evening at God's

GOD: *I should know better than to eat those chili peppers.*
They burn me at both ends.

—from *An Evening at God's*

What it is: a one-minute play King wrote in 1990 to benefit the American Repertory Theater's Institute for Advanced Theater Training. The entire play consists of two-and-a-half typescript pages and was auctioned off on Monday, April 23, 1990.

Chances of finding a copy: don't even try.

In early 1990, Stephen King was asked to contribute a one-minute play to a benefit evening. He jumped at the idea, likening it to "the literary equivalent of a doodle."

King came up with *An Evening at God's.* The manuscript of the play was auctioned off at the Hasty Pudding Theater in Massachusetts on the evening of April 23, 1990.

King was part of an elite contingent of fifteen writers tapped to contribute plays. Other literary luminaries participating included Art Buchwald, Don DeLillo, Christopher Durang, John Kenneth Galbraith, Larry Gelbart, David Mamet, John Updike, and Wendy Wasserstein.

A lengthy interview with King conducted by Gail Caldwell ran in the *Boston Globe* a week before the auction, on Sunday, April 15, 1990. The two-page talk was titled "Stephen King: Bogeyman as Family Man," and in it King discussed the benefit and his play.

King described the plot of the play for Caldwell:

God's sitting at home and drinking a few beers and St. Peter comes in with papers to pass, and God's watching a sitcom on TV. And the earth is sort of hanging in the way of the TV, and he keeps trying to look around the world to see the television.

So I sat down and wrote it. And it may have been a critical comment: The typewriter broke while I was working on this, and I had to redo it.

In the interview King also revealed that he had been following the then-running David Lynch TV series *Twin Peaks* and considered it "the right thing at the right time."

King also told Caldwell that "as a little kid, I was scared a lot of the time. My imagination was too big for my head at that point, so I spent a lot of miserable hours. And I feel like I'm getting back at everybody else now."

What is perhaps most intriguing about the interview is the following admission: "What I'd like to do at some point in the next year—this has never really let go of me—is to write a novel about Jonestown." (In Guyana, in 1978, the messianic religious leader Jim Jones coerced 911 of his followers into drinking Kool-Aid laced with cyanide.)

King gave this interview in 1990, and thus far such a novel has not materialized in the bookstores. King has not publicly commented on the status of this idea, and it remains to be seen as to whether or not he will ever publish a book about the Guyana mass suicide.

An Evening at God's consists of two-and-a-half pages of typescript in standard play format. King provides the stage directions, and there are two characters, God and St. Peter. It is a funny, yet powerful piece and is further evidence of King's incredible storytelling abilities. Throughout the play, we're fascinated by this glimpse into the workings of the divine and are shocked by the nonchalance with which God cavalierly destroys the earth. The most powerful moment is probably God's final question to St. Peter, "My son got back, didn't he?"

There is a knock at the door. God bellows, "Come in!" and St. Peter enters carrying a briefcase. St. Peter, who is leaving on vacation in half an hour, has brought "letters of transmission from hell" for

God to sign. St. Peter inquires after God's health, and God tells him he is feeling better but that he should know better than to eat chili peppers.

God signs the papers, and St. Peter remarks that the earth is still around after all these years. God replies, "Yes, the housekeeper is the most forgetful bitch in the universe."

There is laughter from the television, and God asks St. Peter if that was Alan Alda. St. Peter replies that it might have been but he really couldn't see (because the earth was blocking the set). God then reaches out and with one almighty hand crushes the earth to dust.

God then offers Peter a beer, and as he takes it, the stage lights begin to dim. A single spotlight shines on the remains of the earth.

St. Peter then tells God that he "actually sort of liked that one." God replies that the earth "wasn't bad" but that there were plenty "more where that came from."

As the lights dim, God says, "Maybe I better cut down on my drinking. Still . . . it WAS in the way."

The stage then goes black except for the spotlight on the ruins of the earth.

"My son got back," God then asks Peter. "Didn't he?"

St. Peter tells him that Jesus did indeed get back some time ago, to which God responds, "Good, Everything's hunky-dory then," and the light on the earth goes out.

An Evening at God's is Stephen King literarily "doodling"; even such brief efforts as this one-minute play tackle big issues in an entertaining and engaging way when arising from the mind of King.

PUBLISHING HISTORY

1990: never published. The manuscript was sold at auction on April 23, 1990.

66

"How I Created *Golden Years . . .* and Spooked Dozens of TV Executives"

At some point between 'Salem's Lot, *my second book, and* The Dead Zone, *my sixth, I became America's Best-Loved Bogeyman.*

—from "How I Created *Golden Years*"

What it is: an article King wrote exclusively for *Entertainment Weekly* in which he discusses the genesis of his summer 1991 science-fiction TV series *Golden Years.*

Chances of finding a copy: difficult. *Entertainment Weekly* is not archived in libraries; nor will you will find back issues available from online magazine databases or on the Internet. The only sources, then, are *Entertainment Weekly* itself (see "Sources and Resources" to inquire about the availability of back issues—as always, do not call) or the usual King dealers. The odds on finding the article through a dealer are pretty good, though, since it was an important essay—with pictures— by King (after all, he was writing about his first-ever original TV series), plus this issue contained a review of my first book about King, *The Shape Under the Sheet: The Complete Stephen King Encyclopedia,* plus a review of the video release of *Misery. Three* King-related items in one issue of a magazine usually spurs dealers to buy as many as they can get their hands on, so you might be able to purchase one from some of them. (It'll probably set you back $10–$25 or so.)

King starts off this entertaining behind-the-scenes piece by acknowledging that by the early eighties he had taken over the role in this country that had earlier been played by Boris Karloff, Alfred Hitchcock, and Rod Serling, that of the "ABLB," or America's Best-Loved Bogeyman.

Since 1982, King writes, he had been repeatedly offered his own TV show. One concept would have had him introducing a new tale of terror ("New England horror") each week, à la Rod Serling, and he wouldn't have had to write the shows, just introduce them.

King did not like this idea. ("I *did* want to write. Writing is what I *do*.") He repeatedly turned down similar offers over the years until the notion occurred to him to write a "novel for television," something that "existed as a limited-run TV program *first*." *This* idea excited him because he felt that it "combined the best features of the TV series . . . with the most important feature of good fiction . . . the steady march of events toward a satisfying conclusion."

King had been thinking about writing *Golden Years* as a novel for a year or so when the concept for an original TV series presented itself. He really liked the idea of telling the story of Harlan Williams, an innocent janitor caught up in a secret government experiment who is pursued across the country by a Shop agent determined to eliminate him with extreme prejudice. King describes the Shop agent as "an insane version of *The Fugitive*'s Lieutenant Gerard," an apt comparison, since King had earlier written "As a kid, the only TV series I really liked was *The Fugitive*."

TV executives were flummoxed by King's idea of a TV series that would *intentionally* only run for one year. It would not be a three- or four-night miniseries, like King's very successful ABC miniseries *It*; nor would it be a series that would tell a complete story in one season and then return in the next with the same characters and tell *another* story—similar to the type of three- or four-episode (or occasionally more) story arcs being used today in dramatic series like *ER*, *Homicide*, *Law and Order*, *Chicago Hope*, and *NYPD Blue*.

When King was asked what he would do if the series was a success, he replied, "Then we do it again next year. . . . All new characters. All new situations. All new plot. All new conclusion."

This made the TV executives uncomfortable. The idea was, as King writes, "all new," and "all new"—which many TV people interpret as "untried," "dangerous," and "expensive"—makes TV people nervous.

King compromised his idea by creating a character named Terrilyn

Spann who would be able to continue into the next season if the series was a hit and Harlan's story had been told.

Ultimately, *Golden Years* was not renewed, even though the ratings were respectable. Some critics faulted the show's pace; some could not get through their heads the idea of a self-contained series that was not a miniseries. Personally, I thought it was terrific.

King concludes the piece by admitting that he thinks TV is the perfect forum for "long, complex stories—electronic novels, if you will—that exist in the medium alone and have a beginning, a middle, and an end."

TV is moving toward this, albeit slowly, but it is experimenting with this kind of TV program. The miniseries is back and appears to be quite strong, thanks in great part to the gigantic ratings that all of King's TV miniseries (*The Stand, The Langoliers, The Shining, The Tommy-knockers, It*) have garnered. As noted, the more ambitious TV dramas are tackling story lines that run entire seasons—Jeannie Boulet's AIDS story on *ER*, Sipowitcz's alcoholism on *NYPD Blue,* and Dr. Shutt's divorce-and-stroke story line on *Chicago Hope.*

Then there is *The X-Files,* the show that seems to be closest to King's idea of an ongoing series that tells *completely different stories.* Agents Scully and Muldur are the consistent element; their cases provide the varied stories and plots.

It is probably not a coincidence, then, that Stephen King cowrote, with Chris Carter, an original *X-Files* episode called "Chinga" that aired in February 1998.

PUBLISHING HISTORY

1991: *Entertainment Weekly* (August 2).

67

"Perfect Games, Shared Memories"

This is a story about two boys, both nine years old, and two baseball games—World Series games.

—from "Perfect Games"

What it is: Stephen King's moving and very rare essay about baseball written for the 1991 *World Series Souvenir Scorebook*.

Chances of finding a copy: extremely difficult if not impossible. This kind of publication disappears as soon as it is sold out and when the event it commemorates (in this case the 1991 World Series) ends. (King's written-to-order essay about Bangor for *Black Magic and Music*—see the chapter in this volume—falls into the same category.) Try the usual dealers, though, if you're determined enough. You will have to buy an original if you want to own it, since these publications are rarely, if ever, archived in public libraries. Dealers of baseball collectibles may also be a good source, but you'll have to find those who carry programs and items like this *Scorebook* in addition to baseball cards. (The Baseball Hall of Fame in Cooperstown, New York, may also have this *Scorebook,* but you may not be able to do much more than look at it under glass if they do.)

Stephen King is a baseball fan. Actually, a *huge* baseball fan. He has watched the game almost since he could *see.* He coached his son's Little League team, and in what might be the quintessential illustration of precisely *how the rich are different,* Stephen and Tabitha King footed the bill to build a brand-new Little League field in Bangor, complete with bleachers, lights, and nifty electronic scoreboard.

☠ When he was nine years old, King watched Don Larsen pitch a perfect game in the 1956 World Series. King was alone watching TV in the Stratford, Connecticut, apartment he shared with his mother and his brother David. There was no one there to celebrate with him when Larsen struck out Dale Mitchell with his final record-setting pitch.

King writes about himself in the third person and remembers that "if there was anything to mar the perfect happiness the boy felt at seeing the perfect game brought safely home it was this: he was alone. There was no one there with whom he could share this marvelous, this well-nigh-unbelievable thing."

Thirty years later, King takes his then-nine-year-old son, Owen, to Fenway Park to see the Red Sox play in the World Series. It is Owen's first-ever World Series game, and "his eyes are everywhere, trying to take in everything at once."

Stephen King's father walked out on his family when King was two. Neither he nor David, his brother, have any memories of him. There was never "a Dad in the picture" when King and David were growing up, he remembers, but his single mother "managed to raise Stevie and his older brother pretty well." In 1986, however, in Fenway Park, "there *is* a Dad in this picture," King writes, and we see how his earlier discussion of the "almost ceremonial way in which the joy of the game is handed down from generation to generation" is being played out in the bleachers that day as the Red Sox lose to the Mets, 7–1.

Owen cannot take the depth of sadness he feels over his Dad's favorite team (and therefore *Owen's* favorite team) losing so convincingly, and he starts to cry on the way out of the park.

King brightens his son's mood by telling him about the time he actually saw Don Larsen pitch a perfect game in the 1956 World Series. "[B]y the time we got back to our hotel," King writes, "we had both forgotten that night's bitter defeat."

The passing on of the joys of baseball are what King loves the most about the game, he tells us, concluding this heartfelt essay with a poignant and touching thought:

*I like to think and hope that someday—maybe in 2016—
there'll be three of us—me, Owen, and Owen's nine-year-
old—leaving the park, perhaps to celebrate a Red Sox World
Championship.*

*That would be pretty great, all right, and the only thing
greater than being there would be passing it on.*

"Perfect Games, Shared Memories" is yet one more example of Stephen
King's marvelous touch with nonfiction, especially the personal memoir.
This piece has never been reprinted in any of King's collections, but
one can hope that he will include it someday in one of his anthologies.

It would be a real pity for King's readers not to be able to someday
experience what it feels like to share *a perfect game.*

PUBLISHING HISTORY

1991: *Official World Series Souvenir Scorebook—1991 Fall Classic.*

68

"The Book-Banners: Adventure in Censorship Is Stranger Than Fiction"

As a nation, we've been through too many fights to preserve our rights of free thought to let them go just because some prude with a highlighter doesn't approve of them.

—from "The Book-Banners"

What it is: a guest editorial column King wrote for the *Bangor Daily News* in 1992.

Chances of finding a copy: since this piece has never been reprinted or collected, it will be very difficult to find unless you have access to a library or an online newspaper archive that offers the *Bangor Daily News*. (Most do not.) Of course, most Maine libraries would probably have back issues of many of the state's newspapers, so you could always make a trip up north.

BOOKS BANNED (FROM *USA TODAY*, MARCH 11, 1992)

Stephen King's *The Dead Zone* and *The Tommyknockers* have been banned from the library shelves of Duval County, Fla. middle schools. "This whole book and others of Stephen King I skimmed through are full of filthy language," said parent Louise Reimer in a written complaint about *The Tommyknockers*. King had no comment. Two other King books, *The Stand* and *Christine*, have been targeted for censorship at other schools.

As the news clipping reprinted above reveals, in March 1992 two of Stephen King's books—*The Dead Zone* and *The Tommyknockers*— were pulled from the shelves of a middle-school library in Florida. Following this, there was also talk of limiting access to these books to high schoolers who had specific permission from their parents to check them out of the library.

King wrote the essay that is the subject of this chapter in response to the barrage of press requests for comments about being banned in these Florida schools. King at first turned down requests from several media outlets, including Maine Public Broadcasting, CBS, the Associated Press, and the *Boston Globe,* but then he thought about it and decided that he "didn't like the way that 'the author could not be reached for comment' stuff looked." Thus, "The Book-Banners" was born.

Stephen King addresses three factions in this passionate and discerning editorial. First, he speaks to the kids who attend the middle school where his books were banned. He advises them not to argue with the banners or protest the books' removal. What does he recommend? That the kids go to either the public library or a bookstore, get their hands on the banned books, and read them carefully to learn what it is the censors do not want them to know.

King then speaks directly to the parents in the town where the books were banned. He strongly warns them to be very careful about whom they give the power to decide what their kids can read. These holier-than-thou, know-it-all book banners "don't care what you think because they are positive their ideas of what's proper and what's not are better, clearer than your own."

King's final target for his message is the collective citizenry of the town where the books were banned. He instructs them that "book-banners, after all, insist that the entire community should see things their way, and only their way."

Interestingly, King does not feel that it is his job to defend his own works. "My job is writing stories," he tells his readers, "and if I spent all my time defending the ones I've already written, I'd have no time to write new ones."

Overall, "The Book-Banners: Adventure in Censorship Is Stranger Than Fiction" is a lucid and important essay that makes a critically important point in this era of right-wing attempts at censorship and government-"suggested" ratings systems for popular culture.

The truth is that in a free society no one should be able to control what somebody else can view, read, or say. King acknowledges that certain texts are completely inappropriate for what is essentially the "managed marketplace" of tax-supported middle schools, specifically citing John Cleland's erotic novel *Fanny Hill* and Bret Easton Ellis's incredibly graphic *American Psycho,* but draws the line at these works being deemed unsuitable for any *adult* who wants to read them simply because they are age-inappropriate for ninth-graders.

Stephen King is one of the most published writers in the history of the printed word; he therefore has an enormous stake in his words being available to whoever wants to read them.

Even so, King does not use his powerful global pulpit as an opportunity to launch into a diatribe against the self-appointed censors; instead, he calmly and rationally points out to his readers the dangers of allowing such philosophical atrocities to go unchallenged in a democratic society. Moreover, he winningly and patiently *proves his point,* showing us once again that he is one of the most important defenders of free speech who is writing today.

After reading "The Book-Banners," the fair-minded person—whether a Stephen King fan or not—can not, and will not, deny that there's certainly more to the King of Horror than demonic dogs and haunted cars, no matter what his banners and detractors would have you believe.

PUBLISHING HISTORY

1992: *Bangor Daily News* (March 20).

69

Introduction to
*The Fugitive Recaptured:
The Thirtieth Anniversary
Companion to
a Television Classic*

> The Fugitive *was a groundbreaking television series because
> it featured a hero who was totally powerless.*
>
> —from King's introduction to *The Fugitive Recaptured*

What it is: a brief introduction to a book about a TV series that King
has said was the only series he really liked as a kid.

Chances of finding a copy: excellent. *The Fugitive Recaptured* was
published in 1993 and is still in print and should be available in most
bookstores (especially the large chain stores that have a wide-ranging
TV and film department).

This introduction—even though not really "lost" and still readily accessible—is included in this book because we were afraid it might get overlooked by the majority of King fans. We wanted to be sure that it was
not "lost" to those fans who might not think to look for something by
King in a book about a TV series.

King makes the point in this "introduction" that one of the reasons
The Fugitive so appealed to kids of his generation (the show aired from

1963 to 1967—King was in his mid-teens) was because "kids like me
. . . grew up feeling slightly alienated from the values of our parents. We
felt like fugitives in a sense."

As is often the case when King discusses American pop culture, his
views about *something specific*—a TV show, a movie, a book—become
a penetrating, more wide ranging look at broader issues and sociocultural trends. That happens in this "introduction." King starts out talking about a TV show but ends up discussing the alienation of youth
and the projection of insecurities and feelings of groundlessness onto fictional characters.

The piece is brief—only three paragraphs—but it is well worth tracking down and reading. (You can probably read the whole thing standing in the bookstore if you're not a *Fugitive* fan and don't want to fork
over the moolah to buy the book.) In it Stephen King once again looks
back at his youth. In so doing, he remembers the years and shared influences of many of us who love King's work.

Yes, Stephen King *remembers,* and in pieces like this, he helps *us*
remember, too.

PUBLISHING HISTORY

1993: *The Fugitive Recaptured: The 30th Anniversary Companion to a
Television Classic* (September; Pomegranate Press trade paperback).

70

"The Neighborhood of the Beast"

The band plays music as well as Metallica writes novels.
—Dave Barry

This is the nadir of western civilization. Right here, in our show.

—Al Kooper

What it is: a nonfiction essay about King's experiences touring with the band of writers called the Rock Bottom Remainders.

Chances of finding a copy: not too difficult, since the hardcover was purchased by many public libraries and the trade paperback edition of *Mid-Life Confidential* may still be found in many bookstores.

This lengthy nonfiction essay was King's contribution to an anthology called *Mid-Life Confidential: The Rock Bottom Remainders Tour America With Three Chords and an Attitude.*

   Mid-Life Confidential chronicled the 1993 nine-city tour by the Rock Bottom Remainders, a mediocre rock-and-roll band (sorry, but I've heard the tapes) made up completely of really great writers who are not gifted musicians (plus a couple of truly great "ringers" like Al Kooper).

   King's conversational offering for the book begins: "In the summer of 1971, when I was twenty-three and had been married less than a year, something unpleasant happened to me in Sebec Lake."

As only he can do, King begins his essay about touring with a one-step-above-a-garage-band motley crew of writers with a gripping personal anecdote that could easily have come from one of his novels or short stories.

Because Stephen King is who he is, after he tells us how he almost drowned that day and reveals that the only thing that saved him was realizing that if he panicked, he would die, he them relates the story of an especially nasty diarrhea attack that kept him trapped in a grimy Nashville barroom toilet stall minutes before he had to go onstage and play.

Is Stephen King a piece of work or what?

As is typical of a Stephen King nonfiction piece, his consistently engaging and appealing narrative voice booms through to the reader. We feel as though we're sitting somewhere listening to King talk about whatever's on his mind.

King is a chronicler of the contemporary American landscape, and he is very good at it. In my 1990 book *The Complete Stephen King Encyclopedia,* horror writer J. N. Williamson defines King as a "noticer," an extremely apt description of King's sensibility. In "The Neighborhood of the Beast," King "notices" the graffiti on the toilet-stall walls and also recounts pithy graffiti of the past he couldn't help but remember, such as "Dogs Fuck the Pope (No Fault of Mine)" and "Save Russian Jews, Collect Valuable Prizes."

Speaking of graffiti, the title "The Neighborhood of the Beast" refers to something King saw written on the back of the bathroom door precisely at his eye level: "664/668: THE NEIGHBORHOOD OF THE BEAST." What number sits precisely between "664" and "668?" The ominous numbers 666, of course, the biblical sign of the Beast, a.k.a. Satan.

In his essay, King tells the story of how the band got together and how their first gig was at a bookseller's convention. He does a terrific job of communicating the sheer euphoria the band members felt after their performance.

King also tells of meeting a bouncer in a bathroom who asked him if he was the guy who wrote *The Shining* and *The Dead Zone.* When King acknowledged that he was indeed that guy, the bouncer replied, "Man, I love all your movies." This bouncer's reaction is a constant in the world of King. I have written three books about Stephen King (this is my fourth), and when people ask me what I've written and I mention King as one of the subjects I've published books about, they invariably say either "I love his movies" or "I can't stand his movies." King is a writer first and foremost, but this frequent reaction to King's name indicates that an awful lot of people know King through the film adaptations of his work instead of his books. It is understandable when you consider that, at best, maybe a couple of million people will buy and read an edition of a King book, while anywhere from double to five times that number may see a Stephen King movie, which says something scary about American culture, don't you think?

Here, from *Mid-Life Confidential,* is the official roster of the eighteen members of the musical contingent of the 1993 version of the Rock Bottom Remainders:

1. Dave Barry, *lead guitar, vocals*
2. Tad Bartimus, *Remainderette*
3. Roy Blount Jr., *Critics Chorus*
4. Michael Dorris, *percussion*
5. Robert Fulghum, *mandocello, vocals*
6. Kathi Kamen Goldmark, *Remainderette*
7. Matt Groenig, *Critics Chorus*
8. Josh Kelly, *drums*
9. Stephen King, *rhythm guitar, vocals*
10. Barbara Kingsolver, *keyboards, vocals*
11. Al Kooper, *musical director, guitar, keyboards, vocals*
12. Greil Marcus, *Critics Chorus*
13. Dave Marsh, *Critics Chorus*
14. Ridley Pearson, *bass guitar, vocals*
15. Jerry Peterson, *saxophone*
16. Joel Selvin, *Critics Chorus*
17. Amy Tan, *Remainderette*
18. Jimmy Vivino, *keyboards, vocals*

"I Didn't Get Paid Enough"

by Tabitha King

The essays in *Mid-Life Confidential* are all entertaining, funny, revealing, and extremely well-written—not a real surprise when you consider the caliber of writing talent between the covers of this book.

Stephen King's wife, novelist Tabitha King, accompanied her husband and the Remainders on their 1993 tour and served as official tour photographer. Over one hundred of her behind-the-scenes photos are in *Mid-Life Confidential,* and the title of her *literary* contribution to the project refers to her gripe that she worked as a shutterbug for slave wages and has therefore held back lots of pictures for publication at a later date, "when somebody offers me enough money."

Tabitha King is fully aware that people know that her husband is a money printing press, and she realizes how petty her complaint sounds, considering the size of her family's bank account.

However, Tabitha makes the point that her seemingly mercenary position is not about the money. (Have you ever heard the old adage that goes "When people specifically tell you, 'It's not about the money,' it's about the money"? Just making conversation here.) She addresses this issue in the second paragraph of her essay:

> No doubt there are morons out there demanding to know if I don't have enough money. Well, would you work for diddly-shit? No. You wouldn't. Just what I thought. Probably if you had enough money, you wouldn't work at all. So who's got the work ethic here? I *have* enough money. There's a difference between having enough money and *getting paid* enough to compensate for the work. I knew you'd understand.

Tabitha King's essay then (thankfully) veers away from how much she got paid to take the pictures on the tour and evolves into a fascinating backstage look at life on the road with a bunch of middle-aged writers. Mrs. King also manages to make some insightful points about these writers' "g-g-generation," and one comes away from "I Didn't Get Paid Enough" with the realization that Tabitha King is an absolutely superb essayist. The piece left me wanting more of her non-fiction writing, and I personally think she would make a brilliant weekly columnist, à la Anna Quindlen or Ellen Goodman.

Highly opinionated and scorchingly intelligent, Tabitha King has a lot to say and should do more of this kind of writing. Her fiction has a more literary and stately tone to it; her nonfiction comes across as more accessible and extremely entertaining.

Moreover, "I Didn't Get Paid Enough" is worth reading just for the inclusion of Tabitha's detailed instructions on how to do a constipation-slaying transverse colonic massage. You lie down flat, take the heel of your hand— Well, you should probably read it yourself to get the full benefit of a procedure she describes as "non-invasive, low-tech, free and safe." (*I'm* sold.)

PUBLISHING HISTORY

1994: *Mid-Life Confidential: The Rock Bottom Remainders Tour America with Three Chords and an Attitude* (Viking hardcover).
1995: *Mid-Life Confidential: The Rock Bottom Remainders Tour America With Three Chords and an Attitude* (Plume trade paperback).

71

Introduction to
The Shawshank Redemption: The Shooting Script

I love the movies.

—Stephen King's opening line from his introduction

What it is: Stephen King's warm and flattering appreciation of Frank Darabont's brilliant cinematic adaptation of King's *Different Seasons* novella *Rita Hayworth and Shawshank Redemption,* combined with some fascinating biographical information.

Chances of finding a copy: excellent. Frank Darabont's book *The Shawshank Redemption: The Shooting Script* was published in 1996 and is available in most bookstores. It is a must-own for King fans, since the book also includes Darabont's scene-by-scene discussion of the film, complete with details on why some scenes were eliminated from the final version.

This introduction (included here as a heads-up to fans who may not know of the existence of Darabont's book or King's introduction) is about how *The Shawshank Redemption* went from an option to a "fucking huge screenplay" to an Academy Award–winning film that stunned people who did not know that it was, in essence, a "Stephen King" film.

Frank Darabont—*Shawshank*'s screenwriter and director—had earlier directed a short film based on King's wrenching *Night Shift* short story

"The Woman in the Room," a story King describes in the introduction as having been written "as a kind of cry from the heart after my mother's long, losing battle with cervical cancer had finally ended."

King details Darabont's long and slow journey from that short film to Academy Award winner and, as is often the case with the best of Stephen King's nonfiction, also tells us a great deal about himself as well in the process.

Do you know what the first movie Stephen King ever saw was? It was not a horror flick or a science fiction flick or even a western. It was *Bambi.*

King writes engagingly about his love for the movies and talks about how he sees his books in his head as he's writing them. (He quotes his first editor, Bill Thompson, as remarking, "Steve has a projector in his head.")

This introduction is one of King's most interesting because it is longish (it runs several pages in the book—his introduction to the book *The Fugitive Recaptured* is all of *three paragraphs*)—and also because of his personal involvement with the story.

PUBLISHING HISTORY

1996: *The Shawshank Redemption: The Shooting Script* (March; Newmarket Press trade paperback).

72

Six Stories

Stephen King has his own publishing company and publishing imprint called Philtrum Press. It has a very small catalog of offerings: It has published only four works since its inception in the early eighties. These are King's epistolary novel *The Plant;* the gorgeous limited edition of his *Eyes of the Dragon;* Don Robertson's *Ideal, Genuine Man;* and King's 1997 limited-edition collection of short stories called *Six Stories.*

Essentially, King started Philtrum Press as a means to publish works he believed deserved to see print, with profit motive being secondary.

What it is: *Six Stories* collected four previously published stories ("Lunch at the Gotham Café," "Luckey Quarter," "Blind Willie," and "The Man in the Black Suit") and two brand-new, never-before-published short stories ("L.T.'s Theory of Pets" and "Autopsy Room Four").

Since the previously published stories were never collected until their appearance in this nine-hundred-copy limited edition (eleven hundred copies were actually printed), this chapter looks at all six stories.

Chances of finding a copy: the *Six Stories* collection is not too difficult to find from the usual sources *if* you're willing to spend between $150 and $300, the price on the secondary market in late 1997. (It sold for $80 when it was first published.) A trade edition is rumored to be in the offing sometime around the year 2000 or shortly thereafter, so you can always wait until then.

1

"LUNCH AT THE GOTHAM CAFÉ"

None of us can predict the final outcome of our actions,
after all, and few even try; most of us just do what we do to
prolong a moment's pleasure or to stop the pain for a while.
And even when we act for the noblest reasons, the last link
of the chain all too often drips with someone's blood.

—from "Lunch at the Gotham Café"

What it is: an eerie short story about a man struggling through a painful separation and inevitable divorce who ends up saving his estranged wife's life when the murderously insane maître d' at the Gotham Café goes on a killing spree during a luncheon meeting to discuss the couple's pending divorce.

Chances of finding a copy: relatively easy. The most readily available source would be the Signet paperback edition of *Dark Love,* which came out in 1996 and is still in print.

"Lunch at the Gotham Café" is the first of two stories in *Six Stories* that begin with a husband coming home and finding a note from his wife informing him that their marriage is kaput. ("L.T.'s Theory of Pets" is the other story that begins this way.)

The very effective "Lunch at the Gotham Café" is reminiscent of previous King stories in which some hapless innocent is introduced to madness, shakes its hand, and immediately embraces it as his best friend. He never asks to meet him, but now that he's made his acquaintance, he is more than willing to welcome him into his life.

At the end of his lunch at the Gotham Café, Steven joins that elite fraternity of King characters whose lives change when they meet their dark new friend.

PUBLISHING HISTORY

1995: *Dark Love* (Roc hardcover anthology).
1996: *Dark Love* (Signet paperback anthology).
1997: *Six Stories* (Philtrum Press limited-edition trade paperback).

2

"L.T.'s Theory of Pets"

*Cats are moody, and sometimes they get manic; anyone
who's ever had one will tell you that.*

—"L.T.'s Theory of Pets"

What it is: a dark, atmospheric story about a couple who have different tastes in pets and a departed wife who could very well still be alive; after all, her *body* has not been found: Only her *car* and the body of her dead dog, Frank, a little way off, have been discovered.

Chances of finding a copy: excellent. "L.T.'s Theory of Pets" was initially only available in *Six Stories,* but in November 1997 the story was reprinted in a Plume anthology called *The Best of the Best,* which also included Tabitha King's story "Djinn & Tonic." (This important anthology also contained short stories by Joyce Carol Oates, Nancy Taylor Rosenberg, Sharyn McCrumb, Joy Fielding, Lisa Alther, Erica Jong, Lawrence Block, Ed McBain, Eileen Goudge, Larry Collins, Stephen Frey, Joan Hess, Wendy Hornsby, Jeffery Deaver, Linda Lay Shuler, and E. L. Doctorow.)

"L.T.'s Theory of Pets" reminded me of a couple of early *Night Shift* stories, particularly "Strawberry Spring" and "The Man Who Loved Flowers." A savage serial killer is loose, killing folks (always women) willy-nilly, and no one has a clue as to who he is or when he'll strike again.

As in the *Night Shift* stories, in "L.T.'s Theory of Pets" we immediately wonder about the virtue of the characters we are introduced to in the story. Was L.T. actually the one who did away with Frank or Lulubelle, or could it be the narrator, the dispassionate and sympathetic sidelines observer who sometimes doesn't get along with his own wife and who considers silence marriage's best friend? (King throws in a great line about marriage counselors in the story: He notes that they are always advising troubled and warring couples to talk, but most of the counselors are themselves either divorced or queer.)

We don't know whom to trust in the story, but if the narrator is telling the truth about L.T.'s being at the plant at the time of Lulubelle's disappearance, then it couldn't have been he.

Could it have been the narrator? I suppose it's possible, but King makes it clear that he is a good friend of L.T.'s, and he comforts him when L.T. breaks down on the way home after the dinner party at his home.

Was it the Axe Man who got Lulubelle? And if so, will he strike again? If he does, there's a good chance that this time the authorities *will* find a bunch of bloody body parts in a field by the side of the road somewhere.

This probably still won't convince L.T. that Lulubelle is dead, but I guess that if he wants to believe that she escaped the Axe Man and that she's off blowing truckers somewhere, well, who are we to deny a man whatever small comfort he needs to get through his day?

PUBLISHING HISTORY

1997: *Six Stories* (Philtrum Press limited-edition trade paperback).
1997: *The Best of the Best* (Plume trade paperback).

3

"LUCKEY QUARTER"

> *I'd just checked into a hotel in Carson City, Nevada. My eye caught the housekeeper's "honor envelope" propped up on the telephone, and the whole story just fell into my head.*
>
> —Stephen King, talking about how "Luckey Quarter" came to him during his cross-country *Insomnia* motorcycle tour.

What it is: a short story about a chambermaid in a Carson City hotel who receives a tip—a "luckey quarter"—that changes her life. Or does it?

Chances of finding a copy: pretty good if you're fortunate enough to have a library nearby that archives *USA Weekend*. Many libraries archive the *daily* edition of *USA Today*, but not all of them also have the *USA Weekend* magazine. (Interestingly, a university library I use all the time does the exact opposite: They do not archive the daily edition of the paper but *do* have *USA Weekend* going back to its first issue.) *USA Today* offered a reprint of the summer series of stories which "Luckey Quarter" was a part of, so it might be worth contacting the newspaper and inquiring if the set of all six stories is still available. Also, of course, "Luckey Quarter" appears in *Six Stories,* available as a limited edition from the usual sources.

"Luckey Quarter" and "Dedication" are Stephen King's two stories (so far) specifically about hotel chambermaids.

A single mom receives a single quarter in her room 322 honeypot—the courtesy envelope that all the chambermaids leave for their room guests in case the visitors would "care to leave a little 'extra something' " for them.

Ar first, Darlene Pullen just laughs at the pathetic reality of her life: She works like a slave cleaning rooms for strangers, and she receives a twenty-five-cent tip. But then Darlene finds a note in the honeypot that reads, "This is a luckey quarter! It's true! Luckey you!"

Darlene is skeptical but decides to use the coin in a one-arm bandit in the hotel lobby. She wins a much-needed eighteen dollars in quarters, and from that point on, she cannot do anything *but* win. She stops at a casino on the way home, and before long, she is thousands of dollars richer.

Then she wakes up, so to speak, and we are left believing it was all a fantasy. Or was it?

Could fate have really smiled on her through the gift of an unexpected "luckey quarter?" Does Darlene really win the jackpot?

"Luckey Quarter" is one of King's gentler stories, a tale that asks us to believe in the possibility that every once in a while one of us just might get "luckey."

Publishing History

1995: *USA Weekend* (June 30–July 2).
1997: *Six Stories* (Philtrum Press limited-edition trade paperback).

4

"AUTOPSY ROOM FOUR"

*It's so dark that for awhile—just how long I don't know—
I think I'm still unconscious. Then, slowly, it comes to me
that unconscious people don't have a sensation of
movement through the dark, accompanied by a faint,
rhythmic sound that can only be a squeaky wheel.*

—Howard Cottrell, "Autopsy Room Four"

What it is: a horrifying literary nightmare about a guy who is mistaken for dead and who is fully aware of the preparations for his own seemingly inevitable autopsy.

Chances of finding a copy: "Autopsy Room Four" is available in *Six Stories* (see above); and *Psychos,* which will be much easier to acquire.

It was either an episode of *ER* or *Chicago Hope* (I think it was *Chicago Hope*) that immediately came to mind while I was reading "Autopsy Room Four."

In the episode I remembered, a patient was completely brain-dead and in such good health when he had his accident (it's *always* an accident) that almost all his harvestable organs could have been used to help people in desperate need of a transplant.

The plotline for this episode revolves around a doctor who wants to pull all life support off the guy and harvest the poor sap from stem to stern. This medico is in a nasty battle with others at the hospital who insist on waiting until they can get consent from the guy's long-lost next of kin.

While all this intrahospital bickering is going on, the guy wakes up. What came to mind while reading "Autopsy Room Four" was something one of the doctors said about this whole debacle. Basically he reminded the others (scolded, actually) that the reason more people do not sign up to be organ donors is because they're afraid of being mistakenly cut open and "harvested" while still alive. (Yikes!)

We are in the mind of a man who everyone thinks is dead but who is apparently quite alive. When the story begins, Howard Cottrell is being wheeled into an autopsy room, the apparent victim of a massive heart attack while out on the golf course. The only problem is that Howie is (according to Howie at least) most assuredly *not* dead and is fully aware of everything going on around him.

King takes us through the prep work for an autopsy and also lets us hear what Howard hears: the macabre jokes, the loud music, the flirting among the morgue personnel, and of course the noise of the instruments and equipment being prepared for his autopsy.

Throughout the story, several questions come to mind: Is Howard really dead? If he is dead, is King saying that we are conscious (horrors!) of what goes on after our body expires? Will Howard have to go through his own actual autopsy while apparently fully conscious? If Howie *does* get diced and sliced, will *that* finally terminate his consciousness? If he is really alive, what can he do to make the medicos realize this?

Notably, this story has a very clever sexual subtext—sex being a theme somewhat rare in King's fiction. After all, how many times have you read a line like "Her hand is still holding my cock . . ." in a Stephen King tale? The story concludes with a dark, erotic one-liner that is really very funny.

"Autopsy Room Four" takes place in our beloved Maine hamlet of Derry, as did King's magnum opus *It*. In fact, Howard's dire circumstances are the result of a bizarre and frightening "hobby" of one fellow Derry neighbor.

There are a bunch of King's usual pop-culture references in this tale, but the most dominant one is his use of Rolling Stones songs to mask Howard's feeble attempts to make a sound. It's only rock and roll, but King likes it.

PUBLISHING HISTORY

1997: *Six Stories* (Philtrum Press limited-edition trade paperback).
1997: *Psychos* (Signet mass-market paperback).

5

"Blind Willie"

He has no kids, of course—he wants kids about as much as
he wants kidney stones—and his wife's name isn't
Andrea—but those are things the scrawny, constantly
grinning man will never know.

—from "Blind Willie"

What it is: an odd tale about a man who makes a six-figure income by pretending to be a blind Vietnam veteran—except that he actually *loses his sight* each day as his case fills up with contributions from generous New Yorkers.

Chances of finding a copy: "Blind Willie" is available in *Six Stories* (see above). If you're lucky (or doggedly persistent), you may also be able to find, in a good university library, a copy of the 1993 literary journal *Antaeus* in which the story first appeared.

William Teale is one of the more bizarre characters in King's universe of tales. Teale is literally a trinity of three individual people with three different names, three separate offices (although one of these "offices" is a spot on a New York city sidewalk), three different modes of garb, and three distinctly different personalities.

"Blind Willie" is about identity and artifice and is one of King's more literary works and thematically layered tales. Such a story deserved a debut in an appropriately literary venue, the journal *Antaeus*.

In this reader's opinion, "Blind Willie" weaves its own hypnotic spell and effectively illustrates that even after all of King's self-effacing downplaying of his literary skills (or lack thereof, according to King), he is quite capable of writing stories with depth and an element of literary excellence his naysayers refuse to recognize or even admit that he is able to create.

Publishing History

1993: *Antaeus* (Ecco Press literary journal).
1997: *Six Stories* (Philtrum Press limited-edition trade paperback).

6

"THE MAN IN THE BLACK SUIT"

*I am a very old man and this is something that happened
to me when I was very young—only nine years old.*

—the opening line of "The Man in the Black Suit"

What it is: an award-winning short story about a young boy who has
a fateful meeting with the Prince of Darkness himself one day by the
side of a river.

Chances of finding a copy: excellent, since almost every university
and public library in the United States archives back issues of the
esteemed *New Yorker.* (It's like a *law.*)

"The Man in the Black Suit" is evocative and brilliant and proves once
again just how good a writer Stephen King is. The story won the 1994
World Fantasy Award for Best Short Fiction and the 1994 O. Henry
Award for Best American Short Story. Both accolades were unquestionably well deserved.

PUBLISHING HISTORY

1994: *New Yorker* (October 31).
1997: *Six Stories* (Philtrum Press limited-edition trade paperback).

73

"Everything's Eventual"

I got the call that changed my life just when I thought the combination of Ma and delivering for Pizza Roma was going to drive me crazy.

—from "Everything's Eventual"

What it is: a 20,000-word science-fiction novella that was the final piece of fiction published by Stephen King in 1997.

Chances of finding a copy: very good. The issue of the *Magazine of Fantasy & Science Fiction* in which this novella appeared is of course off the stands by now, but back copies are almost certainly available directly from the magazine (publishers tend to print extras of a "Stephen King" issue; see "Sources and Resources"), or you can get one from any of the usual King merchandise dealers. (the *Magazine of Fantasy & Science Fiction* ran a classified ad in a recent issue offering back issues for sale, "including some collector's items, such as the special Stephen King issue." The ad also said they had limited quantities of some issues going back into the mid-1980s and offered a free list for the asking.)

Stephen King and the *Magazine of Fantasy & Science Fiction* have a long history together, going back to 1978 with the publication of "The Night of the Tiger" and the original appearances of the first five *Dark Tower* "Gunslinger" stories. This relationship continues through today with the late-1997 publication of "Everything's Eventual."

The fairly recent appearance of "Everything's Eventual" would seem to contradict the premise of a book called *The Lost Work of Stephen King,* but since the novella only appeared in a genre magazine and many fans may not even have been aware of its publication, I felt its inclusion would fulfill the purpose of this book, which is to inform King fans about works they may not have seen but may still be available to them with a little hunting (or in this case a quick call to the usual sources).

A teenager named Dinky Earnshaw learns that he is one in 8 million humans who is a *tranny*—a term King uses to describe a person gifted with the paranormal ability to kill by sending personalized letters (or E-mails) containing odd geometric shapes called japps, mirks, bews, smims, and fouders to a selected target.

Dinky is identified and then hired by the Trans Corporation, put through a period of training, and then set up with a house, an allowance, and DINKY'S DAYBOARD, a kitchen chalkboard on which he writes down whatever he wants and voilà! it's there when he returns home from the movies or a walk.

Dinky is told that he is working for the betterment of mankind, and at first he accepts this. Then he begins to learn more about the people he sends DINKYMAIL to and to wonder about the motives of the mysterious organization that takes care of all of his needs—as long as he sits at his computer and performs his E-mail executions.

One day Dinky receives a clandestine message from a fellow tranny, which sets in motion events that may result in even *more* deaths, but not the kind that Dinky is being paid for.

"Everything's Eventual" is science fiction with a touch of the fantastic. Once again, King looks at "wild talents," those humans gifted (some would say cursed) with wondrous abilities that can be used for good or evil. (*Carrie, Firestarter, The Shining, The Dead Zone,* and "The End of the Whole Mess" are other examples of King writing about such "gifted" individuals.)

King is especially good with short fiction, and this novella is no exception. It is definitely worth tracking down, and because of its relatively recent appearance, the price of this back issue of the *Magazine of Fantasy & Science Fiction* should be quite affordable.

PUBLISHING HISTORY

1997: *Magazine of Fantasy & Science Fiction* (October/November).

74

"The Wait is Over . . ."

PART 1: *DARK TOWER RETURNS*

PART 2: *STEPHEN KING MEETS FANS' DEMANDS:*
THE DARK TOWER CONTINUES

I haven't had writer's block since college.

—from "The Wait is Over . . ."

What it is: a two-part interview with King that was published in the November 1997 and December 1997 issues of *The Waldenbook Report.*

Chances of finding a copy: difficult. *The Waldenbook Report* is a free newspaper given out to Waldenbooks' customers. It is not archived in libraries, and if copies do exist, Waldenbooks' corporate offices would probably be the only place to find them. Try writing to the Consumer Relations Department of Waldenbooks (See "Sources and Resources"; do not call) and ask if they have copies available of these two issues. Sometimes book and magazine dealers like Betts Books and The Overlook Connection acquire a quantity of these newsletters and then offer them for sale, but this is a hit-or-miss situation. (If the month in which the issues were published goes by and a dealer has not gotten his hands on any, there are no suppliers he can buy them from.) The usual sources are worth contacting about this two-parter, however, since trying to find a copy of this interview *is* worth the effort. This is an important interview in which King offers some very insightful observations while also picking his favorite book and choosing his five-hundred-year "time capsule" book.

This ten-question interview with Stephen King was conducted by his publicist for Waldenbooks, and the questions are more probing and more *knowing* than the usual journalist's queries King hears every time he agrees to speak to the media.

When asked how many projects he works on at once, King replies two and then explains how he *writes* one thing while *rewriting* another. This reply truly illustrates the old writer's adage that writing isn't *writing*; it's *rewriting*.

After revealing that he hasn't been blocked since college, he then discusses how the process of writing has changed for him over the years and says that he still has to work very hard to "close the door" on everyone and everything—the readers, the critics, people's expectations—and just "try to stick with what makes me happy."

When asked what writers he most admires, his answer is a surprise: He picks as his "Big Daddy" the Providence-born Cormac McCarthy, the southern gothic author of such dark and violent works as *The Orchard Keeper* (1965), *Outer Dark* (1968), *Child of God* (1974), *Suttree* (1979), *Blood Meridian* (1985), and his 1992 National Book Award winner, *All the Pretty Horses.*

King also singles out Ruth Rendell, making special mention of Rendell's own "Richard Bachman," *her* pseudonym, Barbara Vine. He also cites Jonathan Kellerman and Ed McBain and reveals that he still reads Agatha Christie, Dorothy L. Sayers, Charles Dickens, J. R. R. Tolkien, William Golding, and John Fowles. (See the feature on King's *Wimsey,* which was his attempt at writing a tale using Dorothy Sayers's detective character Lord Peter Wimsey.)

Part 1 of this interview ends with King answering the terrifying (for his fans) question "Do you ever think about retiring?" King's response? "What I would like to do is to quit what I'm up to while people are still having a good time with what I write." In other words, he wants to go out a winner. He admits concern about being around "30 years from now, having descended into self-parody." He does state with certainty that he would write even if his work wasn't published—something we all knew already about King. Stephen King writes because he has a *calling,* not because it's his job.

Part 2 starts off with the interviewer asking King why he continues writing the *Dark Tower* series. King admits that one of the reasons he continues the story of Roland is because he knows his fans want him to (and also because the women who work for him put *every single letter* asking about the *Dark Tower* on his desk). "There isn't a day goes by," King says, "that I don't think about Roland and Eddie and Detta and all the other people, even Oy, the little animal. I've been living with these guys longer than the readers have, ever since college, actually, and that's a long time for me."

When asked which of his books is his favorite, King hedges, comparing his books to children, noting that even if all your kids are different, you love each one of them and try not to pick a favorite. Then he caves in and *does* pick a favorite, and it is the book that many (including this writer) consider his best work of all time: *It*.

The interviewer then asks King a very interesting question. Which of his works would he put in a time capsule, to be opened in five hundred years?

Have you got a guess? Could it be his first book, *Carrie*? Or perhaps his favorite book, *It*? Could it be the one book that may be his most personal statement about being a successful writer, *Misery*?

"No" to all of the above.

Stephen King's time-capsule novel is the only book he thought enough of to republish years after its initial appearance with deleted text reinstated, making this book, finally, "complete and uncut": King picked *The Stand*.

This fascinating interview concludes with King talking about the most satisfying experience of his career. It was not signing a multi-million-dollar contract or having three or four books on the bestseller lists at the same time. It was receiving a telegram informing him that *Carrie* had sold to Doubleday at a time when he had just had his phone taken out for lack of payment.

"The Wait is Over . . ." is a very interesting look at America's most popular writer as well as one of King's most candid interviews to date.

PUBLISHING HISTORY

1997: *The Waldenbook Report* (part 1; November).
1997: *The Waldenbook Report* (part 2; December).

75

The "Almost" Stories

Stephen King is incredibly prolific, but you already knew that. In the case of a writer who churns out terrific work year after year the way King does, the idea factory upstairs in that Maine head of his works incessantly, and sometimes King has more ideas than he realistically has time to write. Sometimes he has ideas that just don't pan out, or he loses interest in them.

This feature—The "Almost" Stories"—looks at a handful of Stephen King ideas that *almost* became short stories or novels. King had talked about these ideas and had even begun developing some of them, but in the end, he abandoned them for one reason or another. You'll have no chance of getting them because they exist only in King's macabre mind.

Whether or not these ideas ever become full-blown works, it is still fascinating to review them and see how a mind like King's works.

"The Rats Are Loose on Flight 74"

In Douglas E. Winter's marvelous 1985 collection of interviews with horror writers, *Faces of Fear,* Stephen King discussed with Doug a short story he had actually conceived and essentially written in his mind but had not set down on paper:

> *I worry about airplanes. I can remember being on a transcontinental flight and getting to the halfway point—which the stewardesses always announce with great cheer—although what they are saying is that you are now too far to turn back. You either have to go ahead or die. And I thought, what if somebody said, "I need a pillow," and the stewardess opened the overhead rack and all these rats came out into her face, and she started to scream,*

*and the rats were biting off her nose and everything else, and one
of the people in first class opened up a pouch to get an airsick
bag because this was so gross, and rats came out of there, rats
came out of everywhere. And the name of this story was going to
be "The Rats Are Loose on Flight 74." I just haven't gotten
around to writing it yet, but I probably will."*

Stephen King *has* written about rats ("Graveyard Shift") and airplanes and the fear of flying (*The Langoliers*), but so far "The Rats
Are Loose on Flight 74"—if it *is*, of course, actually written—has not
seen its way into print.

THE "KIDDIE RIDE" STORY

In a January 31, 1988, interview with Julie Washington for the *Cleve-
land Plain Dealer* titled "If You're Scared Silly, Then Stephen King Is
Happy," King talked about an idea that had more than likely come to
him while walking through a mall one day. "You know those kiddie
rides in malls?" he asked Washington. "Well, what would happen if a
mother put her kid inside a ride, dropped in a quarter and watched the
thing spin a few times, and when it stopped, she discovered her son
had disappeared?" This story idea echoes the "magical" disappearance
of David Brown in *The Tommyknockers,* but a story with this exact
plotline has not yet surfaced.

THE "AIRPORT LADIES' ROOM" STORY

King described a second story idea in the Julie Washington interview
that we can call the "Airport Ladies' Room" story.

"Or how about this?" he began. "Husband and wife are at the airport to board a plane. The woman has to go the ladies' room, so the
man waits outside for her. And waits. She never comes out. Pretty soon
he notices that other women are going in but not coming out.
Boyfriends and husbands accumulate outside the bathroom, all feeling
uneasy but reluctant to talk to each other. Eventually they alert airport
security, then the governor and ultimately the president, in an effort to
deal with the mystery."

This sounds like another fun story, one in which King toys with the
idea of setting a tale in a bathroom. King *has* used a bathroom setting
in other works, most notably the "exploding toilets" scene in *It*; the

haunted toilet stall in "Sneakers"; and the monster in the bathroom sink in "The Moving Finger," but so far we have not seen an "Airport Ladies' Room" story (although some of *The Langoliers is* set in an airport lobby).

THE "WEREWOLVES IN CONNECTICUT" STORY

On Wednesday, October 26, 1988, the *New York Times* published an interview with Stephen King called "Writer Eats Steak Before It Eats Him." The interview was conducted by Bryan Miller, the *Times*'s food columnist. The dinner party consisted of Stephen King, his business manager, Arthur Greene, and Miller. King had a Bloody Mary and split the house-special steak with Arthur Greene. The steak came with fried potatoes and creamed spinach, and as they ate, King discussed the many uses of food in his works, specifically mentioning *Thinner, Carrie, 'Salem's Lot, The Shining, Cujo,* and *Pet Sematary.*

King also revealed that he often cooked for his children and that one of his specialties was "ground chuck with canned spaghetti, jazzed up with cayenne and other peppers."

The talk then turned to King's always being on the alert for new story ideas, and Miller wrote that King "even devised one on the spot when I mentioned that I had once worked for a newspaper in Connecticut":

> *I can see it now. You go up there and take this job because, well, either your wife died or you had some terrible debilitating illness. That's when the werewolves show up. You know it, but nobody else will believe you and your editor won't publish any of these things.*
>
> *"It was a quiet little New England town until he came."*

This sounds like *Tarker's Mills comes to 'Salem's Lot,* doesn't it? King had already had werewolves wreak havoc on a small town in 1983's *Cycle of the Werewolf,* so he probably didn't have much interest in having them all move to Connecticut.

"STEPHEN KING'S DESERT ISLAND"

This "almost" story was actually written in part for the July 1990 issue of the magazine *Condé Nast Traveler.*

In "Stephen King's Desert Island," King discussed the oft-asked question "If you were stranded on a desert island, what one book would you take with you?" King concedes that his survival skills are essentially nonexistent and that "the concept of living off the land belongs only in robust, self-congratulatory novels like *Robinson Crusoe,* allegories like *Lord of the Flies,* or those mindlessly cheerful novels of boys' adventures written in the last quarter of the nineteenth century and the first quarter of the twentieth."

King then provides three paragraphs of flawless literary imitations of these types of novels, describing the exploits of three characters: Richard, Thomas, and Little Toby. In the brief scene of the story, Thomas suggests, "If we stretch our shirts over those fallen logs . . . we shall catch each morning's fall of dew! We can drink that!" Richard exclaims, "Rather!" and tells the others that he can make a "whizzer heliograph" with a piece of broken mirror because he, of course, remembers his "Morse from the Scouts."

This excerpt from King's nonexistent novel ends with: " 'Hurrah for the adventure!' cried Little Toby, causing them to all laugh indulgently."

THE CENSORED SCENE OF '*SALEM'S LOT*

In his June 1983 *Playboy* interview, Stephen King talked about just how far he would go when it came to the horrors he would depict and how *his* vision of a story sometimes clashed with what the less daring powers-that-be at publishing companies would be willing to see in print:

> *Anyway, though I wouldn't censor myself, I was censored once. In the first draft of* 'Salem's Lot, *I had a scene in which Jimmy Cody, the local doctor, is devoured in a boardinghouse basement by a horde of rats summoned from the town dump by the leader of the vampires. They swarm all over him like a writhing, furry carpet, biting and clawing, and when he tries to scream a warning to his companion upstairs, one of them scurries into his open mouth and squirms there as it gnaws out his tongue. I loved the scene, but my editor made it clear that no way would Doubleday publish something like that, and I came around eventually and impaled poor Jimmy on knives. But, shit, it just wasn't the same.*

The Sequel to 'Salem's Lot

After 'Salem's Lot was published in 1975, King repeatedly said that he wanted to write a sequel to this classic contemporary vampire novel.

In a 1982 interview with Fangoria magazine, King had this to say about the possibility of things not being over in the haunted town of Jerusalem's Lot:

> When I wrote "One For the Road" [in Night Shift] I knew that things weren't over in Jerusalem's Lot, the same way that I know they aren't over now. I think about a sequel a lot. I even know who would be in it and how it would launch . . . it's Father Callahan. I know where he is. People ask me, "You see Father Callahan [leave on] that Greyhound Bus; what happened to him?" Well, I know what happened to him. He went to New York City and from New York he drifted across the country and he landed in Detroit. He's in the inner city and he's running a soup kitchen for alcoholics, mostly black, and he's been attacked a couple of times and he's been in the hospital and people think he's crazy. He doesn't wear the turned-around collar anymore, but he's doing this anyway and he's trying to get right with God. So one day this guy comes in. He's dying and he says, "I have to talk to you, Father Callahan." And Callahan says, "I'm not a Father anymore and how did you know that?" Finally, the guy is actually dying and coughing up blood and the last thing he says as he grabs Callahan by the shirt and pulls him down into this mist of beer and whiskey and puke and every-thing else is, "It's not over in the Lot, yet." Then he drops dead. . . .

In 1983, King sat for a lengthy interview with Eric Norden for Play-boy magazine. Norden wrote in his introduction: "Of all of his books, 'Salem's Lot remains King's personal favorite and he is planning a sequel."

However, King's feelings regarding the idea of a sequel changed sometime after 1983, and in 1989, at a lecture at the Pasadena Library, when King was asked about this second installment of the story of the Lot, he said that he felt the time had passed and that he would not be writing a follow-up.

Interestingly, there was even talk for a time of King's wife, Tabitha, a respected novelist in her own right, penning a sequel to 'Salem's Lot or possibly collaborating with her husband on the book. That, too, did not come to fruition.

In 1997, King was interviewed by Edward Gross for *Fangoria* magazine. Gross wrote, "One novel King will not be writing is *'Salem's Lot II*." Gross then quotes King, who says, "It has been too long. The kid's all grown up now, and the only way to do it would be to slug it back in time and set it up in 1980. At one time, that was something I wanted to do very much, but the time has gone by. It always does after a while. You either write it, or the time passes."

THE "JONESTOWN/JIM JONES" NOVEL

In 1989, in an interview with *W·B* (Waldenbooks' magazine of reviews, author interviews, and book news), King said, "I've got an interest in writing a novel about what happened at Jonestown."

A year later, in 1990, King gave an interview in which he said, "What I'd like to do at some point in the next year—this has never really let go of me—is to write a novel about Jonestown." Almost a decade later, nothing of this potential project has been seen.

THE "WESTERN" NOVEL

In 1989, King said, "A few years ago, I did try very hard to write a western, because it's a form I like. I wrote about 160 pages and the only scene that really had any power was when this old guy got drunk outside this farmhouse and fell into the pigsty, and the pigs ate him. That one scene has some real drive and punch. This is what turned on my lights, for reasons I don't understand."

There are, of course, elements of the western in *The Dark Tower* series (most notably in the "Gunslinger" stories) and in King's college serial *Slade* (see the feature on *Slade*), but so far we have not been gifted with a full-blown western by Stephen King. For what it's worth, in 1997, during a lecture and reading in Australia, King told his audience that the Australian outback reminded him of how the American West was meant to be.

STEEL MACHINE

In *The Dark Half* there are excerpts from three novels by Thad Beaumont's "dark half," George Stark: *Machine's Way, Riding To Babylon,* and *Steel Machine*. *Steel Machine* was the novel Thad was forced to "coauthor" with George Stark, and parts of it appear in manuscript form in King's novel.

In King's 1989 interview with *W·B*, the horrormeister said, "My editor at Viking, Chuck Verrill, is now suggesting to me that I write one of the Stark novels that's brought up in the book. And so I'm actually thinking about writing the one called *Steel Machine*, the book that Stark is working on at the end. If I were to do that, it would be published as *Steel Machine* by Richard Bachman, not by George Stark. Because George Stark doesn't exist but Richard Bachman does."

There is little likelihood of seeing *Steel Machine* until at least sometime after the year 2000, since King's 1997 contract with Simon & Schuster was for three books: the novel *Bag of Bones*; a collection of short stories; and *On Fiction*, the nonfiction book on writing, all of which would be published sequentially, beginning with *Bag of Bones* in 1998. After that, who knows? Richard Bachman did, after all, resurface in 1996 with *The Regulators*, so the manuscript for *Steel Machine* may very well be sitting in the same trunk where Claudia Inez Bachman found the manuscript for *The Regulators*.

THE "BASEBALL" NOVEL

In the aforementioned 1989 *W·B* interview, King told his interviewer, "There is a baseball novel in me. I didn't mention it [earlier] because that's the one that's closest to happening."

In April 1990, King published in the *New Yorker* a lengthy nonfiction article called "Head Down," which was about his son Owen's Bangor Little League team.

A few months later, at the October 1990 press conference for the film *Graveyard Shift*, King confirmed that he was still thinking about writing a baseball novel.

This comment notwithstanding, King has not said anything lately about the baseball novel, so he may have satisfied his urge to write about baseball with the Little League essay. Only time will tell.

THE "EVANGELIST" NOVEL

King also told *W·B*, "I'd like to write a novel about an evangelist, not necessarily an Elmer Gantry novel, but I'd like to write about religion."

King's 1996 novel *Desperation* is about an ancient evil power named

Tak that is awakened from beneath a mining town. In the story, the only person Tak seems to have no power over is a young boy who just might have a direct line to God.

THE "CHRIST" NOVEL

King also told *W·B*, "I'd like to write a novel about Christ." In *Desperation*, the character of prayerful young David Carver *could* be interpreted as a Christ figure, although it sounds from King's comment that he was talking about writing about the actual historical figure Jesus Christ, something he has not yet done, or if he has, it has not yet been published.

THE "AUSTRALIAN" SHORT STORY

In October 1997, after touring the Australian outback on a Harley, King gave a lecture and a reading in which he told his audience that there was a possibility that he would someday write a short story set in Australia but that he needed time for all the myriad influences of the outback and the country to "settle" in him before he tried writing about it.

THE *EYES OF THE DRAGON* SEQUEL

During the aforementioned 1997 Australian lecture and reading, King was asked if he was writing a sequel to *The Eyes of the Dragon*. King's reply? "Go and read the *Dark Tower* books."

Make it so.

76

King.com: Stephen King on the Internet

Stephen King is an important presence in cyberspace. This feature looks at (1) the two times he has posted on Internet newsgroups; (2) the Usenet newsgroups devoted (pun intended) solely to him and his work; (3) Stephen King web sites; and (4) how to write to King. (Hint: It *ain't* by E-mail!)

STEPHEN KING'S TWO INTERNET NEWSGROUP POSTINGS

King has only posted publicly twice.

Posting number 1 was from Cornell University in 1994 during King's Harley-Davidson book-signing tour of independent bookstores to promote *Insomnia*. Here is the text of what King sent out from a computer at Cornell.

Someone wondered if I ever get into these electronic bulletin boards. I got a peek into this one while preparing to do a speaking gig at Cornell University, in Ithaca, on October 6th, 1994. I haven't been in Colorado buying Slurpies at any 7-11s lately, but I was in a Christie's in Hoosick, New York yesterday. The new book is INSOMNIA, and that's what I'm promoting. I'm glad so many people liked Frank's version of SHAWSHANK, and I hope to see many of you on my tour ... if the Harley doesn't break down ... or if I don't break down. The question that occurs is whether or not the people reading this will believe I'm me. It really is, but if I put in something only I would know in order to prove it, everybody would know it. It's the only catch, Catch-22. In closing, the big cahunas and cahunettes here at Cornell want

me to tell you that I don't have an account or an electronic post-
box here. In fact, I don't really know what the f—— I'm doing.
Oh, I think I DO know how to prove I'm me. First, the next
book is called ROSE MADDER—June of 1995 from Viking.
Second, it will be Eddie, not Roland, who saves the party of trav-
ellers from Blaine the Mono. Joe Bob sez "Check it out." Check
ya on the flip-flop,
    Stephen King

The comment about the Slurpie had to do with a previous newsgroup poster who claimed to have seen King walk into his 7-Eleven
store in Colorado and buy a Slurpie.

Stephen King Internet posting number 2 addressed the fan uproar over
the 1996 Christmas *Desperation/The Regulators* promotion in which
anyone who bought both books would receive a two-chapter preview
booklet of *The Dark Tower IV: Wizard and Glass*.

When *Desperation* and *The Regulators* were initially released, they
were packaged as a set that came with a "Keep You Up All Night
Light."

When the night light sets ran out, Stephen King came up with an
idea he thought would satisfy the disappointed fans who were planning
on buying both books, anyway, but who would now be deprived of
their own little bonus.

King decided that anyone who bought *both books* at the same time
would receive a two-chapter preview booklet of his forthcoming *Dark
Tower* book, *Wizard and Glass*.

He thought that this would make *everybody* happy, but in reality,
he really didn't think this through. After all, if you, as a Stephen King
fan, had a choice between a cheesy, battery-powered night-light and the
first two chapters of the next *Dark Tower* book in a special limited-
edition preview booklet, what would *you* choose?

There was an enormous outcry on the alt.books.stephen-king newsgroup from people who had bought the packaged set when it first came
out and were now *not* entitled to something everyone felt was much
more special—something that the Johnny-come-latelies totally lucked
into.

King's constant readers and biggest fans bitched to high heaven that
they were the ones who had scurried out to buy the *Desperation/The*

Regulators set when it first came out, and now *they* were being shafted for their devotion because those who had waited were getting this wonderful bonus.

The whining and carping and complaining and crying went on for quite a while until one day, this post from a Penguin employee showed up on the asbk newsgroup:

> I work at Penguin USA (Viking) and Stephen King has asked me to post the following note to you all. Please feel free to copy and disseminate this. For those of you who are wondering, this is only the second time there has ever been a message from Steve in this newsgroup. The first time was when he was on his motorcycle tour cross country for INSOMNIA (two years ago) when he posted from a bookstore at Cornell U. Please don't flood us with responses to this letter. Steve will not be reading them. Any responses to this AOL e-mail address will just be going to the publisher.

This "introduction" of sorts (which was really a "hold on to your hats" kind of warning, because King was undeniably pissed off when he wrote his own little missive) was followed by this open letter to his fans from Stephen King himself:

November 21, 1996

> *Gentle Readers: It's reached my attention that there's been a fair degree of pissing and moaning about the WIZARD AND GLASS booklet which comes with a dual purchase of DESPERATION and THE REGULATORS. I swear to God, some of you guys could die and go to heaven and then complain that you had booked a double occupancy room, and where the hell is the sauna, anyway? The major complaints seem to be coming from people who have already bought both books. Those of you who bought the double-pack got the light, right? A freebie. So whatcha cryin' about?*
>
> *The booklet was my idea, not the publisher's—a little extra for people who wanted to buy both books after supplies of the famous "Keep You Up All Night" light ran out. If you expect to get the booklet IN ADDITION to the light, all I can say is sorry, Cholly, but there may not be enough booklets to go around. If you bought the two books separately, because there weren't any*

gift packs left (they sold faster than expected, which is how this booklet deal came up in the first place), go back to where you bought them, tell the dealer what happened, show him/her your proof of (separate) purchase, and they'll take care of you. If they get wise witcha, tell 'em Steve King said that was the deal.

If you're just jacked because you want to read the first two chapters of Wizard and Glass, *wait until the whole thing comes out. Or put it on your T.S. List and give it to the chaplain. In any case, those of you who are yelling and stamping your feet, please stop. If you're old enough to read, you're old enough to behave.*
STEVE KING

So there.

Usenet Newsgroups

There are currently two Internet newsgroups *solely* devoted to Stephen King and his work. They are:

> alt.books.stephen-king
> alt.fan.authors.stephen-king

The newsgroup alt.books.stephen-king (known as "asbk" among frequent posters and lurkers) is the more popular of the two newsgroups, and the postings there are frequent and very often authoritative.

I know for a fact that Tabitha and Stephen King monitor this newsgroup, but they never post publicly. (Information that the Kings would like leaked is sometimes posted under different names on asbk, though.) There are, of course, the occasional off-topic postings (as there are on any Usenet newsgroup), but they make up a small part of the daily dialogue on the group.

The serious King fan will want to check out the postings on asbk on a regular basis. Not only will you often find out hitherto-unknown bits of Stephen King fact and lore; you will also have access to dealers, collectors, and countless others intimately involved with the entire Stephen King universe.

Stephen King Web Sites

I won't even make an attempt to list any or all of the web pages devoted to Stephen King. On a recent Stephen King World Wide Web expedition, my search engine came up with 8,698 web pages on which the name "Stephen King" appeared.

In addition to fan pages, there are official sites set up by King's publishers (two recent sites were a *Green Mile* page and a *Dark Tower IV* page), plus sites maintained by book dealers, private collectors, and libraries on which King and his works are prominently featured and actively discussed.

There are Stephen King "FAQ"s available ("Frequently Asked Questions" files) that are often linked to other King-related sites as well as sites devoted to first lines of King's works, King dedications, King movies, and more.

My suggestion is to do your own Stephen King search on the Internet and visit the sites that sound interesting to you.

Although there are many efficient and powerful search engines out there, my personal favorites are Yahoo (http://www.yahoo.com), Infoseek (http://www.infoseek.com), and Excite (http://www.excite.com).

These search engines offer power searches, Boolean searches, and the ability to search within the located web sites and also to modify searches in progress with more specific qualifying terminology. They also offer a "More like this" feature which will search based on the characteristics of the selected web site.

Start by doing a search for stephen-king. The hyphen tells Infoseek to only find pages on which those two words are sequential, thus giving you *only* the pages on which our boy is mentioned specifically.

A word of caution: Searching for the name "Stephen King" without a hyphen will find you every web page containing either the word "Stephen" or the word "King"—with the *case* of the word not being considered. Thus, Infoseek (or any other search engine for that matter) will find every web page with the *noun* "king" as well. You do not want to do this. Believe me.

STEPHEN KING'S E-MAIL ADDRESS

Stephen King's E-mail address is . . . *Yeah, right.* That's all I'd have to do is publicly reveal the address of Stephen King's electronic mail box. I don't think the Internet could handle the volume of E-mail messages King would receive if that information were made public.

If you want to write to Stephen King, write him in care of his publishers (Penguin, Simon & Schuster, and Doubleday all forward his fan mail to him). Be forewarned, though: Stephen King has stated publicly that he does not read the vast majority of his fan mail. He simply *cannot* and continue to write books.

When I interviewed King's secretary, Stephanie Leonard, back in 1989 for my *Complete Stephen King Encyclopedia,* she told me that King was at that time receiving over 500 pieces of unsolicited mail a week "and probably 450 expected a reply." It's anybody's guess how much mail he gets now, but a revealing indicator is that he now has *three* people reading and answering his mail, "and a lot of times," he said in a 1997 interview, "they don't tell me what's going on with the fan mail, except for the stuff that I pick up myself."

So write to King if you must, but the odds on a reply from the man himself are slim, although there have been postings on the newsgroups from fans who have received replies from one of his assistants.

THE FINAL WORD

The genre exists on three basic levels, separate but interdependent and each one a little bit cruder than the one before. There's terror on top, the finest emotion any writer can induce; then horror, and, on the very lowest level of all, the gag instinct of revulsion. Naturally, I'll try to terrify you first, and if that doesn't work, I'll try to horrify you, and if I can't make it there, I'll try to gross you out. I'm not proud; I'll give you a sandwich squirming with bugs or shove your hand into the maggot-churning innnards of a long-dead woodchuck. I'll do anything it takes; I'll go to any lengths, I'll geek a rat if I have to—I've geeked plenty of them in my time. After all, as Oscar Wilde said, nothing succeeds like excess. So if somebody wakes up screaming because of what I've wrote, I'm delighted. If he merely tosses his cookies, it's still a victory but on a lesser scale. I suppose the ultimate triumph would be to have somebody drop dead of a heart attack, literally scared to death. I'd say, "Gee, that's a shame," and I'd mean it, but part of me would be thinking, Jesus that really worked!

—Stephen King, *Playboy*, June 1983

APPENDIX A

HOW TO BECOME A STEPHEN KING COLLECTOR

How does one become a Stephen King collector? Simple: Hit the lottery. Only kidding, folks. Actually, there are several layers to that question and, as might be expected, several answers. First, one must decide what he or she wants to collect. This is no easy task. The following listing details some of the "Stephen King" items available for collecting.

Unpublished SK (Stephen King) manuscripts
Signed SK manuscripts
Unsigned SK manuscripts
Signed letters from SK
SK autographs
Publishers' advance reading copies (galleys, etc.) of SK's books
Signed, lettered limited editions of SK's books
Signed, numbered limited editions of SK's books
Numbered limited editions of SK's books
U.S. hardcovers of SK's books
U.K. hardcovers of SK's books
U.S. trade paperbacks of SK's books
U.S. paperbacks of SK's books
U.S. movie tie-in paperbacks of SK's books
"Richard Bachman" paperbacks
Unabridged audiotape versions of Stephen King's books read by
    Stephen King
Unabridged audiotape versions of Stephen King's books read by
    someone other than Stephen King
Abridged audiotape versions of Stephen King's books
Video games based on Stephen King stories

CD-ROM games based on Stephen King stories
U.K. paperbacks of SK's books
Foreign-language hardcovers of SK's books
Foreign-language paperbacks of SK's books
Magazine appearances of SK stories or articles—English language
Magazine appearances of SK stories or articles—foreign language
Newspaper appearances of SK stories or articles—English language
Newspaper appearances of SK stories or articles—foreign language
U.S. anthology appearances of SK stories
U.K. anthology appearances of SK stories
Miscellaneous publications related to SK (programs, catalogs, etc.,
    containing writings by or about SK)
Signed photographs of SK
Unsigned photographs of SK
Movie scripts written by SK
Movie scripts of SK stories written by others
Posters from SK movies
Press kits from SK movies
Soundtracks of SK movies
Stills from SK movies
Miscellaneous movie memorabilia (caps, mugs, etc.) from SK
    movies
Laser discs of SK movies
Videos of SK movies
Videos of TV episodes written by SK
Videos of TV episodes based on an SK story written by someone
    else
Videos of SK talk-show appearances
Videos of SK lectures
Tabitha King (TK) hardcovers signed by TK
TK paperbacks signed by TK
TK hardcovers
TK paperbacks
Signed, numbered, limited editions of books *about* SK
Limited editions of books about SK
Trade hardcovers of books about SK
Trade paperbacks of books about SK
Books (non–SK) by authors of books about SK (Beahm's *Anne Rice*
    Companion; Spignesi's *Italian 100*; Collings' *Matrix*, etc.)

Magazine articles about SK—English language
Magazine articles about SK—foreign language
Newspaper articles about SK—English language
Newspaper articles about SK—foreign language
Newsletters devoted to SK (*Castle Rock, SKIN, SKEMERS*, etc.)
Books by authors SK likes or recommends (Richard Matheson,
    Clive Barker, Don Robertson, etc.)
Books published by SK (*The Ideal, Genuine Man, Six Stories*, etc.)
Catalogs offering SK material (The Overlook Connection, Betts
    Bookstore, etc.)
SK miscellanea (the *Year of Fear* calendar, the Rock Bottom
    Remainders videotape, etc.)

As you can see from this list, the world of Stephen King collecting is wide-ranging, eclectic, and seductive: One *must* draw a line (in the gore, as it were) as to what one wants to own and how much one is willing to spend on a collection.

There are a few ways to get started collecting Stephen King:

1. *Start buying stuff*: Most new fans who get turned on to King by a friend usually start by making a trip to the bookstore and picking up a bunch of paperbacks. They then work their way through these and will then often buy King's next book in hardcover. Thus begins the chase!

2. *Get on some mailing lists*: In this book you will find the addresses for some truly noble folk who specialize in Stephen King. Write them and ask to be sent their catalogs. Peruse them when they come and consider buying some of the oddities that interest you, like an early magazine appearance by King or a movie press kit. Focus on what appeals to *you*.

3. *Become familiar with some of the books about King and his work*: These include my books, George Beahm's books, Douglas Winter's *Stephen King: The Art of Darkness*, Michael Collings's exhaustive references, and many others. These volumes will teach you more about King and his career and will often steer you in the direction of what you find most interesting about King's work. One fan I know read my *Complete Stephen King Encyclopedia* and decided he wanted to specialize in Stephen

King interviews. He now collects interviews with Stephen King almost exclusively (outside of owning King's books, of course).
4. *Network*: Get to know some other King fans. They are often a good source of information about King and his work.
5. *Monitor the Internet*: Subscribe to the King newsgroups; join the Internet King organization SKEMERs and get their newsletter E-mailed to you; browse the thousands of web sites about King. Get familiar with the CyberKing.

Stephen King collecting is an exciting and fascinating avocation; how deep you want to get into it is up to you.

You can literally spend as little as ten dollars a year or so collecting King by only buying his latest paperback and subscribing to free newsletters, or you can commit hundred of thousands of dollars to your hobby. One collector I know has conservatively estimated that the value of his collection is in the low- to mid-six figures. His latest acquisition? A lettered copy of the asbestos-bound *Firestarter*. He is now one of the twenty-six people in the world who own one of these extremely rare and exceptional volumes, valued in the high four figures. His current want list includes a first edition of the U.K. edition of *Danse Macabre* and a few advance reading copies of early King books, post-*Carrie*.

I know this guy very well, and I'm betting he'll find what he's hunting for, too. In the meantime, though, you, too, can also collect King. Just set your sights on what appeals to your tastes and what your wallet can afford and then get moving.

However, there's one thing you must remember: Do not forget that King writes to be *read*. I own a first edition of *The Dark Tower: The Gunslinger*, a relatively rare and valuable book. I know other collectors who also have this book and yet have never opened it. They don't want to risk creasing the spine or defiling its pristine state.

I shocked a lot of these people when I bought my copy. How? I actually *read* it. And I'd do it again. Because that, my friends, is why Stephen King wrote it. In the end, *that* is the most important thing to remember when you collect Stephen King.

THE ROYAL LIBRARY

A Reader's Guide to the Work of Stephen King, from *Carrie* to *Bag of Bones* 1974–2000

This Reader's Guide is a complete listing of everything King has written that is considered his mainstream work—books that the average fan can easily find either in any bookstore in the land or in even more public and academic libraries.

This guide begins with King's debut 1974 novel *Carrie* and concludes with his most recent publication, the 1998 novel *Bag of Bones* (as well as a preview of the books in his three-book Simon & Schuster deal, *On Fiction,* his first book of nonfiction since 1981).

By the way, my reviews of some of King's works are my opinion and mine alone. I am certainly aware of the fact—and I completely understand this, believe me—that many fans will not agree with my opinions about certain King works. Tough.

Please do not write me and try to convince me of how great *The Tommyknockers* or "Head Down" are. I did not like them, but I'm *really* glad that you did.

Carrie (1974)   Carrie White, the beleaguered psychokinetic daughter of a religious-fanatic mother, gets tortured and ridiculed one too many times and finally uses her mighty powers to wreak death and fiery destruction on her high school classmates.

As might be expected, Carrie is constantly tormented and ridiculed at her high school. Partly as a joke, Carrie is invited to the prom, where she is subjected to the brutal humiliation of being crowned queen and then having a bucket of pig's blood dumped on her as she stands onstage, smiling and wearing her crown. This is the ultimate betrayal ("you tricked me you all tricked me"), and Carrie mercilessly unleashes her mighty powers. Over four hundred kids end up dead, and the school is burned to the ground.

Carrie meets an equally tragic fate, and "the Black Prom" becomes part of Maine's history.

The story goes that King originally wrote *Carrie* as a short story. He based the tale on a girl he knew from the school where he taught but found himself stalled and threw the pages away. King's wife, Tabitha, came home from work, fished the pages out of the trash, read them, and insisted that he finish the story. King decided to lengthen the story by making up and inserting fake news reports, book excerpts, journal entries, etc. This creative "trick" worked beautifully, and *Carrie* became King's first published novel. He received a $2,500 advance for the book but ultimately scored a $400,000 movie deal, of which he kept half. Thus, *Carrie* was the book that allowed Stephen King to quit teaching and write full-time.

King's ability to communicate the mind-set of the typical teenager in a high school environment is amazing. His years as a teacher were well spent observing the cruelties and rigid, often unforgiving caste structure so prevalent during high school years.

The scenes at the prom are riveting, as are the subsequent devastation and grisly dispatching by Carrie of her enemies.

I especially like the way Carrie kills her mother: She mentally slows Margaret White's heart until Mama's dead ("Full stop."). The final segment of the novel—"Wreckage"—is also extremely well done. King neatly sums up the aftermath of Prom Night, and we also read a letter from Amelia Jenks in which she tells her sister, Sandra, that her two-year-old niece, Annie, can make marbles fly up into the air just by looking at them. ("They were mooving around all by themselfs.") Carrie's legacy lives on, but thus far we have not had the pleasure of a *Carrie* sequel.

Also worth mentioning is the astonishingly mature narrative tone present in the novel. (Remember, King was only in his mid-twenties when he wrote *Carrie*.)

In terms of technique, the interjection of article and book excerpts, court transcripts, news reports, and even a death certificate—items that have since become commonplace but were extremely rare when King wrote *Carrie* in the seventies—lend an air of veracity to the novel.

Carrie was made into a Broadway musical in 1988 starring Betty Buckley and Linzi Hateley. It closed after five performances and is now known as the biggest failure in the history of the Great White Way.

'Salem's Lot (1975)   A vampire comes to a small New England town in the twentieth century. *'Salem's Lot* was King's attempt at modernizing Bram

Stoker and succeeded wildly in depicting what would happen if a monster from antiquity surfaced in twentieth-century America.

The Shining (1977)   A disgraced, alcoholic former teacher takes a job as winter caretaker at a Colorado hotel. He ends up becoming possessed by the demonic forces residing there and goes on a murderous rampage against his wife and son, a young boy gifted with psychic powers.

King's first two novels, *Carrie* and *'Salem's Lot,* served as the genesis of his spectacular, "brand-name" megacareer; *The Shining*—King's first universally acknowledged *masterpiece*—elevated him to the position he still occupies today, that of the world's King of Horror.

King finds inspiration everywhere. In the mid-seventies, King and his wife, Tabitha, checked into the Stanley Hotel in Estes Park, Colorado—exactly when the hotel was preparing to close for the season. They ended up essentially alone in the hotel (along with a "skeleton crew"), and since King's mind works the way it does, the story of the Torrances came to him, and—lucky for us—he decided to write it down. Many of the elements of the novel—the fire hose, the long corridors, the ballroom, etc.—are derived from King's stay at the Stanley.

The Shining is one of King's most literary novels. His writing is superb, and the book is structured as a five-part tragedy (it was originally conceived as a play): *Prefatory Matters, Closing Day, The Wasps' Nest, Snowbound,* and *Matters of Life and Death.* Each section has several titled chapters, and King pulls you through the story with amazing deftness and skill. Since *The Shining* is a brilliantly rendered, contemporary Gothic horror novel, it is one of the few Stephen King novels that professors of literature are not averse to teaching in class. *The Shining* is also one of the King works that most experts and fans believe will still be read fifty years from now.

King's strong use of interior monologues for Jack Torrance reflects the claustrophobia of being locked up in a hulking haunted hotel all winter. Just as Wendy and Danny are confined to the Overlook, we and Jack are trapped in the nightmare landscape of Jack's mind—a very effective device and one which King uses for maximum shudders.

The Shining is about as important as it gets: It is one of those rare books *about which* a book—*The Shining Reader* by Anthony Magistrale—has been written. The undeniable gravitas of the novel has also spawned some fairly serious literary criticism, including such essays as "The Redrum of Time: A Meditation on Francisco Goya's 'Saturn Devouring His Children' and Stephen King's *The Shining*" by Greg Weller, and "The Red Death's Sway: Setting and Character in Poe's 'The Mask of the Red Death' and King's *The Shining*" by Leonard Mustazza.

In *The Shining,* King tackled his own personal feelings regarding occasional anger toward his children and used the writing of the novel and the development of the Jack Torrance character to try to understand those inexplicable outbursts of rage we all have felt toward our children from time to time. Born of frustration, impatience, and exhaustion (as well as, for some people, liberal doses of alcohol), these episodes need to be handled so that things don't get out of hand and result in a child's getting hurt. In *The Shining*, Jack Torrance breaks his son's arm when he comes home and finds that Danny has made a mess of his papers. Jack is drunk at the time, and when he pulls Danny up off the floor, he uses just a wee bit too much strength, and little Danny ends up in a cast. This is one of the primary catalysts for Jack to give up drinking.

As Jack explores the hotel's basement, King interweaves the history of the Overlook into the story, dramatically illustrating the hotel's sordid past and setting us up for Jack's complete surrender to the evil powers running the show.

King's use of "redrum" ("murder" backwards, of course—not a crimson alcoholic beverage) as a totemic portent sent to Danny by his alter ego, Tony, is clever and has become an oft-cited part of our culture.

The Shining was Stephen King's first bestseller. Today, over twenty years later, it is still in print and has been translated into dozens of languages.

Rage (1977)   A disturbed high schooler named Charlie Decker shoots his algebra teacher and then holds the entire class hostage.

Rage, originally published as a Richard Bachman novel, is a book Stephen King now seems to regret having published. Over the years, deranged high school students have re-created the deadly scenarios King describes in the book and have cited the novel as their inspiration.

The Stand (1978)   King's most beloved novel. This epic tells the postapocalyptic story of two bands of survivors, one led by the Dark Man, the diabolical Randall Flagg, the other by the spiritually gifted Mother Abagail. Stu Redman, Trashcan Man, Larry Underwood—*The Stand* contains some of King's most memorable characters. The final violent confrontation between the two factions takes place in Las Vegas and is one of King's most dramatic and powerful finales.

Night Shift (1978)   King's first short-story collection and an important book that is still considered, twenty years after its initial publication, a classic compilation of horror, science fiction, and dark fantasy stories. The stories in this collection still hold up; there are many tales in *Night Shift*, in fact, that are better than some of the genre stories being written and published today.

"Jerusalem's Lot"   In October 1850, Charles Boone moves into his ancestral home, Chapelwaite, in Jerusalem's Lot and begins a correspondence with his friend "Bones." Over a period of weeks, Boone begins to discover the dark secrets of the tiny village of Jerusalem's Lot, especially the horrifying "Worm That Doth Corrupt," awakened when Charles burns one of only five copies of the forbidden book *The Mysteries of the Worm.* Told in epistolary form, "Jerusalem's Lot" provides a dark "back story" to King's later novel about the same place, *'Salem's Lot.*

King would again revisit the nasty environs of Jerusalem's Lot in the *Night Shift* short story "One for the Road," in which he describes the Maine town as a place that "went bad."

Interestingly, there is a character in "Jerusalem's Lot" named Mr. Thompson, a man King describes as "a besotted pulp-logger" with five sons. *Bill* Thompson was the editor who first accepted *Carrie* for publication.

"Graveyard Shift"   In a fall 1990 interview with Philip Nutman for *Fangoria* magazine, King spoke about this short story, describing it as "a Marxist short story. It's about the proletariat and the overclass that exists on the sweat of the proletariat's brow, and it puts them into an intense class struggle, and there's a monster underneath the mill that's sort of this cannibalistic creature, so it's all there. But when you take away all this Marxist gobbledygook, it's basically a story about 'Take this job and shove it.' "

"Night Surf"   Several teenagers muddle through a postapocalyptic nightmare in this short story that serves as a very effective prequel to *The Stand.*

"I Am the Doorway"   A deep-space astronaut named Arthur returns from a mission to Venus "infected" with creatures who burrow up through the skin of his fingers and grow eyes with which they view our world.

"I Am the Doorway" was the story chosen as the source of the cover illustration for the Signet paperback edition of *Night Shift.* The (uncredited) cover drawing shows a right hand half-wrapped (unwrapped, actually) in gauze, the top half of the hand revealing eight beautiful blue eyes scattered across the fingers and palm.

Even though "I Am the Doorway" has all the trappings of science fiction—spaceships, travel to other planets, malevolent aliens, etc.—King deftly uses these genre elements to write an unabashed *horror* story, brilliantly blurring the barrier between the two genres and creating the memorable hybrid genre of sci-fi/horror.

"I Am the Doorway" was written in 1971, and King postulates earthlings landing on Mars in 1979. As you know, man did finally land a controllable vehicle on Mars in 1997—the exploration craft *Sojourner*—but as of yet a manned mission to the Red Planet has not been possible.

King has Arthur fearing that the early manifestations of his "infestation" is actually leprosy, utilizing the theme of the horrors of physical "decay"—a leitmotif that King will return to again and again in his work. King will later metaphorically make very effective use, for instance, of cancer as an alien creature eating a person up from the inside out. In "I Am the Doorway," he actually has the enemy alien creatures *living* inside Arthur and using him as a host for their murderous deeds.

"The Mangler" A demonic industrial-laundry shirt-pressing machine comes to life and kills to satisfy its satanic urges. Inspired by King's real-life experiences working in an industrial laundry when he and Tabitha were first married. (Interestingly, his mother also had once worked in a similar laundry when she was raising King and his brother David alone.)

"The Boogeyman" A troubled father confides his fears to a psychiatrist who may ultimately be the manifestation of the patient's worst nightmares.

"Gray Matter" One bitter January night, Timmy Grenadine comes into Henry's Nite-Owl in Bangor, Maine, during one of the worst blizzards in years. Timmy has a horrible story to tell about his father, Richie. It seems that Richie polished off a case of bad beer a few months back and has now changed into something terrible—a huge mass of putrid gray "jelly" (the gray matter of the story's title) that eats dead cats and lately has taken to killing and eating people, too.

"Gray Matter" was one of King's "skin mag" stories, those wonderfully gruesome tales that King churned out by the dozen during the seventies for very little money. The checks for these stories, however, often arrived just when King and Tabitha needed money for an antibiotic for one of their kids' ear infections or to pay the phone bill.

Although King was in his early twenties when he wrote "Gray Matter," the narrative tone of the piece is that of a much older, much more mature writer. It was clear even at this early stage in King's career that here was a writer of exceptional talent.

When *Night Shift* was being compiled back in the early seventies, King at first wanted to cut "Gray Matter" from the collection in lieu of "Suffer the Little Children." His editor, Bill Thompson, won, and "Gray Matter" was included in the book. King has never commented on why he preferred the one over the other, but he did ultimately include "Suffer the Little Children" in his 1993 collection, *Nightmares & Dreamscapes*.

"Gray Matter" is another story set in King's hometown of Bangor. A character named George Kelso is mentioned in the story, but it isn't said if he is related Carl Kelso, the voted-out-of-office sheriff of *The Dead Zone*.

"Battleground" Toy soldiers come to life in this darkly comic tale that could easily make you suspicious of your kid's toy chest.

"Trucks"   Sentient, malevolent vehicles. (Haven't you always felt that cars and trucks had *faces?*)

"Sometimes They Come Back"   A teacher is haunted by monsters from his past.

"Strawberry Spring"   A serial killer is murdering women on the campus of New Sharon Teachers College. The story of the terrible "strawberry spring" (a false spring, a winter warm spell that taunts with the promise of spring that is nothing but a lie) of 1968 is told by a narrator who we later learn may have been the one responsible for the murders.

"Strawberry Spring" first appeared in the University of Maine literary magazine *Ubris* in 1968, when King was a student at the school. A substantially revised version was later published in the men's magazines *Cavalier* and *Gent* and was ultimately collected in *Night Shift*.

The atmosphere and tone of this story perfectly evoke not only the weird, otherworldy feel of the fog-laden strawberry spring itself but also that of the sociocultural climate of a college campus in the late sixties: "The jukebox played 'Love Is Blue' that year," King writes. "It played 'Hey Jude' endlessly. It played 'Scarborough Fair.' "

One especially nice touch in the story is King's use of a *Lord of the Rings* metaphor. After the narrator exits the campus eatery called the Grinder and walks into the damp and all-encompassing fog, he muses thusly: "You half expected to see Gollum or Frodo and Sam go hurrying past." With this simple image, King evokes all the magic and dark wonder of J.R.R. Tolkien's Middle Earth and places us squarely in the ambience of its environs.

"Strawberry Spring" powerfully evokes the Jack the Ripper mythology (even mentioning Jack in the text), with King effectively creating his own homegrown version of the elusive serial killer. (By the way, "Springheel Jack" was the name given in London in 1837 to a mysterious humanoid who would appear suddenly from alleys or doorways, try to scratch his victim's face with claws, and then leap away, often clear across a street in a single bound. Jack was also alleged to sometimes spray his victims with an anesthetic gas and was also spotted flying over Aldershot, England, in 1877. Sightings of Springheel Jack have occurred since 1837, the most recent in 1975 in London's East End.)

"The Ledge"   Stan Norris, a thirty-six-year-old tennis pro, gets involved in an affair with Marcia, the wife of a mob lord known only as Cressner, who soon learns of the affair. The powerful—and homicidal— husband invites Norris to his apartment to propose a "wager." (Gentlemen never "bet"; they always *wager.*) If Stan can walk around the five-inch-wide ledge of Cressner's building—forty-three stories up above the ground—then he can have $20,000 in cash, his freedom, and Marcia.

If he refuses the wager, then the police will find six ounces of heroin in his trunk, and he'll spend the next forty years in prison.

"The Ledge" is Stephen King in his "crime fiction" mode. This tale does not have even a whit of the supernatural in it, and yet it establishes and maintains a nerve-racking level of suspense throughout its entirety. "The Ledge" fits nicely with King's other nonsupernatural crime stories, including, "The Fifth Quarter," "Man With a Belly," "Dolan's Cadillac," *Rita Hayworth and Shawshank Redemption*, "The Wedding Gig," "The Doctor's Case" (an honest-to-goodness *new* Sherlock Holmes story), and "Umney's Last Case" (King's homage to Raymond Chandler).

"The Ledge" was originally written over thirty years ago, and it is fascinating to compare how things have changed during this period. As part of the wager, Cressner offers Stan $20,000, and to Stan this was an enormous amount of money. Today, for the money to be a pivotal plot element, the amount would have to be something like a half a million dollars for it to carry any clout. Also, Stan, at the age of thirty-six, had the sum total of only $200 in his savings account.

"The Ledge" was written for the screen by King himself and included as one of the segments of the film *Cat's Eye*.

"The Lawnmower Man" A suburbanite inadvertently hires a minion of Pan to mow his lawn, ultimately becoming a sacrifice to the apparently malevolent God.

"Quitters, Inc." A man goes through the ultimate quit-smoking program, one that involves electric shock and amputation.

"I Know What You Need" A short, skinny weirdo who doesn't wash his hair too often and who wears mismatched socks approaches Liz Rogan one evening in the library as she's desperately cramming for her sociology final. The first thing Edward Jackson Hamner Jr. says to Liz is "I know what you need," and it turns out he's not kidding.

"I Know What You Need" is one of King's "college" stories—those handful of tales with college students as the main characters and a college campus as the setting. These stories reflect King's interest in creating stories using familiar, real-world elements of his life at the time. Others of this "genre" include "Strawberry Spring" and "Cain Rose Up."

Throughout his career, King has also used grammar school and high school settings (as well as teachers as main characters) for several other stories, including *Carrie*, *The Shining*, *Rage* (especially), "Sometimes They Come Back," *The Dead Zone*, *Christine*, "Here There Be Tygers," and "Suffer the Little Children."

I like this story, especially the tone and the flawless portrayal of the college student's angst over grades.

One nice touch is Liz's roommate, Alice, lying in bed reading the erotic novel *The Story of O*. That blatant acknowledgment of Alice's sexuality, plus her enterprise in finding out the truth about Ed Hamner, made me want to know more about the smart and confident, "comes-from-money" Alice. So far, this character has not popped up in any later King works, but there's always hope.

One of the eeriest and most effective scenes in the story is Liz's "lying in an open grave" nightmare.

"Children of the Corn"   A hapless young couple unwittingly kill a young boy with their car and end up trapped in a Nebraska town where the children willingly give their lives to a malevolent God of the Corn, a "pagan Christ" who demands blood sacrifices when the children turn nineteen.

"The Last Rung on the Ladder"   A sister's suicide spurs memories of their childhood together.

"The Man Who Loved Flowers"   A young man buys flowers for his one true love, Norma. However, she has been dead for the past ten years. When each woman he comes upon tells her she is not Norma, he kills her with a hammer and moves on, hoping the next one will be his beloved.

"One For the Road"   A family is stranded in a snowstorm in an abandoned town known as The Lot in this prequel to *'Salem's Lot*.

"The Woman in the Room"   A young son helps his dying mother commit suicide.

The Dead Zone (1979)   A high school teacher—a hapless Everyman named John Smith—awakens from a coma with the ability to see the future and learns a horrible truth about a presidential candidate who will ultimately plunge the world into the nightmare of total nuclear destruction.

The Long Walk (1979)   This is one of my all-time favorite Stephen King novels, a psychologically dense story that takes place in the near future, when government-sanctioned competitions to the death are enthusiastically enjoyed by a blood-hungry populace.

The Long Walk is an annual endurance test in which one hundred Walkers begin a nonstop Walk from northern Maine to Boston. The Walkers must maintain a pace of four miles per hour; if they do not, they are given a Warning. After three Warnings, the Walker is executed on the spot by soldiers following the troupe in radar-equipped jeeps.

The winner is the last Walker left alive.

Gripping and suspenseful, *The Long Walk* (originally published as a Richard Bachman novel) is a deft display of narrative skill, all the more impressive when we take into account the fact that King was only nineteen or so when he wrote it.

Firestarter (1980)   A young girl with pyrokinetic powers as a result of government drug experiments performed on her parents is pursued by The Shop for exploitation as the ultimate biological weapon.

Roadwork (1981)   When the city decides to demolish George Dawes's home and the place where he has worked for twenty years in order to build a new freeway ramp, Dawes resists and ends up barricaded in his house with a load of explosives and a real bad attitude toward civic improvement.

Stephen King's Danse Macabre (1981)   In his only book-length work of nonfiction, King takes an insightful and comprehensive look at the entire horror genre (books, movies, and TV shows), revealing many of the early seminal influences on his own work.

Cujo (1981)   A demonic St. Bernard holds a terrified mother and her young son prisoners in a stalled Pinto; mayhem ensues.

The Running Man (1982)   In this Richard Bachman novel, Ben Richards and his wife live a woefully poor existence in the year 2025. Ben is unemployed; his wife works as a hooker to earn whatever money she can. Desperate, Ben agrees to appear on a TV game show called *The Running Man*. The object of the game is to survive one month while being hunted by Network hunters and citizens, all of whom will shoot to kill if they spot Ben. The prize is $1 billion, except that no one who has attempted the game has lived beyond eight days. Ben hooks up with an antigovernment underground, takes a housewife as a hostage, and ultimately manages to commandeer a jet, which he uses to exact his final revenge on the Network.

Creepshow (1982):

"**Father's Day**"   A vicious father "wants his cake!" And he gets it.

"**The Lonesome Death of Jordy Verrill**"   A comic adaptation of the short story "Weeds." (See the chapter on "Weeds.")

"**The Crate**"   An ancient monster lying dormant in a crate under a stairway at a quiet university is awakened; mayhem ensues.

"**Something to Tide You Over**"   A cuckolded husband exacts a watery revenge on his cheating wife and her new husband, only to have his vengeance backfire on him when the couple comes back from the dead.

"**They're Creeping Up on You**"   Cockroaches run rampant in a clean freak's apartment; mayhem ensues.

Different Seasons (1982)   King's first novella collection, the book that was the source of one of the finest film adaptations of a King story, *The Shawshank Redemption*.

Rita Hayworth and Shawshank Redemption   A wrongly convicted banker escapes from a maximum-security prison.

Apt Pupil   A young boy forces a Nazi war criminal—on threat of exposure—to tell him about the "gushy" stuff.

The Body   Four young friends embark on a journey to see a dead body and during the trip come of age in more ways than one.

The Breathing Method   "Headless Lamaze." That about sums this one up, wouldn't you agree?

The Dark Tower: The Gunslinger (1982)   The first book of King's legendary *Dark Tower* epic, a series of novels that will eventually total seven or eight books, and that will probably be completed between now and 2010.

"The Gunslinger"   Roland begins his search for the Man in Black. The desert town of Tull gets in his way, and everyone there must die before he can continue his quest.

"The Way Station"   Roland meets Jake and senses death in him.

"The Oracle and the Mountain"   Roland and Jake continue their journey, and Roland learns from an Oracle that three is the number of his fate, that Jake is his gateway to the Man in Black, and that the Man in Black is his gateway to the Three.

"The Slow Mutants"   Roland tells Jake of his childhood under the tutelage of Marten. In an underground cave they are attacked by the Slow Mutants, forcing Roland to decide between saving Jake or continuing his pursuit of the Man in Black.

"The Gunslinger and the Dark Man"   The Man in Black tells Roland's future and reveals to him that his master is Maerlyn, the servant of the beast that is Keeper of the Dark Tower. Roland falls asleep, and when he awakens, ten years have passed. The Man in Black is a skeleton and Roland moves toward the ocean . . . and the drawing of the three.

Christine (1983)   A haunted car possesses its new teenage owner; mayhem ensues.

Cycle of the Werewolf (1983)   A werewolf terrorizes a small town; a crippled young boy in a wheelchair is the only one who knows the truth about the monster's identity.

Pet Sematary (1983)   A grieving father buries his son in a graveyard that can resurrect the dead, but when the dead come back, they're *changed*.

The Eyes of the Dragon (1984)   In the kingdom of Delain, the death of King Roland results in the King's son Peter, the true heir to the throne, being falsely imprisoned due to the machinations of the evil sorcerer Flagg. Will Peter escape and restore order to the kingdom—against the malevolent doings of his brother Thomas, who is under the spell of Flagg (whom we first met, of course, in *The Stand*)? Even though *The Eyes of the Dragon* is ostensibly a children's fantasy, it easily engages adult readers and adds more detail to the sordid story of the apparently eternal Flagg.

The Talisman (with Peter Straub; 1984)   An epic quest in which young Jack Sawyer (the nod to Twain is not accidental) travels through horrible landscapes and alternate worlds on his way to the Black Hotel. An amalgam of horror, science fiction, and fantasy, *The Talisman* is a brilliant achievement that evokes the narrative grandeur of *The Stand, Insomnia,* and the entire *Dark Tower* series. Supposedly, *The Talisman* will someday be a Steven Spielberg film.

Thinner (1984)   In this final Richard Bachman novel (before the pseudonym was discovered), Billy Halleck, an overweight lawyer with a thriving practice and loving wife and daughter, kills an old Gypsy woman by running her down with his car as his wife is masturbating him while he's driving. Billy is exonerated by his cronies in town, and the dead woman's outraged husband scratches his cheek and says one word: "Thinner." When Billy begins losing weight at a terrifying rate, he realizes he has been cursed.

Skeleton Crew (1985)   King's second short-story collection. *Skeleton Crew* contains some major pieces by King as well as some oddities, like the two poems and the two excerpts from the unpublished and incomplete novel *Milkman*. *Skeleton Crew* is somewhat less satisfying then *Night Shift* but is an important collection with some rare early stories—"The Reaper's Image" and "Here There Be Tygers," for instance—unavailable elsewhere, as well as a major novella, *The Mist.*

The Mist   After massive thunderstorms finally break "the worst heat wave in northern New England history," an enormous mist covers Long Lake, Maine, and environs, and there are *creatures* in the mist—big, hungry, apparently prehistoric creatures that were somehow transported to our time, possibly due to a secret government project known only as the Arrowhead Project. *The Mist* tells the story of Dave Drayton and his ill-fated trip to the supermarket following the storm.

Dave, his son Billy, his neighbor Brent Norton, and a bunch of other area folks are trapped in the market when the Mist completely covers the parking lot, and anyone who ventures out into it is never seen or heard from again.

Will Dave and company escape the market and successfully make it through the Mist to safety? Will the survivors be able to elude the giant monsters from the past?

We ultimately don't know what happens to Dave and his son (giving us what Dave describes in the story as an "Alfred Hitchcock ending"), but the last word of the tale *is,* after all, "hope."

King originally wrote this story for an anthology called *Dark Forces* that was being put together by his then-agent Kirby McCauley. Originally, King came up dry in the "short story" department when trying to find something to write about, and then *The Mist* came to him exactly as he described it in the "Notes" section of *Skeleton Crew.* King being King, however, he described the flash of inspiration by telling us, "In the market, my muse suddenly shat on my head." At a lecture in Truth or Consequences, New Mexico (cited in George Beahm's *Stephen King Story*), King expanded on his *Skeleton Crew* notes by remembering that he specifically thought to himself, "Wouldn't it be funny if a pterodactyl just came flapping up this aisle and started knocking over Ragu and Hunt's and all this other stuff?"

Kirby McCauley remembers expecting a short story of a few thousand words from King for the *Dark Forces* anthology and being stunned when King ultimately turned in a 40,000-word novella.

In George Beahm's aforementioned *Stephen King Story,* King authority Michael Collings makes a convincing case for comparing *The Mist* to *Beowulf.* I won't perfunctorily butcher Collings's analysis here by trying to paraphrase it: Get George's book and read Collings's introduction, "The Persistence of Darkness—Shadows Behind the Life Behind the Story."

There are all kinds of "real world" references in *The Mist*. King and his family have a house on Long Lake in Bridgton, Maine, where *The Mist* takes place; Dave Drayton's wife's name is Stephanie, which is the name of Tabitha King's sister (Stephanie Leonard, the founder and editor of the King newsletter, *Castle Rock*); like Dave Drayton, King attended the University of Maine; Selectman Mike Hatlen is named after King's University of Maine professor Burton Hatlen; and the next-door neighbor, Brent Norton, is really King's Long Lake neighbor Ralph Drews, although King makes it clear that, unlike Brent, Ralph is a nice guy.

The Mist has been adapted for other media three times: Once as a killer ninety-minute, 3-D sound adaptation; once as an unabridged, 4 1/2-hour, audiocassette recording; and once as a computer game by Mindscape Software. A film version by Frank Darabont (*The Shawshank Redemption*) is currently (late 1997) in the talking stages.

In a 1997 interview with the *World of Fandom,* King spoke about the eventual film adaptation of *The Mist*: "As far as *The Mist,* it's very much alive. Frank and I have talked a lot about it. Right now I think, and he thinks, that there has to be an ending that works in terms of the story, but that will also please people in Hollywood, who are really uncomfortable with the way the story ends. It just sought of trails off into the mist. No one is necessarily looking for a sugary ending, but what I think they're looking for is some real closure, which the story doesn't provide."

"Here There Be Tygers" A third-grader finds a hungry tiger in the boys' room but manages to survive, even though a classmate and his teacher do not.

This story was written when King was in college and first appeared in the University of Maine literary magazine *Ubris,* along with King's "Cain Rose Up" and the poem "Harrison Park '68." (See the chapters on these works.)

"Here There Be Tygers" is a surrealistic piece in which an event of extraordinary *unreality*—a man-eating tiger just *appears* in a grammar school bathroom—is presented within the context of a third-grader's often daunting daily reality. Is the tiger real? We don't know. King just tells us that he is there, and the story and its deadly conclusion proceed from this bizarre and possibly supernatural occurrence.

Michael Collings makes the point in his *Annotated Guide to Stephen King* that "Here There Be Tygers" is an early foreshadowing of King's more ambitious Richard Bachman novel *Rage* in which once again a student and a teacher are in conflict. Both works include the dispatching of the authority figure in a grisly manner.

Although "Here There Be Tygers" is quite short, with very few words King quite effectively takes us inside a third-grade classroom, a deserted grammar school hallway, and a basement bathroom using images and language to not only draw realistic characters but to let us *see* the "thumbtack-stippled bulletin board" and the red fire-alarm box.

"The Monkey" When Hal Shelburn is a young boy, he finds an old windup monkey in the back of a storage area in his Aunt Ida's house in Maine. The monkey is in a Ralston Purina cereal box, and Hal doesn't think it even works anymore. He puts it on a shelf in his bedroom and forgets about it.

The monkey, however, is not really a toy; it is actually a cursed demonic murderer that can kill at will just by banging together its worn brass cymbals.

King got the idea for the monkey during a visit to New York. He passed a street merchant who had a battalion of little toy windup monkeys lined up on a blanket on a street corner, and the sight so frightened him that he returned to his hotel room and wrote almost the whole story in longhand.

Hal Shelburn and his family lived in Arnette, Texas, the place where Charles Campion "touched down" at Hapscomb's Texaco Station after he was infected by the Project Blue virus in *The Stand.*

The newspaper that ran the story "Mystery of the Dead Fish" was the *Bridgton News*. Bridgton was the Maine town where Dave Drayton and his family lived in *The Mist* and is also the real Maine town where King and his family have a house on Long Lake.

"The Monkey" is not one of my favorite King short stories, only because I feel it could have been shorter. The story did, however, strike a chord with horror fans: Prior to its 1985 *Skeleton Crew* appearance and after its 1980 *Gallery* debut, "The Monkey" was reprinted no less than four times. It appeared in *Modern Masters of Horror* (reprinted three times!—1981, 1982, 1988); *The Year's Best Horror Stories, Series IX* (1981); *Horrors!* (1981); and *Fantasy Annual IV* (1981). After its *Skeleton Crew* appearance, it was again reprinted in David Hartwell's important *Dark Descent* series (1987, 1990, 1991) and in *The Mammoth Book of Short Horror Novels* (1988).

"The Monkey" was adapted by horror writer Dennis Etchison for a radio performance to benefit UNICEF on Halloween night, October 31, 1985. It has not yet been adapted as a film.

The original manuscript of "The Monkey" is in the Stephen King Archives in the Special Collections Library at Stephen King's alma mater, the University of Maine at Orono, Maine.

"Cain Rose Up"   A depressed college student named Curt Garrish succumbs to the frustration of college life by randomly shooting people with a rifle from his dorm window.

"Cain Rose Up" fictionalizes the real-life, murderous rampage of Charles Whitman, a former marine and academically overloaded college student who went on a shooting spree from a twenty-seven-story tower on August 1, 1966, at the University of Texas at Austin. Whitman ultimately killed twelve people and wounded thirty-three others. King had been fascinated by Whitman's story (I've even heard he kept a scrapbook of newspaper clippings about it) and decided to try his hand at putting himself in the mind of a student pushed just a tad too far. He was, as the story reveals, extremely successful at "understanding" Whitman and those like him.

This story, originally published when King was in college, was revised somewhat for its *Skeleton Crew* appearance. The new version is more visceral and effectively communicates Garrish's completely delusional state of mind, which actually rationalizes his brutal murders as a fulfillment of a mandate from God found in Genesis: "God made the world in His image, and if you don't eat the world, the world eats you." The story concludes with Garrish murmuring to himself, "Good God, let's eat."

Maine horror writer and fellow University of Maine student Rick Hautala remembers reading "Cain Rose Up" in *Ubris* in 1968 and thinking that "this story—and this King-fella—were somehow . . . different." "Cain Rose Up" was the first Stephen King story Hautala had ever read, and he was instantly hooked on everything King wrote from that point on. (King and Hautala later became friends, and King wrote favorable blurbs for Hautala's first two novels, *Moondeath* and *Moonbog*.)

In "Cain Rose Up," Garrish's father was a Methodist minister. This fact, combined with Garrish's twisted interpretation of the Bible, suggests some kind of subtle psychological damage caused by religion, a theme King would later revisit in *Carrie* (remember Margaret White?) and other works.

The locales in "Cain Rose Up" parallel real landmarks and buildings on the campus of the University of Maine. In the story, "Carlton Memorial" was actually Androscoggin Hall on the university's campus.

Some of the pop-culture references in "Cain Rose Up" include Humphrey Bogart, *Playboy* magazine, Howdy Doody, Pig Pen, and a Ford station wagon. There is also a reference in the story to Rodin's classic sculpture *The Thinker*.

"Mrs. Todd's Shortcut"   Homer Buckland is the caretaker for the Todds' Maine home. Worth Todd and his second wife are "summer people," those visitors to Maine who arrive on Friday and leave on Sunday and who are never really as interesting to the locals as are their own neighbors.

To Homer, though, the *first* Mrs. Todd—Ophelia was her name—was special. She drove a champagne-colored, two-seater Mercedes sportster and was absolutely rabid about finding shortcuts, especially to Bangor and back.

One day Homer took 'Phelia up on her offer and rode with her to Bangor. The trip would change Homer's life.

"Mrs. Todd's Shortcut" reads like a fable and is something of a departure for King. He has said that he is especially fond of this story, mainly because he loves the sound of Homer's voice in the tale.

King's wife, Tabitha, is the real Mrs. Todd, although so far she has not traveled to Olympus. (If she has, she has not yet admitted it.) It seems that Mrs. King is always looking for a shortcut, and that's where King got the idea for the story.

In the "Notes" to *Skeleton Crew*, King revealed that this story was repeatedly rejected by women's magazines specifically because of the line "a woman, who will pee down her own leg if she does not squat!"

In "Mrs. Todd's Shortcut," the cadence of Homer's narrative takes a little getting used to, but the payoff is worth it. The ending elevates the story to another level, and it becomes transcendent. King takes his time building to the climax—Homer and Ophelia's departure for Olympus—

and leaves us with a palpable sense of what it feels like to be left behind. While not as powerful as "The Reach," this story nevertheless proves that King has a sensitive side that he can call upon to tell a story that does not require severed limbs to engage its readers.

"The Jaunt" A daring young boy stays awake while being transported via the teleportation device known as the Jaunt and ends up actually experiencing the horrifying eternity of the universe and coming out the other side completely insane.

"The Jaunt" is one of Stephen King's infrequent forays into hard science fiction, and considering the results, he should write more of it.

The dreadful climax of "The Jaunt" is horrifying, and I, for one, would love to see this story adapted as a short film. It is probably one of the best *Twilight Zone* episodes that was never on *Twilight Zone*.

It's always fascinating when authors postulate what the future will be like and it doesn't even come close to their vision. In the "energy crisis" years of the late seventies and early eighties, 1987 seemed like a long way off, and King decided to set the discovery of Jaunting during that year. We should have been so lucky.

King is very good at really fleshing out his ideas: The mechanics of the Jaunt—complete with the Nil button to erase all the emergence portals—are completely believable and realistic.

I also like the inclusion of details from a book written about the Jaunt called *The Politics of The Jaunt*. This device gives King the opportunity to delve even more deeply into the story and provide a lot of exciting background of the discovery of teleportation and the sometimes tragic events surrounding its early use.

Although "The Jaunt" is not that long, King creates an entire history for the story, complete with a wide array of characters and an enormous time span. "The Jaunt" is a virtuoso performance by the Man from Maine.

"The Wedding Gig" An Irish mobster books a jazz band for his sister's wedding in the year 1927, a period of gangland hits and detestable Jim Crow laws.

"The Wedding Gig" is King in his crime-fiction mode, a genre he has visited now and then throughout his career ("The Fifth Quarter," "Man With a Belly," etc.) and which, it is clear, he has a special knack for. He is superb at communicating the whole "gangster" gestalt, and when he adds period touches—such as the elements of Prohibition and racial discrimination in "The Wedding Gig"—there's no one better.

Though this story is ostensibly about a crime-family wedding, King also subtly tackles racism in "The Wedding Gig." Billy-Boy, the piano player in the jazz band, is black, and Mr. Cornet Player tells us what it was like to be black in the South in the 1920s:

> *In the south was the worst, of course—Jim Crow car, nigger heaven at the movies, stuff like that—but it wasn't that great in the north, either. But what could I do? Huh? You go on and tell me. In those days you lived with those differences.*

The narrator also tells us: "In those days nigger was a word I hated and kept saying." He casually and thoughtlessly throws the word around, realizing later that he has said it but unable to completely eliminate it from his vocabulary. (In one telling moment, he tells the band he won't play "Camptown Races." He says, "We don't play that nigger stuff till after midnight," in full earshot of Billy-Boy.)

King parallels discriminating against Maureen Scollay for being grotesquely obese with prejudice against Billy for being black, noting that "fat people can always stop eating."

Maureen is yet another of King's "monstrous" women—overwhelming female characters who are grotesque and frightening. Mrs. Leighton in "The Blue Air Compressor" and Annie Wilkes in *Misery* are two more examples of King's thematic use of this type of character.

King beautifully nails the lingo and the slang of the Roaring Twenties in "The Wedding Gig," tossing off phrases and words of the period with an ease that would make you think he lived during that tumultuous time. Englander was a "good joe" and that made him "aces to work for"; Mike was a "pretty tough egg"; a cigarette was "a fag"; and Maureen was fat and ugly, but she was not "hoity-toity."

As of 1997, "The Wedding Gig" had not been adapted to film.

"Paranoid: A Chant"   This precisely hundred-line poem takes us inside the mind of a man who is utterly mad and completely paranoid.

The poem's narrator sees people watching him and knows that "men have discussed me in back rooms." His mother has been investigated, the FBI is monitoring him, and the old woman who lives upstairs from him is radiating him with a suction-cup device attached to her floor. His mail contains letter bombs, he's seen UFOs, waitresses are poisoning his food, and "a dark man with no face" has surfaced in his toilet to listen to his phone calls.

King effectively communicates madness with his superb use of language and disjointed, free-form lines, taking us inside the mind of a man who has created a bizarre, fully realized interior reality that must, for the reader, coexist with the mundane details of the narrator's *exterior* reality. This is a literary high-wire act, and yet King pulls it off masterfully.

King uses some very powerful, surrealistic images in this poem, especially that of the black crows with black umbrellas and silver-dollar eyes standing at the bus stop looking at their watches. Very Magritte.

"The Raft"   Four teenagers are trapped on a raft by a floating monster that has an appetite for human flesh.

"Word Processor of the Gods"   A man receives a magic word processor from his beloved dead nephew and sets about repairing his life.

"The Man Who Would Not Shake Hands"   A man is cursed after killing an Indian holy man's son. Anyone he touches will die.

"Beachworld"   A living sand planet devours invading astronauts.

"The Reaper's Image"   Anyone who sees the image of the Grim Reaper in a haunted mirror isn't long for this world.

"Nona"   A man whom we know only as The Prisoner meets a woman named Nona in Joe's Good Eats one night and goes on a bloody, murderous rampage with her. Nona, a gorgeous creature who transforms into a giant rat while embracing The Prisoner, may or may not be real, and the whole story of the killing spree is told by The Prisoner from his jail cell just before he plans on killing himself.

"Nona" is an atmospheric tale in which King blends the supernatural with a realistic setting and leaves it to the reader to determine if The Prisoner is insane and has completely created Nona from his delusions or if he has actually been visited, possessed, and controlled by a demonic being.

"Nona" is one of King's "Castle Rock" stories. The Prisoner's mother came from Castle Rock, and The Prisoner grew up in Harlow, a town we are told is across the river from Castle Rock.

"Nona" marked King's first use of his haunting "Do you love?" leitmotif. In the story, Nona, the rat thing, asks The Prisoner this question in the Castle Rock graveyard. Four years later, in the story "The Raft" (which was first published in *Gallery* magazine in 1982), Randy asks the malevolent, devouring thing in the water the same question.

In "Nona," The Prisoner mentions seeing the GS&WM railroad trestle off in the distance. In what might be the quintessential "Castle Rock" story, *The Body* (which appears in the collection *Different Seasons*), this railroad trestle plays a very important role.

"For Owen"   In this thirty-four-line poem, a father walks his son to school.

Although this poem is brief, King manages to pull together several powerful images and elicit an emotional response by dramatically illustrating the fears and burdens of a little schoolboy who is fat and is teased by his classmates.

Michael Collings, writing in *The Shape Under the Sheet,* astutely analyzes another theme in this surprisingly gentle poem:

> "For Owen" soothes and expands metaphorically to suggest the universal experience of death, not in terms of the terror defined in the more horrific stories in *Skeleton Crew*—"The Mist," "Gramma," "The Raft," or "Nona"—but rather in terms of the gentle awakening and understanding that Stella Flanders attains in "The Reach." The poem is admittedly cryptic, reaching for meaning through references to schoolchildren as fruit: watermelons, bananas, plums. But by the final lines, the speaker penetrates the metaphors and deals with death, noting that just as a schoolchild must learn to write, he must also learn the art of dying.

In his annotated bibliography *The Work of Stephen King,* Collings also noted: "[P]art surrealism, part symbolist poetry, the piece is less graphic than is usual with King; horror is implicit rather than explicit in either content or language."

"Survivor Type" A drug dealer named Richard Pine ends up stranded on a desert island with four gallons of water, a first-aid kit, a lifeboat-inspection log, two knives, a combination fork and spoon, and two kilos of pure heroin. After a month or so, a starving Pine resorts to anesthetizing himself with the heroin, amputating parts of his own body and eating them to survive, all the while slowly descending into shock and total madness.

"Survivor Type" is the type of Stephen King story people who say they hate King (but have never read him) are talking about. All the anti-King zealots have to do is hear the *premise* of this story and they'll nod their heads solemnly and say, "See? I *told* you that guy was twisted!" The truth is, as grisly as "Survivor Type" undoubtedly is, it still has the King touch, and that means tight writing, realistic details, and marvelous characterizations. If you can get past the "self-cannibalism" theme, then "Survivor Type" is just like any other King short story. (Yeah, right.)

King has written—as only King could write it—about how he got the idea for this tale: "I got to thinking about cannibalism one day—because that's the sort of thing guys like me sometimes think about—and my muse once more evacuated its magic bowels on my head." King's thinking led him to the inevitable question (for King, anyway) as to how much a person could eat of himself before he died. He thought this idea was "so utterly and perfectly revolting" that at first he was hesitant to actually try writing the story; he was afraid he wouldn't do the idea justice. He later discussed the specifics of self-cannibalization with a doctor-friend of his, and after learning that it was indeed possible for a person to eat himself—to a point—he sat down and wrote "Survivor Type."

King has a refreshingly self-effacing (and often overly harsh) attitude about his work and his place in the annals of American literature. In the "Notes" section at the back of *Skeleton Crew,* he concludes his discussion of "Survivor Type" with these words: "I guess Faulkner never would have written anything like this, huh? Oh, well." Perhaps not. But I'll bet more people have read "Survivor Type" than *Light in August.* I'm not saying that this is a good thing or a bad thing. I'm just making a point: People like to read Stephen King, and I'll bet there aren't too many people who read William Faulkner for entertainment. This must mean *something,* don't you think?

"Uncle Otto's Truck"   A haunted truck begins creeping slowly across a field, moving toward the house of the man who once killed his business partner—the very same man who owned the advancing truck.

"Morning Deliveries (Milkman #1)"   A milkman named Spike leaves death on people's doorsteps in this bizarre segment from the unpublished novel *Milkman.*

"Big Wheels: A Tale of the Laundry Game (Milkman #2)"   Another chapter from King's aborted novel *Milkman* in which two drunken laundry workers visit a gas station in search of an inspection sticker. Ramsey Campbell called this tale King's "strangest story," and he was probably speaking specifically of the stunning shift in the story's narrative flow from naturalism to surrealism when Leo reveals that dripping rain has drilled a hole in his back and that his coworker Rocky keeps his rocks in the hole. The story is strange and compelling, and one finishes reading this and "Morning Deliveries" wishing King would complete *Milkman* and publish it—and as soon as possible, you know?

"Gramma"   Eleven-year-old George Bruckner has to stay home alone with his grandmother, an eighty-three-year-old invalid, while his mother goes to visit his injured brother in the hospital.

Gramma is obese, blind, and bedridden, and it is Georgie's job to make her tea and attend to any of her other needs *if* she wakes up when his mother is gone.

George is afraid of Gramma, and although he isn't sure exactly *why* she terrifies him, we learn that his fear is for a good reason. Gramma practiced black magic before she became ill, and her family knows the dark secrets of her powers.

"Gramma" is based on King's years living in Durham, Maine, when his mother, Ruth, took care of her aged parents. In an interview I did with King's childhood friend and collaborator Chris Chesley for *The Complete Stephen King Encyclopedia,* Chris talked about the roots of this tale:

> When I first knew Steve, his mother was . . . taking care of his grandparents. They lived in the house with Steve and his mother, and Steve's story "Gramma" from *Skeleton Crew* came out of that.
>
> In that story, the grandmother has been transformed into a supernatural thing about which a child has to make a decision. Should I give this . . . what seems to be a monster . . . should I give this creature the tea? Well, that giving of the tea is based directly upon his life at that time, when he was a boy between ten and twelve. The grandparents lived in the downstairs front room. The grandmother was invalided. She was not able to talk. And for kids that age, someone who is invalided and very old is kind of a horrifying presence.
>
> And so Steve had that experience, and it was borne home on him, and you can see the connection between that experience, and how affected he must have been by that situation to be motivated to later turn it into such a powerful story.
>
> When I read the story—sitting there by myself in the night—it raised the hackles on my neck, even though I knew from whence the story was derived. And I thought to myself at the time, think of how much he took in. Think of how affected he was by that in order to have the psychological motivation to spit it back out by writing this hair-raising story.

"Gramma" is another of King's "Castle Rock" stories. The Castle Rock Strangler's mother, Henrietta Dodd (from *The Dead Zone*), makes a cameo appearance, as does Joe Camber from *Cujo* (his hill is mentioned) and Cora Simard from *The Tommyknockers*. (She gossips with Henrietta on George's party line.)

"Gramma" has been recorded twice for audiocassette adaptations and was also adapted (by no less a horror luminary than Harlan Ellison) for the CBS-TV series *The New Twilight Zone*. (See the feature on the TV adaptation in this volume.)

"The Ballad of the Flexible Bullet"   A one-book novelist descends into madness—taking his editor with him—when he realizes that Fornits are living in his typewriter.

"The Reach"   Ailing Stella Flanders walks across the frozen Reach to her final destiny. One of King's most touching stories.

It (1986)   King's magnum opus; a multiple-time-line, multiple-character epic that tells the history of Derry and the timeless and evil thing that lives in its sewers.

Misery (1987)   An obsessed fan holds hostage the injured author of her favorite series of romance novels and forces him to write a new book in which he resurrects the "Misery Chastain" character he killed off in his last book.

The Dark Tower II: The Drawing of the Three (1987)   Roland continues his quest for the Tower and while walking north on a beach is attacked and injured by a lobstrosity, a giant lobster that bites off his right index finger—his trigger finger—and infects him with a strange poison. Farther up the beach Roland comes upon freestanding doors labeled the Prisoner, the Lady of Shadows, and the Pusher. These doors open onto other worlds and deliver Eddie, Odetta, and Detta to Roland—the drawing of the foretold three. Ultimately, Detta and Odetta merge into a single personality—Susannah Dean. This installment concludes with Roland affirming to the others his pledge to find the Dark Tower no matter what it takes.

The Tommyknockers (1987)   Writer Bobbi Anderson finds an ancient alien spacecraft buried in the woods and begins digging it up; mayhem ensues.

The Dark Half (1989)   Bestselling novelist Thad Beaumont's pseudonym, "George Stark," comes to life when Beaumont "kills him off": Stark *does not want to be dead.*

The Stand: The Complete & Uncut Edition (1990)   King added backloads of material originally cut from the first version of this novel, making for a richer, more fully developed, just plain *better* novel. *This* version is how *The Stand* should have originally been published.

Four Past Midnight (1990)   King's second novella collection, containing some of his most powerful "long short stories."

The Langoliers   A red-eye flight from Los Angeles to Boston goes terribly wrong when the passengers realize that the United States they know is no longer below them and that there is something waiting for them in the dark.

Secret Window, Secret Garden   A writer is accused of plagiarism, a charge that takes him into a nightmare he thought was dead and that he had buried many years before. One of King's more layered and textured novellas; a gem that reveals more and more of itself as you read and ponder.

The Library Policeman   A nightmare inspired by King's son's fear of returning a book to the library late. This novella combines otherworldy horrors with all-too-real *real-life* horrors.

The Sun Dog   A Castle Rock story in which a young boy takes a picture that inexorably changes as the sun dog begins its slow creep toward the world *outside* the photograph.

The Dark Tower III: The Waste Lands (1991)   A complex novel which utilizes multiple time frames, multiple narrative viewpoints, false histories, and premonitions and also introduces exotic new characters like Oy the Billy-Bumbler, the Tick-Tock Man, and Blaine the sentient and insane train that promises to kill the three unless they can solve his riddles. Too intricately plotted to synopsize in the space here, suffice it to say that *The Waste Lands* is yet another chapter—another step forward—in what may turn out to be one of King's most important (and transcendent) works.

Needful Things (1991)   The Devil opens an antique shop in Castle Rock; mayhem ensues.

Gerald's Game (1992)   A woman is trapped handcuffed to a bed in a deserted cabin after her husband dies of a heart attack during kinky sex. Suddenly, she is not alone.

Dolores Claiborne (1993)   Dolores Claiborne is accused of murdering her employer; years earlier, Dolores had been suspected of killing her husband. Did she kill either of them? Both of them?

Nightmares & Dreamscapes (1993)   King's third short-story collection and his most eclectic to date: In addition to short stories, it also includes poetry, a screenplay, nonfiction, and a fable.

Dolan's Cadillac   A betrayed husband exacts revenge on Dolan, the man who's been having an affair with his wife, by burying him alive in his Cadillac in the desert.

"The End of the Whole Mess"   A fascinating end-of-the-world tale that reminds us of *Flowers for Algernon*.

"Suffer the Little Children"   A teacher begins to suspect that her young students are actually monsters.

"The Night Flier"   A vampire pilot hops from small airfield to small airfield, dining on the help and leaving behind maggot-riddled mounds of dirt. A tabloid reporter becomes obsessed with finding out who "Dwight Renfield" actually is and ultimately pays an extremely high price for his knowledge.

"Popsy"   A vampire grandpa rescues his kidnapped grandson from a kidnapper for hire.

"It Grows on You"   A house adds on to itself every time somebody in town dies.

"Chattery Teeth"   A sentient pair of windup joke teeth saves a man who foolishly picks up a psychopathic hitchhiker, even though he knows he's making a mistake as the guy gets into the car.

"Dedication"   The premise of this short story is a major gross-out. ("All right!" I can hear the hard-core gore hounds cheering. "Tell me more!")

The work of Stephen King has always appealed to me vicariously; horror and terror seem to exist in my mind rather than my gut. However, the first time I read "Dedication," I got physically sick.

The premise is neither terrifying nor horrifying: The publisher's blurb described the tale thusly: "A desperate woman is driven to witchcraft to change the natural father of her unborn child."

But the way she goes *about it* . . .

"Dedication" is a terrific story. Just accept the fact that you'll want to skip dinner the evening you read it. Small price, I would say.

"The Moving Finger"   Howard Mitla discovers a finger poking up out of his bathroom sink drain, and he's the only one who can see it. The finger grows to a grotesque length of *seven feet*, and there *are* five fingers on a hand, right?

"Sneakers"   "Sneakers" is about a haunted toilet stall. King has said that he figured since he had written about haunted houses, it was now time to write about a haunted *shithouse*. King acknowledges the black humor in this brainstorm by having John Tell muse to himself that "gruesome as the story had been, there was something comic in the idea of a ghost haunting a shithouse."

"Sneakers" contains some terrific music puns: The three main characters of the story are John, Paul, and George. (Alas, King did not deign to work a "Ringo" into the mix.)

King made an interesting revision when he reprinted "Sneakers" in *Nightmares & Dreamscapes*. In the original appearance of the story (in the limited-edition *Night Visions 5,* edited by Douglas E. Winter), King has Paul Jannings describe The Dead Beats by saying, "These guys make The Dead Kennedys sound like the Beatles." In the *Nightmares & Dreamscapes* version, King changes "Dead Kennedys" to "Butthole Surfers."

"Sneakers" seems to be King's rehearsal for his longer, more ambitious rock-and-roll story "You Know They Got a Hell of a Band," which was first published in the anthology *Shock Rock* in 1992.

King has Paul and John mix a new Roger Daltrey album and even mentions a "new" Roger Daltrey song called "Answer To You, Answer To Me."

"Sneakers" is King having fun with music—something he would do for real five years later when he toured with his band the Rock Bottom Remainders. (Roger Daltrey was not in the Remainders, though.)

"You Know They Got a Hell of a Band" A couple makes a detour to rock-and-roll heaven, where dead rock stars live on and perform. The only problem is that because this supergroup always needs an audience, once you arrive, you can never leave.

"Home Delivery" A written-to-order zombie story about a dead Maine fisherman who comes back to visit his wife.

"Rainy Season" Killer toads rain down (literally) on a small Maine town every seven years, and the only way for the deadly downpour to stop is for two outsiders to be sacrificed to the razor-toothed amphibians.

"Rainy Season" was originally submitted to the dark fantasy magazine *Midnight Graffiti* by King for whatever they were paying at the time for short stories, allowing the editors to build an entire "Stephen King" issue around the story.

This story is, in King's words, "pretty gross" and makes no pretenses toward being anything other than a fast-paced, exciting tale about razor-toothed toads who eat people alive. King sets up the premise, and in no time, it seems, John and Elise are being eaten by the toads. "Rainy Season" is one of King's most tightly constructed stories. Metaphorically, he gets on, delivers his speech, and thanks the audience before they even realize he's started talking. Truly a fun piece.

"My Pretty Pony" An independent hit man remembers back to a more halcyon period in his life when his grandfather taught him about the fluid nature of time. One of six chapters of an abandoned novel called *My Pretty Pony,* this short story (complete unto itself) was originally published in an overpriced limited edition produced by the Whitney Museum. King ultimately included it in *Nightmares & Dreamscapes,* describing it as "just another short story, a little better than some, not so good as others."

"Sorry, Right Number" A widow receives a warning phone call from the future, but is it too late to save her husband's life?

"The Ten O'Clock People" The truly strange premise for this story is that horrible batlike creatures with oozing tumors on their face and a taste for humans (especially eyeballs, it seems) have infiltrated the highest levels of American business and culture with a plan to take over the world, ultimately using the human race as their own personal all-you-can-eat buffet. The only ones that can see these bat creeps in their true form are the "Ten O'Clock People."

Why is it that these certain folks—including the hero of this tale, Brandon Pearson—are gifted with the ability to see the bats' malformed, tumor-ridden, grayish-brown, hairy visages? Because they are all Ten O'Clock People: smokers who are in that anxious, unpleasant area between smoking like a chimney and quitting completely. The Ten O'Clock People have restricted their smoking to between five and ten cigarettes a day, and that seems to be the intake range within which their brains develop the ability to see the bats.

King got the idea for "The Ten O'Clock People" while wandering around Boston one morning and noticing the groups of smokers gathered in front of their buildings having their "ten o'clock" nicotine fix.

"The Ten O'Clock People" is one of the few stories King has ever written that has a black hero. Duke Rhinemann is described as "a good-looking young black man." Other than this initial description, Pearson's race is never mentioned again.

"Crouch End"   An American couple looking to find the home of their English friends get lost in London's Crouch End, a Lovecraftian realm where "Him Who Waits" feeds on hapless and ultimately doomed trespassers. (Peter Straub lives in the Crouch End section of London, and this story was inspired by Stephen King and his wife actually getting lost while trying to find Straub's house.)

"The House on Maple Street"   A wicked stepfather is sent into what King describes as the "Great Beyond" when his house literally takes off into space.

"The Fifth Quarter"   A hard-boiled crime tale (which King published in *Cavalier* under the pseudonym "John Swithen") in which an ex-con seeks revenge for the double-cross death of his friend during a Brinks truck robbery.

"The Doctor's Case"   King's very own "Sherlock Holmes" tale.

"Umney's Last Case"   An extremely well done crime story in the tradition of Raymond Chandler.

"Head Down"   This lengthy (around twenty thousand words) non-fiction essay tells the story of the Bangor West All-Star Little League team's attack on the 1989 Maine Little League State Championship. It is dense with detail and at times can be tedious to read, especially if you do not like sports or sports writing.

As some critics have acknowledged, though, King literarily draws the real-world players on the team (including his son Owen) with the same kind of textured nuance that he does so well and that he is so well known for in his fiction.

The truth is that this piece may be tough going if you (1) don't actually know any of the people King writes about (which is the majority of us, I would assume) or (2) you don't like sports.

Reading "Head Down" is like being shown a scrapbook jam-packed with photos of another family's vacation. Some people are into things like that; others are not.

King considers "Head Down" to be "the best nonfiction writing of my life" but reveals that he hesitated about including it in *Nightmares & Dreamscapes,* admitting that "it doesn't really fit in a collection of stories which concern themselves mostly with suspense and the supernatural."

"Brooklyn August" As King acknowledges in the "Notes" to this poem, "Brooklyn August" is about as uncharacteristic as he can get, and that is why it has been reprinted so many times in baseball anthologies. Along with "Head Down," the piece illustrates just how fond of baseball King actually is—both the Little League *and* Major League varieties.

The poem's three opening stanzas all have the same rhyme pattern and metric structure:

> *In Ebbets Field the crabgrass grows*
> *(where Alston managed) row on row*
>
> *In Ebbets Field the infield's slow*
> *and seats are empty, row on row*
>
> *In Ebbets Field they come and go*
> *and play their innings, blow by blow*

The meter of these three stanzas is reminiscent of two important poetic works: "The Love Song of J. Alfred Prufrock" by T. S. Eliot, and "In Flanders Fields" by John McRae.

The Eliot masterpiece begins:

> *In the room the women come and go*
> *Talking of Michelangelo*

The McCrae poem begins:

> *In Flanders fields the poppies blow*
> *Between the crosses, row by row*

Both of these important works seem to have influenced King while writing "Brooklyn August," a work dedicated to Jim Bishop, one of King's University of Maine instructors.

King's career-long use of specific names, places, and cultural references is very evident in "Brooklyn August." In the space of just over forty lines, King refers to Schlitz beer; Mail Pouch chewing tobacco; Flatbush, Harlem, and Brooklyn; and baseball players Walter Alston, Gil Hodges, Jackie Robinson, Stan Musial, Don Newcombe, Carl Erskine, Johnny Podres, Clem Labine, Sandy Amoros, Pee Wee Reese, and Roy Campanella.

"The Beggar and the Diamond"   This short fable is King's rewriting of a Hindu parable originally told to him by a man named Surrendra Patel. King replaced the Lord Shiva and his wife, Parvati, from the original with God and the archangel Uriel.

King does not comment on the inclusion of this story in the collection except to tell the reader, in an "Author's Note" preceding the text, about hearing the story from Patel. He also apologizes for changing it to those who knew the original.

"The Beggar and the Diamond" is an interesting Zen-like piece that each reader must interpret for him- or herself and find the meaning most appropriate for them. Its ambiguity brings with it a sensibility that almost transforms it into a *koan*—one of those intriguing little Zen riddles, the most famous of which is probably the classic "What is the sound of one hand clapping?"

Insomnia (1994)   In this massive epic, King links his novels *The Stand, The Talisman, It, The Eyes of the Dragon,* and the *Dark Tower* series through one stunning scene in which *Insomnia*'s hero, the elderly—and increasingly sleepless Ralph Roberts—suddenly (and irrevocably) understands that existence is like a skyscraper and that humans only occupy the first two levels of a dark tower stretching into eternity. Stately and profound, *Insomnia* is one of King's most important novels, one that serves as a nexus around which the great epic of Roland and his quest is being told.

Rose Madder (1995)   For years, one of the major complaints about Stephen King's characterizations was that he could not create a realistic female character older than twelve or younger than seventy. Frankly, there was merit to that criticism. Even King himself has admitted that he honestly had trouble invoking a woman in her twenties, thirties, or forties.

With his 1995 novel *Rose Madder,* that was no longer the case.

Rose Madder is extraordinarily successful. After a somewhat slow start (which is absolutely necessary to set the tone and establish the subtext for the later events), *Rose Madder* flies along *on fire*. *Rose Madder* is one of the first King novels in several years that I quite literally could not wait to get back to after putting it down.

King immediately sets the tone with the lyrical and ominous first line of *Rose Madder*:

> *She sits in the corner, trying to draw air out of a room which seemed to have plenty just a few minutes ago and now seems to have none.*

Rose Madder is about a thirty-something woman named Rose McClendon Daniels who is married to an abusive cop named Norman. Norman is the kind of guy who gives all men a bad name. He is sadistic and often uses sexual torture as a gruesome means of controlling his wife (including one particularly nasty incident with a tennis racket).

One day, Rose Daniels makes a decision. A single drop of blood on a bed sheet is her catalyst, and before she even has time to talk herself out of it, she has stolen her husband's ATM card and left town.

Rose just gets on a bus and goes. Before long she is eight hundred miles from home, just one of dozens of female fugitives living at a battered women's shelter, astonished and unbelieving that she actually made a break for it—and succeeded.

Or did she?

Stephen King has obviously worked diligently over the past decade at understanding the sensibility of women and re-creating them realistically in his fiction. Rose McClendon in *Rose Madder* seems to be the latest character in a creative evolution that began with Bobbi Anderson in *The Tommyknockers* and includes Annie Wilkes in *Misery,* Jessie Burlingame in *Gerald's Game,* and Dolores Claiborne in *Dolores Claiborne.*

I have often said that Stephen King was writing one gargantuan book and just breaking it up into annual installments. In *Rose Madder,* several characters and places from previous King works show up unexpectedly, adding a frisson of familiarity that is quite engaging. These "crossovers" include Paul Sheldon, Lud, Susan Day, and Misery Chastain.

Rose Madder is a great book, and I, for one, can not wait until they cast the movie. (It was in preproduction in early 1998.) The role of Norman will likely be one of the most sought after male leads of the decade (I think Bruce Willis would excel in this role, or—is this a stretch?—perhaps Robin Williams would consider taking on a dark role like that of Norman. Might be good to get him away from the Mouse for a while?). And speaking of the movie version of *Rose Madder,* in Hollywood a powerful role is often described as one in which the actor can "chew the scenery."

As you know if you've read *Rose Madder, this* time that cliché is accurate.

The Green Mile (1996)   Retired prison guard Paul Edgecombe tells the story from his nursing home of the murder of two little girls many years ago. This serial novel (one installment was published each month for six months) is a brilliant exercise in "cliffhanger" writing and was one of 1996's biggest publishing successes.

Part 1: "The Two Dead Girls" (March)   A hulking and physically intimidating but surprisingly subdued black man is convicted of horribly killing two little girls and is sent to the Green Mile—the Death Row at Cold Mountain Penitentiary.

Part 2: "The Mouse on the Mile" (April)   A mouse who may be more than he appears to be arrives at E Block.

Part 3: "Coffey's Hands" (May)   Can convicted murderer John Coffey heal with his hands?

Part 4: "The Bad Death of Eduard Delacroix" (June)   A nightmare takes place when an electrocution goes wrong—deliberately.

Part 5: "Night Journey" (July)   Paul Edgecombe asks John Coffey to use his healing powers to help a woman dying in agony. Is Coffey capable of such healing?

Part 6: "Coffey on the Mile" (August)   We learn the truth about John Coffey *and* about Jingles the mouse in this stunning concluding installment.

Desperation (1996)   An ancient evil power named Tak is awakened from beneath the mining town of Desperation, and anyone who passes through this dark place is snared in its demonic grip—except for a young boy, who just might have a direct line to God.

STEPHEN KING ON WHAT IT'S LIKE TO BE RICHARD BACHMAN

I use to have these activity books that I played with on rainy days when I was a kid. They had this trick where you could get an interesting look at your face, a different look of your face, by placing a mirror perpendicular to half of your face. It makes a reflec-

tion that is a whole face. In a way that is what The Regulators *and* Desperation *are. Obviously, I'm Richard Bachman, and when I write as Richard Bachman it opens this part of my mind. It's like this hypnotic suggestion where I become my idea of who Richard Bachman is. It frees me to be somebody who is a little bit different. In a way* The Regulators *and* Desperation *are really different books, however what makes them interesting isn't the differences but the similarities.*

—Stephen King, from a 1997 interview with
Joseph Mauceri for *The World of Fandom*

The Regulators (1996)   An autistic child named Seth has his imagination taken over by Tak, the evil power from *Desperation*. Suddenly, "Power Rangers"–like monsters are terrorizing our heroes; the Regulators are on their way; mayhem ensues.

Six Stories (1997)   See *The Lost Work*.

The Dark Tower IV: Wizard and Glass (1997)   The fourth of a proposed six or seven *Dark Tower* novels. This installment tells of Roland's proposal of a desperate bargain to the insane Blaine the Mono and its consequences. Also, Roland and none other than Randall Flagg interact; Oy wears red slippers; Susannah gets some gravid news; we learn what Thinnies are and who Sheemie is, *'Salem's Lot* rears its head; and *The Stand, The Eyes of the Dragon, Insomnia*, J.R.R. Tolkien's *Lord of the Rings* trilogy, and *The Wizard of Oz* all seem to now be a part of the increasingly *epic* and engrossing *Dark Tower* epic. (And by the way, King uses the phrase "essential weirdness" to describe the writing of the *Dark Tower* series and also admits that Roland's story is his "Jupiter"—his biggest story in a universe of imagination.)

Bag of Bones (1998)   This 1998 novel—King's first authentic ghost story since *Pet Sematary*—revisits Castle Rock and Derry (the setting of *It*) and centers on a bestselling writer's grief over his wife's death, a tragedy which is somehow related to some strange doings at their summer lakeside place, Sara Laughs, in western Maine.

Bag of Bones boasts an ancient curse, dazzling sequences of mind-boggling and horrifying paranormal activity, and a couple of the most memorable villains King has ever blessed us with.

Once again (as in *The Dark Half, Misery*, "Secret Window, Secret Garden," *Desperation, The Tommyknockers, The Shining*, etc.), King has as his main character a writer, this one a bestselling author of mysteries who has been a fixture on the bestseller list for years. Michael Noonan and his wife, Jo, have had a blessed life: His books have made them wealthy, and their love has fulfilled them in ways neither of them could have ever dreamed was possible.

Then one day, while running across a shopping-center parking lot to help an accident victim on the hottest day of the year, Jo Noonan suffers a brain aneurysm that kills her instantly, making Mike Noonan one of the youngest widowers in Maine.

Jo Noonan's death also saddles Mike with one of the worst cases of writer's block imaginable. Following Jo's death, he has immediate and paralyzing panic attacks whenever he sits down to write. However, bestseller Mike Noonan is no fool. Even though he published *one* book a year, he wrote *one and one-half*, resulting in a bank safe-deposit box containing five unpublished novels, labeled simply I, II, III, etc.

Mike begins plundering his stash, providing his publisher—and his bottom-line fixated agent—with their one bestseller a year, keeping his career alive temporarily while trying to cope with being suddenly alone.

Mike Noonan decides to move to his lakefront house, Sara Laughs, and see if a change of scenery inspires him. As soon as he arrives in town, he meets a divorced young girl with a young daughter. Her wealthy father-in-law is conspiring to wrest custody of the little girl away from her mother, and Mike is inexorably drawn into the struggle, during which he learns some dark secrets about the old man and about the town and its past.

According to King, "*Bag of Bones* contains everything I know about marriage, lust, and ghosts." The novel is King at the top of his game, and the last three hundred pages contain some of the best writing King has produced.

Untitled short story collection (1999)   The second book of King's much-ballyhooed 1997 Simon & Schuster three-book deal.

On Fiction (2000)   This is Stephen King's first book of nonfiction since 1981's *Danse Macabre.* (We're not counting *Nightmares in the Sky,* since that was essentially a photo book for which King wrote an essay.) *On Fiction* is the third book of King's 1997 three-book deal with Simon & Schuster after he left Viking, his publisher for twenty years. (The first was 1998's *Bag of Bones*; the second was a collection of short stories scheduled for 1999.) In a November 1997 interview with America Online's "Book Report," King said, "My next big risk is a book called *On Fiction,* which is a book about writing stories. It is also a book about my own past, and that feels very risky to me."

APPENDIX C

THE KING OF HOLLYWOOD

Stephen King Movies, from 1976's *Carrie* to 1998's *Storm of the Century*

Horror films are films that exist primarily to scare the shit out of the audience. I have a real simple definition of that.

—Stephen King, from an interview
with Linda Marotta in *Fangoria*

Like "The Royal Library," this feature, "The King of Hollywood," is eccentrically annotated: Some of the film adaptations of Stephen King's tales get extensively reviewed, while some receive no more than a line or two.

In the spirit of *The Lost Work of Stephen King,* there *are* a few oddities in this feature that we think you'll find interesting and entertaining.

For instance, there is a lengthy look at the "lost scenes" of Frank Darabont's brilliant film *The Shawshank Redemption,* along with excerpts of interviews with Tim Robbins, Morgan Freeman, and Frank Darabont.

Moreover, prior to my review of Mark Pavia's terrific movie *The Night Flier,* I include my review of his *Night Flier* screenplay, which I read three years before the movie went into production and reviewed for SKIN, a Stephen King newsletter that has since ceased publication. I found it intriguing to read what I had thought of the script before a single scene had been shot and then to see the movie and compare my two reactions. I hope you find this side-by-side review interesting as well.

"The King of Hollywood" reviews short film adaptations of King's stories ("The Woman in the Woman" and "Gramma," for instance), as well as a few extremely rare, very low budget adaptations of King stories, such as

"The Last Rung on the Ladder"; "The Lawnmower Man" (which uses King's original story instead of making one up and slapping King's title on it the way the 1992 film *The Lawnmower Man* did); and "Disciples of the Crow" (a twenty-two-minute adaptation of "Children of the Corn.")

I conclude this filmography with a list of my ten favorite Stephen King movies of all time. I'm sure that many of you will disagree with my choices, and I'd love for you to tell me why. Write to me in care of my publisher and perhaps we'll include a section of fan comments in the next edition of this book. Just keep your comments as brief as possible. Better yet, just send me *your* Top Ten list with a short note telling me why you picked the flicks you picked and we'll use what we can in the next edition.

A Note on Criteria: What makes for an excellent adaptation of a Stephen King film? Even though King's writing is viscerally visual, adapting his books is like squeezing his stories through a funnel. The key, then, is a good adaptation; one that retains the essence of King's plot but doesn't bog down in unnecessary material and scenes that just don't work in a movie. The best King adaptations—*Misery, The Dead Zone, Stand by Me, The Shawshank Redemption*—capture the spirit of the tale and present the drama in a lean, mean form that engages the viewer and crystallizes King's story. The worst King adaptations—*Children of the Corn, The Running Man, Trucks*—fumble the ball big time by coming across as *parodies* of King's stories. It's almost as though horror were not taken seriously by the makers of these films, and thus a kind of tongue-in-cheek attitude comes across in the script and acting. Of course, fine performances are an absolute must, but that's true for any film adaptation of a book or short story. I think a successful King movie solely depends, then, on who is doing the adapting, how seriously they take the source material, and how much respect they have for King's writing. There are only a handful of screenwriters who seem to have this sensibility down pat, and they include Frank Darabont (*The Shawshank Redemption* and *The Green Mile*); William Goldman (*Misery*); Raynold Gideon and Bruce A. Evans (*Stand by Me*); Jeffrey Boam (*The Dead Zone*); Lawrence Cohen (*Carrie, It*); and Stephen King himself (*Pet Sematary, The Stand, the Shining*).

A Note on Availability: The vast majority of the films listed in this section were originally released theatrically and are now readily available on video and often on laser disc. Some of the shorter films reviewed were initially released on video but are now out of print; the student films were never released commercially. Our best suggestion for finding any of these flicks would be to start with your local video rental store. (Of course, the big guys—Blockbuster et al.—will have a wider selection than many of the smaller outlets.) The out-of-print short films occasionally show up in the catalogs of places like The Overlook Connection and Betts Bookstore. Keep your eyes open and your antennae up if you're interested in some of those oddballs. Also, do not forget that King's films often show up on cable and are thus easy to collect by taping. One of the Stephen King newsgroups actually posts all of the Stephen King movies scheduled for broadcast in the coming week. This can be helpful.

Carrie (1976)   Stephen King was lucky: The very first film adaptation of King's first published novel was not only successful; it was a great movie, a marvelous adaptation of his novel, and perhaps one of the ten best screen versions of his books to date. Sissy Spacek is superb; John Travolta makes his screen debut.

'Salem's Lot (1979)   This wasn't too bad an adaptation, but it wasn't something I have wanted to see again over the past few years. It exists in two forms on videotape: the edited version and the complete miniseries. The complete version is the better of the two and the one you should rent if you haven't seen it yet.

The Shining (1980)   King was never really thrilled with this original, lavish Stanley Kubrick adaptation of what some consider to be one of his three best novels of all time. Kubrick took liberties with King's story and did not seem to pay much attention to his feelings about these changes. King remade *The Shining* as a TV miniseries in 1997.

Creepshow (1982)   a garish Stephen King/George Romero tribute to the old *EC Comics*. Lots of fun if you watch it in the right frame of mind. It ain't *Citizen Kane,* but it sure is a hoot to watch.

Cujo (1983)   Dee Wallace is trapped in a Pinto by a killer St. Bernard. An excellent adaptation of one of King's most intimate novels.

The Dead Zone (1983)   *The Dead Zone* is one of the finest cinematic adaptations of a Stephen King work to date. The script is taut but still remains faithful to King's story. The acting is of the highest caliber; the direction, classic Cronenberg. The cinematography is breathtaking; this may be one of the most visually stunning adaptations of a King work.

Cronenberg and screenwriter Jeffrey Boam have crafted a dark, supernatural thriller that ultimately is about the *people* in the story, which is rare for a "horror" movie and simply proves that when King's tales are given the respect they deserve and all the plot devices and scare tactics of the horror genre are used as tools for character development instead of *as* the story (the *Friday the 13th* films and others of their ilk come to mind), then the result is a magnificent movie experience. (*Misery* is another example of how to do a "Stephen King movie" correctly.)

The "winter in New England" feel to the film is quite effective. Truly great movies communicate more than just a story; they also let viewers lose themselves in what is often referred to as the *mise en scène,* a French term for the environment of the "play." In David Cronenberg's *Dead Zone,* we feel the Maine cold; we see the visible breaths of the characters; we hear the crunch of the snow. All of this wonderful texture works to fully define Johnny Smith and his figurative and literal isolation because of his horrible "gift" of precognition.

Christopher Walken's performance in this film is extraordinary. Walken did a great many films between 1983 and 1994, but I really think that the next time he achieved such extraordinary heights as an actor was in Quentin Tarantino's *Pulp Fiction.* Walken, however, did not receive an Academy Award nomination for his performance in *The Dead Zone,* which is reprehensible.

Colleen Dewhurst, Brooke Adams, and Martin Sheen should all likewise be singled out for their excellent performances.

There are some real frights in this flick, especially during the scenes when Johnny Smith has his visions and we get to see him lying in a burning bed or standing on the gazebo watching Frank Dodd murder one of his victims. These are very powerful and very dramatic moments.

Another religious-fanatic mother: Like Margaret White in *Carrie,* Johnny's mother, Vera Smith, is a good old-fashioned, Bible-thumping, vision-seein' religious nut. King writes these characters very well, and one wonders who in his life inspired these types of loonies. It certainly wasn't his mother, Ruth. In an interview I did with King's brother, David, for my *Complete Stephen King Encyclopedia,* David said that their mother went to church and believed in God but was certainly nowhere near as fanatical as some of King's more "devout" characters.

Christine (1983)   Haunted car possesses new teenage owner; mayhem ensues—in Technicolor and stereo! A pretty good version of a kick-ass novel.

The Woman In The Room (1983)   The Frank Darabont short film that convinced King to allow Darabont to option *Rita Hayworth and Shawshank Redemption.* We all know how *that* film turned out, so obviously *Woman in the Room* is definitely worth tracking down. Try your favorite video-rental places first; occasionally, The Overlook Connection will have tapes for sale. After seeing this short film, King said that *The Woman in the Room* is "clearly the best of the short films made from my stuff."

Disciples of the Crow (1983)   a short film adaptation of "Children of the Corn." Now out of print, although you might be able to find a rental copy as part of the *Stephen King Night Shift Collection* videos.

Children of the Corn (1984)   a dreadful adaptation of one of King's better short stories. The best part of the movie (and all that makes it worth watching) is Linda (the *Terminator* movies) Hamilton's performance.

Firestarter (1984)   Even though Stephen King called *Firestarter* a "resounding failure as a film" in the book *The Shawshank Redemption: The Shooting Script,* the movie *is* considered watchable and can justifiably be called an "average" translation of a King novel to the screen. (*Firestarter* director Mark Lester once hung up on me from his car phone when I called to tell him I wanted to interview him about *Firestarter* for my Stephen King encyclopedia. I guess he had heard King's review, eh?) Drew Barrymore is not very good, but Martin Sheen and George C. Scott deliver fine performances and make up for the little Drew's painfully lame one. If you haven't seen it, *Firestarter* is worth a rental, but one viewing, I think you'll find, is more than enough.

Cat's Eye (1985)   This was Drew Barrymore's second King film. It is a watchable anthology of three King tales, "Quitters, Inc." "The Ledge," and a wraparound story called "General," which was published as a screenplay in Richard Chizmar's *Screamplays* in 1997. Alan King is especially good, and so are the special "ledge" effects.

Silver Bullet (1985)   the film adaptation of *Cycle of the Werewolf.* Average. No more, no less.

The Boogeyman (1986)   a chilling short adaptation of one of King's most Freudian short stories.

The Word Processor of the Gods (1985)   Bruce Davison (*Short Cuts, Six Degrees of Separation*) stars as failed writer, dad, and husband Richard Hagstrom in this worthy adaptation of one of Stephen King's *Skeleton Crew* short stories.

Originally aired on November 19, 1985, as a *Tales From the Darkside* episode, this twenty-two-minute version of King's fantasy was written by acclaimed horror writer Michael McDowell and also starred Karen Shallo as Richard's repulsive wife, Lina; William Cain as the knowing Mr. Nordhoff; and Jonathan Matthews as Richard's doomed nephew (and the son he *should* have had) Jonathan.

The word processor Richard receives after his brother and his wife Belinda and son Jonathan are killed in a car accident was a birthday gift from Jonathan, and it greets him with a "Happy Birthday" message on its opening screen. As in the story, as Richard begins fooling around with it, he realizes that the machine can make whatever he types come true by using the crudely labeled EXECUTE and DELETE buttons. Richard uses Jonathan's gift from beyond to "repair" his life. First he deletes his slug of a son, and then he marries Belinda, who gives birth to Jonathan, the young man Richard always felt was more like him than his own son.

McDowell does a lot with the brief time allotted for this episode, including a scene in which Jonathan appears to his uncle Richard and tells him that he'll build him a word processor but that he'll have to hurry, because he doesn't have much time.

The Word Processor of the Gods ("The" was not part of King's original *Skeleton Crew* short-story title) was originally released on a seventy-minute videotape from Laurel around the time the episode originally aired (or some time thereafter) but may now be out of print. You may still be able to find a copy for rental at some video stores, or you can try the usual dealers who specialize in King material (Betts Bookstore, The Overlook Connection, etc.) for possible purchase of the tape.

Maximum Overdrive (1986)   Stephen King's directorial debut (he wrote the script based on his short story, "Trucks") and the movie that King himself describes as a "moron movie." He's right.

Stand by Me (1986)   a brilliant adaptation of one of Stephen King's most moving stories. Rob Reiner directed this coming-of-age tale that became one of the most beloved cinematic versions of a Stephen King story, featuring up-and-coming stars River Phoenix and Corey Feldman. Four years later, Reiner proved that his prowess interpreting a King story was not a fluke when he directed the best King film to date, *Misery*.

Gramma (1986)   an excellent *New Twilight Zone* episode scripted by none other than Harlan Ellison. Micky Hart of the Grateful Dead provided the music, and Barret Oliver played Georgie, a little boy left home alone with his grotesque (and ultimately dead) Gramma. Darlanne Fluegel played Georgie's mother and would go on to star in *Pet Sematary 2,* a sequel that King had nothing to do with.

Creepshow 2 (1987)   Not as good as *Creepshow,* this sequel is nonetheless watchable. "The Raft" and "The Hitchhiker" segments are probably the best. (The other segments are a wraparound story and "Old Chief Wood'nhead.") Look for Stephen King in a cameo as a trucker in the "Hitchhiker" segment and his secretary, Shirley Sonderegger, as crocheting Mrs. Cavanaugh in "Old Chief Wood'nhead."

The Last Rung On The Ladder (1987)   In Frank Darabont's 1996 book *The Shawshank Redemption: The Shooting Script,* Stephen King wrote:

> *I have made the dollar deal, as I call it, over my accountant's moans and head-clutching protests sixteen or seventeen times as of this writing. Stories filmed include . . . "Last Rung on the Ladder" from* Night Shift.

King is talking about Jim Cole's eleven-minute short film, which Jim discusses in the essay "Why Kitty Absolutely *Had* To Die," which he wrote especially for *The Lost Work of Stephen King.*

I first saw Jim Cole's short film back in the late eighties when I was putting together my King *Encyclopedia*. I did not see it again until this year, eight years after my initial viewing.

My thoughts almost a decade later? I still liked what I had *originally* admired about the movie: Jim's tight screenplay, his direction, the performance of Melissa Whelden as Kitty.

This time, though, I definitely did not like the music and thought that the unknown actor who played the father was woefully lacking.

Nevertheless, the film still moved me, and I once again marveled at what Jim Cole (now one of my closest friends) was able to do with a Super-8-mm camera and sixteen hundred bucks.

The Lawnmower Man (1987) a student adaptation (another "dollar baby") of one of King's most mythical short stories. Yes, this version shows a naked fat guy crawling behind a lawnmower eating the clippings. That scene alone is worth the price of admission, but it's a moot point, because this entertaining short film has never been released commercially.

Sorry, Right Number (1987) a *Tales From the Darkside* episode in which a widow receives a warning call from the future. This one works quite effectively, and the performances do King's original screenplay justice.

The Running Man (1987) a lame nonadaptation of one of King's Bachman novels that makes us wonder how they can get away with putting King's name on a movie when the final film has almost nothing to do with his original story.

Pet Sematary (1989) one of the better adaptations of a King novel due in great part to the fact that King wrote the screenplay himself. Dale Midkiff and Denise Crosby are very good as Louis and Rachel Creed, but it is Fred Gwynne who truly shines in the role of Jud Crandall.

Tales From The Darkside: The Movie (1990) This an anthology of four stories—a wraparound story written by Michael McDowell; "Lot 249," written by McDowell from an Arthur Conan Doyle story; "Cat From Hell," written by George Romero from Stephen King's short story; and "Lover's Vow," written by McDowell. The King story is slow-paced, and we never feel any real emotional involvement with the characters.

Stephen King's Graveyard Shift (1990) Great sets and decent performances by Kelly Wolf and Brad Dourif do not wholly redeem this slow-paced adaptation of one of King's most horrifying short stories.

Misery (1990) probably the best King film of all time. Kathy Bates brought Annie Wilkes to life with a visceral reality that made her screen presence utterly authentic and absolutely terrifying. Okay, so they made some concessions to the sensibilities of the audience (changing Annie's ax to a sledgehammer for the "hobbling" scene was one of them), but William

Goldman did with his screenplay what many others could not: successfully bring a Stephen King novel to life.

Stephen King's It (1990)   a terrific miniseries adaptation of the novel many consider King's magnum opus, that is chilling and original in its execution. Scripters Lawrence D. Cohen and Tommy Lee Wallace, by cutting the story down to its bare bones, were able to squeeze a massive doorstop of a book through the funnel of television and produce a gripping and faithful version of *It*. Annette O'Toole was especially good as Beverly Marsh, and John Ritter was surprisingly effective as Ben Hanscom. (After *Three's Company*, who knew the guy could really act?) Richard Thomas played Bill Denbrough with sensitivity and depth, and overall this must be considered as close to an unqualified success as a King adaptation (especially one on *TV*) can be.

Sometimes They Come Back (1991)   a decent made-for-TV adaptation of one of King's *Night Shift* stories. It starred Tim Matheson and Brooke Adams (who also starred in *The Dead Zone*).

Stephen King's Golden Years (1991)   King's first original TV series. Personally, I loved it, but the ratings did not warrant renewal. Pity. (See the chapter "How I Created *Golden Years*. . .").

Stephen King's Sleepwalkers (1992)   an entertaining film based on an original King screenplay. *Sleepwalkers* is about feline vampire creatures who suck the life force out of unsuspecting victims. Mädchen Amick is irresistible; and watch for cameos by Joe Dante, John Landis, Clive Barker, Tobe Hooper, Mark Hamill, and King himself.

The Tommyknockers (1993)   a miniseries that starred *NYPD Blue*'s Jimmy Smits as alcoholic poet Jim Gardener and Marg Helgenberger as the novelist Bobbi Anderson who discovers the buried alien ship containing the still-frisky spirits of the long-dead Tommyknockers. A decent adaptation, but the pace only moves during Smits and Helgenberger's scenes together. I thought the scenes involving the Hilly Brown disappearance subplot were boring. Good special effects, though, and worth a rental if you haven't seen it.

The Dark Half (1993)   a nice and gory adaptation of one of King's "writer" novels. Directed by *Night of the Living Dead* and *Creepshow* genius George Romero.

Needful Things (1993)   Max von Sydow plays the devil who comes to town in this adaptation of King's final Castle Rock tale. It starred the always-terrific Ed Harris, with Bonnie Bedelia and Amy Madigan. This was Fraser Heston's (Charlton's son) directorial debut.

Stephen King's The Stand (1994)   An eagerly awaited miniseries of King's most beloved novel, this adaptation mostly works and includes some terrific performances and some grisly (by TV standards) scenes. It is terrific to see big-screen vets Molly Ringwald and Laura San Giacomo in this six-hour version of *The Stand*. Watch for cameos by Ed Harris, Kathy Bates, Kareem Abdul-Jabbar, and Stephen King. Mick Garris (*Sleepwalkers, Desperation*) directed.

The Shawshank Redemption (1994)   *The Shawshank Redemption* is probably one of the best prison movies ever made. It harkens back to the classics of the genre, with characters who are brilliantly brought to life by Tim Robbins, Morgan Freeman, and the rest of the amazing cast.

This movie once again proves that Stephen King is much more than a horror writer. *The Shawshank Redemption* does have its horrors, but they are all based on the cruelty man can inflict upon his fellow man.

Well plotted and faithfully adapted for the screen by Frank Darabont (*The Woman in the Room*), *The Shawshank Redemption* is one of those "Stephen King" movies you should show to people who say they hate Stephen King movies.

The Shawshank Redemption did not do very well at the box office, and many blamed this on what they considered to be a terrible title. Alternate titles for the film included *Conviction!*; *Walls of Hope*; *Hope Springs Eternal*; and *Zihuatanejo*. Personally, I like *The Shawshank Redemption* just fine. It is evocative and clever, and the alternate titles considered for the film are clichés and lame. Interestingly, Morgan Freeman (who played Red) wanted to use King's original novella title, *Rita Hayworth and Shawshank Redemption*. In an interview on Showtime, he said, "Word of mouth sells movies. And you can't sell what you can't say." In the same interview, Tim Robbins revealed that during auditions a transvestite sent in a picture and a resumé: He wanted to play Rita Hayworth.

Tim Robbins said, "[*The Shawshank Redemption*], more than any other movie I've ever done, has affected people to the degree where they come up on the street and have to talk about it. I mean, all over the place, wherever I go. And there's something about the movie that has touched a chord in people. A lot of people are saying how important it was to them and how great it was to see a movie about friendship." Morgan Freeman agreed, noting: "A surprising number of men have [told] me the ending just grabbed them and shook them. And I find that very gratifying, because this was a scene where two men came together like that. These two men had great love for each other."

Writer-director Frank Darabont said, "I think the thing about the film that has touched people is really what touched me so deeply about the book. There's a very basic message that I think people really want to hear. Some people find it unforgivably corny, but I think most people want to hear it, and that is that we have value. Every human being has value, every human being has potential, and every human being has dignity."

During the aforementioned Showtime interview, Darabont and company showed and discussed two "Lost Scenes" that were cut from the final film:

Lost Scene 1   This scene takes place as the newly released Red is working in a grocery store as a bagger. He asks permission from the manager to go to the bathroom and is scolded that he need not ask every time. In the bathroom we then hear Red talking to himself:

> *Forty years I've been asking permission to piss. And I can't squeeze a drop without say-so. Women, too. That's the other thing. I forgot they were half the human race. There's women everywhere. Every shape, Every size. I find myself semi-hard most of the time, cursing myself for a dirty old man. Not a brassiere to be seen, nipples poking out at the world. Jesus pleeze-us. Back in my day, a woman out in public like that would have been arrested and given a sanity hearing.*

The scene shifts to Red walking through the park as the song "Season of the Witch" plays on the soundtrack.

> *They're calling this the Summer of Love. Summer of Loonies, you ask me.*

Back at the grocery store now, Red cannot keep up with the bagging. A little white kid shoots a toy gun at him, and the customers give him dirty looks. Red ends up having a panic attack and fleeing into the bathroom, where he collapses, panting. The scene then shifts to Red walking the street after work and we hear his sad, resigned realization:

> *There's a harsh truth to face. No way I'm gonna make it on the outside.*

Of this cut scene, Morgan Freeman said, simply, "Should've been in the movie. Couldn't have everything, though."

Frank Darabont explained: "The reason it was pulled out—it was not an easy decision for me to make—sometimes you just have to [do what] William Goldman calls 'murdering your children.' Sometimes you *have* to murder your children. Morgan was very understanding. He knows that you have to look at the overall effect of the movie."

In Frank's 1996 book *The Shawshank Redemption: The Shooting Script,* he explained at length why these scenes (actually scenes 282 through 287 in the shooting script) were cut:

> It was an amazing experience to sit through these scenes with a live audience. They were good scenes, don't get me wrong. They played beautifully in and of themselves (especially 282, with Red checking out the women; hell, the audience loved that scene). But here's the odd contradiction: though the audience enjoyed what they were seeing scene by scene, the *sequence itself* made them terribly impatient. Why? *Because it spent three minutes telling them something they already knew.* . . . It shows that moviegoers can sometimes be far more intuitive than a filmmaker thinks.

Lost Scene 2   This scene (225–227 in the script) actually takes place before Lost Scene 1 in the film. In this scene, Andy's escape route has been discovered, and they decide to send a young guard down into the hole to see what he can learn. We then hear Red in his cell:

> *And then came the unmistakable sound of Rory Tremont losing his last few meals. The whole cellblock heard him. I mean, it echoed [Red begins laughing hysterically] I laughed right into solitary. Two-week stretch. . . . Andy once talked about going easy time in the hole. Now I knew what that meant.*

Morgan Freeman on Lost Scene 2   "Red is listening to the screams coming out of the hole and realizes that his friend has made good. . . . I miss that scene because it was so hard to shoot. . . . I had to do it about four or five times."

Frank Darabont on Lost Scene 2   "The reason the scene didn't work is not necessarily because there was anything wrong with the scene but because it didn't belong in the narrative flow of a movie. You don't want to take a two-and-a-half minute detour down an air shaft with a character you've never met before." He also noted: "I'd never seen a man laugh for two-and-a-half minutes on cue."

In his book, Darabont had this to say about these scenes:

> This has always been one of my favorite sequences in Stephen King's story; it made me laugh until tears were rolling down my cheeks when I first read it. And because it's also the movie's

best example of a terrifically written sequence dropping dead on a screen with a dull thud, it points up the fundamental difference between a book and a movie. . . . [O]nce we see Norton discover a tunnel behind the poster, once we realize that Andy has actually by-God *escaped*, we want the movie to *deal* with that revelation.

Actors' Dialogue   It seems that Tim Robbins and Morgan Freeman enjoyed a good-natured, pugnacious relationship throughout the shooting of Shawshank, as this exchange from the Showtime interview reveals:

TIM ROBBINS (on Morgan Freeman): Morton Freedman? Excellent actor.

MORGAN FREEMAN (on Tim Robbins): Was he in it?

TIM ROBBINS (on Morgan Freeman): I had to carry him along.

MORGAN FREEMAN (on his role in the film): Actually I was more powerful than Tim. If you look at it carefully, you'll see that I was much, much more powerful than Tim.

MORGAN (on the hiring of Tim Robbins): They said Tim Robbins is going to do the role, and I thought, Perfect, you can't get better than that.

TIM ROBBINS: You see? Once in a while Morgan tells the truth.

FRANK DARABONT (on Tim Robbins): With Tim, what's interesting about him as an actor is that he doesn't show much. You kind of have to peer at him and figure what's going on in this guy's mind, and *that's* Andy Dufresne—the man who is cerebral and hidden in a lot of ways.

TIM ROBBINS (on preparing for his role): There is a lot of truth to be found in animal behavior, and for me, going to the zoo, you can find out an awful lot about what it's like to be incarcerated; and looking in those animal eyes; and seeing the pacing wild animals . . . just this kind of caged intensity.

During the interview, Frank Darabont talked about how in the *book* the character of Andy Dufresne was short and in the *script* Andy Dufresne was short, but in the *film* Andy is 6 feet 4 1/2 inches tall because "Tim was the best choice for the part." He also laughed about how in the book the character of Red was a white Irishman, but when they got Morgan Freeman to play the role, he rewrote accordingly.

FRANK DARABONT (on what the movie's about): It's really a movie about a man who learns how to hope. That's really what the movie's about. He learns how to hope by the example of another man who struggles against every odd that is thrown in his face to not forget how to hope. . . . Ultimately I wouldn't change a thing about *Shawshank*. I think we may have caught that lightning in a bottle, I don't know. Ask again in about forty years. Let's see how people feel about it then.

Dolores Claiborne (1995)   One of my ten best. Once again, Kathy Bates brings to life a Stephen King "heroine," and she does it with depth and an emotional gravity often missing from other female King characterizations. Jennifer Jason Leigh is brilliant as Dolores Claiborne's estranged daughter. A must-see (if you haven't already).

The Mangler (1995)   A not-so-terrific Tobe Hooper (*'Salem's Lot*) adaptation of a *Night Shift* story that ends up long on blood and guts and short on story and characterization. It starred Robert Englund (Freddy Krueger of *Nightmare on Elm Street* fame) and Ted Levine (the cross-dressing psycho in *The Silence of the Lambs*).

Stephen King's The Langoliers (1995)   *Crash and Burn* (almost). I was hopeful while watching the first half of *The Langoliers*. It had a very "Twilight Zone" feel to it, and I was looking forward to the second half, but by the time part two was over and the credits rolled, I was disappointed.

The second half seemed rushed and perfunctory, and I wasn't thrilled with the special effects. I do, however, like director-screenwriter Tom Holland's work. He's done *Child's Play, Fright Night*, and *The Temp*, and *The Langoliers* was his first stab at a Stephen King flick. He wrote the adaptation and directed it, and I think he might have been better off if he had just handled the directing chores and left writing the screenplay to someone else.

All that aside, there was a lot to like in this miniseries. As I mentioned, the opening hour or so had a nice, weird tone and feel to it. Let's face it: Airports and airplanes are bizarre places. There's something almost surrealistic about them, and *The Langoliers* captures that "edge" we all feel when boarding and waiting for the plane to take off.

Bronson Pinchot was astoundingly over the top in his performance as Toomey, but you couldn't take your eyes off him (which, I suppose, is the ultimate test of an effective acting job, right?)

The remainder of the cast was just okay, and I am especially grateful that *thirtysomething*'s Patricia Wettig turned in a relatively understated performance. With some of the lines she was given, she could have easily made *viewers* reach for the airsick bags, if you know what I mean.

As to the special effects: Hey, it's television, right? With a limited budget and limited time, there's only so much you can do. The Langoliers themselves reminded me of turds with teeth from a rear view and clams with teeth from the front. And some of the airplane shots looked blatantly phony. The chief value of this miniseries lies in the undeniable strength of the source material. King's novella is scary and macabre, and most of this TV version comes very close to capturing that feeling.

Now about Stephen King's performance: I know that his cameos have become something akin to Hitchcock's predilection for appearing in every single one of his films. And, hey, if Big Steve wants to be in his movies, who's going to stop him, right?

However, I wish that now and then he would tone down his deliberate attempt at camp. His performances often come across as *parodies* of the Stephen King persona, and I, for one, would love to see him play something totally straight instead of this "boogeyman" shtick. I also think fans would absolutely love to see King appear in one of his films not as a character but as Stephen King himself. (I don't know how the real King could be worked into a script; I'm just saying it would be great fun if he did a cameo now and then.)

Stephen King's Thinner (1996)   A decent version of one of King's more entertaining Richard Bachman tales. The "fat" special effects are terrific.

Quicksilver Highway (1997)   *Quicksilver Highway* was a Mick Garris project that adapted a Clive Barker short story ("The Body Politic") and a Stephen King short story ("Chattery Teeth" from *Nightmares & Dreamscapes*) and presented the two one-hour adaptations as a two-hour movie, connected by a wraparound story written by Garris.

The wraparound story focuses on a strange traveler named Aaron Quicksilver who goes from town to town in his Airstream trailer pulled by a Rolls-Royce Silver Cloud. He is the owner and curator of a museum of oddities, one of which is a genuine Hand of Glory—a five-fingered candle that is an actual human hand cut off a man executed on the gallows and dipped in wax.

The "Chattery Teeth" portion of the movie is a fairly faithful adaptation of the King story and is the stronger segment of the two. Mick Garris is *very* good at adapting Stephen King for the screen, and he does a terrific job with a story that could have easily disintegrated into farce in the hands of a lesser writer.

In the case of "The Body Politic," Garris does his best with a story that is blatantly ridiculous (not to say that the idea of vengeful, chattery joke teeth is the height of narrative sophistication), but one has to try *real hard* not to laugh out loud as Matt Frewer's possessed hands communicate by waving their fingers at each other as Frewer sleeps.

"Chattery Teeth," on the other hand, still retains a welcome frisson of horror (in a story that has a blatantly funny premise as its jumping-off point) and overall just works *better.*

Stephen King's The Shining (1997)   In the June 1983 issue of *Playboy,* Stephen King said, "I'd like to remake *The Shining* someday, maybe even direct it myself if anybody will give me enough rope to hang myself with." Well, in 1997, a remake of *The Shining*—with King's own script but not his direction—aired over three nights as a six-hour miniseries.

Was this shiny new *Shining* a vanity project, green-lighted by ABC because King's previous miniseries for the network were, for the most part, successes? If so, are we to believe that King, for almost two decades, has been so annoyed and offended by Stanley Kubrick's version of *The Shining* that he simply *had* to do his own version, even though there are countless other unfilmed novels and stories of his that he could have adapted instead?

Whatever. I did like this version (which starred Steven Weber of *Wings* and Rebecca DeMornay) probably only because it was truer to the novel. Visually, it doesn't even come *close* to Kubrick's version.

The Revelations of 'Becka Paulsen (1997)   A short film version of a segment of *The Tommyknockers* that was directed by Steven Weber (star of *Stephen King's Shining*) for Showtime's *Outer Limit* series. Average.

Trucks (1997)   A somewhat boring USA Network original movie adaptation of King's *Night Shift* story "Trucks," which King himself had already adapted as *Maximum Overdrive.* Maybe it's time to admit this story just isn't suitable for the movies? Just asking.

Stephen King's The Night Flier (1997)   [an HBO original movie]

I've seen a rough cut. They keep promising me they're going to show me a second cut, but they haven't yet. I think it's wonderful, in a way that the movies have integrally missed with my work. This is like Dawn of the Dead. It really goes beyond the limits and renders discussions of "good taste" meaningless. I don't feel that right now it's a ratable picture, other than "NC-17" and I'd love to see it stay that way.

—Stephen King talking about *The Night Flier* before
the movie's release in a 1997 interview
with Joseph Mauceri for *The World of Fandom*

Written After Reading the Screenplay

FOOMP!

"*Foomp*" is a word *Night Flier* screenwriter and director Mark Pavia uses in his script (written with Jack O'Donnell) to indicate a smash cut to a startling image or scene, usually of a mutilated corpse.

If Pavia manages to translate his written words onto the screen, then *The Night Flier* may be one of the most frightening Stephen King film adaptations to date.

The screenplay is based on a King short story that first appeared in Doug Winter's wonderful 1988 anthology *Prime Evil.* It tells the story of tabloid reporter Richard Dees and his relentless pursuit of an exquisitely malevolent vampire pilot. Our bloodsucker flies from small airport to small airport, landing only long enough to "have dinner."

Pavia's script is a faithful adaptation of the story as well as an expansion of it. He takes some liberties with the ending, adding some scenes and plot developments that change the original ending of the tale but, in my opinion, do work quite well overall.

King has often used the metaphor of viewing adaptations of his books and stories as children whom a parent is sending off to college: You do your best to raise them right, but once they're out of your circle of influence, there's nothing more you can do. Selling film rights necessarily turns over story power to the screenwriters who are adapting the tale for the movies. Movies, being the strictly visual medium that they are, often mandate changes to the original text and story lines. Such is the nature of the cinematic beast. As a writer, you hope that the screenwriter is up to the task of the translation.

Mark Pavia and Jack O'Donnell have done a superlative job with *The Night Flier.* My usual reaction when I read a terrific screenplay is: "Sweet fancy Moses, I hope the director doesn't screw it up!" With Pavia himself directing, I'm hopeful that what's on the page will end up on the screen.

Stephen King is reportedly quite high on this project. It's a Richard Rubinstein Production under the aegis of Laurel Entertainment, so it's already got a great lineage. The tag line for the film's poster reads: "Never believe what you publish. . . . Never publish what you believe," an axiom that figures prominently in both the story and film.

After reading the screenplay, I am really looking forward to seeing *The Night Flier.* I won't give away the ending, but I will tell you that there's a scene at the conclusion of the film that takes place in Dees's mind (or does it?) that, if it's done well, will leave viewers horrified and spent.

Stay tuned.

Written After Seeing the Movie

Stephen King's The Night Flier is one of the ten best adaptations of a Stephen King story to date. Everything the script promised was ultimately delivered in Mark Pavia's final version, and man, oh, man, is this one scary movie.

At first, I didn't think Miguel Ferrer was right for the part of Richard Dees. After ten seconds of seeing Ferrer in the movie, though, my opinion changed completely. Ferrer plays the pilot/tabloid journalist with an edge that is unrelentingly *mean*. I really didn't pick up as much of a "I hate the world and go fuck yourself" vibe from the Dees character in the story, but Ferrer ruthlessly expands Dees's cynicism and transforms it into a vicious "fuck you and your family and your dog and cat and your ancestors and get out of my way or I'll bury you" attitude that is truly mesmerizing.

The movie is loaded with King references that will delight his fans. It seems that several of *Inside View*'s cover stories were about Stephen King short stories, including "The Mangler," *Thinner*, "Children of the Corn," *The Breathing Method*, and "Strawberry Spring," just to name a few.

The movie is graphic and explicitly violent, and we don't get to see Dwight Renfield (except from behind, black cape billowing) until near the end, and then we get a good glimpse of his disgusting and horrifying visage. Renfield the vampire is *much* scarier physically than Barlow the vampire from the film version of *'Salem's Lot*.

Overall, a real achievement for newcomer Pavia and company.

Storm of the Century (1998)   A made-for-ABC miniseries based on an original Stephen King screenplay.

STEPHEN KING MOVIES IN THE WORKS
AS OF DECEMBER 1997

Apt Pupil
The Green Mile
Rose Madder
Desperation

STEPHEN KING MOVIES NOT BASED ON KING WORKS
BUT USING HIS TITLES OR CHARACTERS

Return to 'Salem's Lot
The Lawnmower Man
The Lawnmower Man 2: Beyond Cyberspace
Sometimes They Come Back . . . Again
Sometimes They Come Back . . . For More
Children of the Corn 2: The Final Sacrifice
Children of the Corn 3: Urban Harvest
Pet Sematary II

STEPHEN J. SPIGNESI'S PICKS OF THE TEN BEST
STEPHEN KING MOVIES OF ALL TIME (SO FAR)

1. *Misery* (1990)
2. *Stand By Me* (1986)
3. *The Shawshank Redemption* (1994)
4. *The Dead Zone* (1983)
5. *Carrie* (1976)
6. *Dolores Claiborne* (1995)
7. *Stephen King's The Night Flier* (1997)
8. *Cujo* (1983)
9. *The Shining* (1980)
10. *Christine* (1983)

WHY KITTY ABSOLUTELY HAD TO DIE,
OR
HOW I MADE A MOVIE OF A STEPHEN KING SHORT STORY FOR A BUCK

by James Cole

Just over a decade ago, I joined a club made up of about seventeen members. This club has never held a meeting, most of us have never met, and I don't know the names of the majority of its members, but we have one thing in common: We are all "Dollar Babies." Rather, our films are Dollar Babies.

The term "Dollar Babies" was coined by Stephen King. It refers to his allowing student filmmakers to adapt his short stories to film. Since 1977, King has endorsed this arrangement so long as he controls the rights and the finished product is not exhibited commercially without his approval. The cost of this deal is, as you may have guessed, one dollar. I still have my canceled one-dollar check with Stephen King's signature on the back.

Completed in 1987, my film version of King's *Night Shift* short story "The Last Rung on the Ladder" got more attention than I could ever have hoped for.

What inspired me to take on such a project, and why did I choose this particular story? I think it comes down to what makes Stephen King such a phenomenon and what his work means to me.

In the summer of 1981, I was staying with friends at Little Sunapee

Lake, New Hampshire. As I scanned their bookshelf, a paperback with a yellow cover caught my eye. It was the movie tie-in version of *The Shining*. I'd heard of the film but hadn't seen it, and I knew nothing of the story.

For the next couple of days, I sat on a deck with the warm sun on my face but chilled to the bone as a blizzard raged outside the Overlook and Danny Torrance "pulled the shower curtain back." That's all it took: I immediately became a full-blown Stephen King junkie.

Just what was it that made me want more of the King?

Even at fourteen, I understood that it wasn't King's monsters or "gross-outs"—it was his characters. When the paperback of *Different Seasons* appeared in the summer of 1983, the novella "The body" made me yearn for a boyhood that I was just beginning to realize I'd lost. "The Body" was also the first story I fantasized about making into a movie. I found it wonderfully appropriate that *Stand by Me* was playing the summer I was shooting my first Stephen King film.

Getting that film off the ground took more than a year. After moving to Cape Cod in 1984, I met Dan Throin, a fellow Stephen King addict, and we decided to make *Last Rung* together. We started shooting in the summer of 1985 and then stopped after just one day.

Our two young actors were not ready for the demands of such a project, and we couldn't locate a real barn, which was crucial to the story. That was the end of *Last Rung,* or so we thought.

In the spring of 1986, I came across the video *Stephen King's Night Shift Collection,* which contained two short King adaptations, *The Woman in the Room* and *The Boogeyman*. Encouraged, I figured it was time to try again. Armed with a new script, a genuine barn, and the same actors, production on *Last Rung* resumed in June 1986. As you can imagine, the challenges were enormous. We were a crew of two dealing with the limitations of Super-8 and two child actors. Yet after a mere nine days of shooting, we were done.

Postproduction—editing, sound work, scoring—took a year. Most of the technical problems we faced during filming were overcome, and the final film was transferred to video in the autumn of 1987. However, Dan and I did not consider our adaptation truly complete until the day we mailed off a tape to Stephen King.

Months went by without a word. Finally, King's secretary responded, saying Stephen had received the film, but she didn't know if he'd watched it yet. We continued to wait and hope.

In September 1988 my account of making the film, "The Good and Bad of Film Adaptation," was published in *Castle Rock: The Stephen King Newsletter,* and four months later the newsletter gave the film a glowing review. Then, in the spring of 1989, *Last Rung* was shown at the Horrorfest Convention at the Stanley (Overlook!) Hotel in Colorado. Dan and I were thrilled. That our film was getting noticed, even seen, was a dream come true.

In 1991 I moved to Los Angeles to pursue a career in Hollywood. That same year, an excerpt from my *Castle Rock* article was featured in Stephen Spignesi's first book about Stephen King, *The Shape Under the Sheet: The Complete Stephen King Encyclopedia*. Even though *Last Rung* was undoubtedly a "name" project, Super-8 mm just wasn't professional enough, nor did it convey the full scope of the story—the adult lives of Larry and Kitty—so it got little notice in the industry.

Then I got an idea: Remake our short adaptation but do it right. I worked on a new thirty-page script and sent a query letter to King. King's secretary responded, telling me that Stephen did not wish the film remade. Truthfully, I was relieved. It was madness to even consider it, and that was the end of it, or so I thought.

By the summer of 1992, an original script I was working on was stalled, and I realized I needed to focus on something different, something I could get excited about.

Then I had an even more outrageous idea: Do *Last Rung* again, but this time as a full-length feature film.

As exciting as this idea was, I knew I was walking into a potential legal minefield. Adapting the story as a feature would require my making a deal with King, and as an unrepresented, unproduced writer, that seemed highly unlikely.

Putting aside legal worries, though, I focused on nailing the story, a daunting task. How could I get a 120-page script out of a 12-page story? I reread the story countless times, spent weeks writing notes and outlines, and discovered something surprising. Except for the incident in the barn, much of King's story is a beautifully written outline. All the events between the ladder incident and Kitty's jump from a building are painted in broad strokes. ("we grew up.") There are some wonderful specifics, like Kitty winning a beauty contest and marrying one of the judges, but I would have to fill in the blanks and create the Larry and Kitty that weren't on the page.

Sticking close to the story, I used the Vietnam-to-Watergate era as a backdrop as I helped Larry and Kitty navigate their junior high and high school years. Then I got stuck.

Kitty's troubles and eventual death are partly due to Larry's not being there for her. Every time Kitty writes and asks, "Can you come, Larry?," he writes back and says he can't. Then he stops writing altogether.

Heart-wrenching, sure, but useless in a screenplay. The essence of good characters are those that grow—or don't—through conflict, but how could there be conflict if Larry and Kitty never even appeared in the same scene?

This taught me an important lesson about adapting: Change the specifics to remain faithful to the intent of the story. A great example is David Cronenberg's *Dead Zone*. Although little more than the basic plot of King's novel ended up in the film, its tone and "feel" are exactly right.

After much thought I changed the dynamics of the relationship. Instead of Larry's never being there for Kitty, he rescues her again and again, determined to never let her "fall." In my version, this commitment almost costs Larry his marriage. In King's story, Larry is divorced from his wife, Helen, but I knew I needed Helen as a character, as a competitor for Larry's attention.

I completed my first draft in October 1992 and then passed it along to friends for their reaction. The verdict? Thumbs down.

Among the story's problems, the worst was my decision to let Kitty live. Worried about the script's marketability, I had changed the ending and let Larry save her. This move totally violated the theme of my adaptation: Larry has to let go. Disappointed, I started over, this time remaining true to the intent of King's story: I let Kitty die. My second draft was completed in the summer of 1993.

This version was close but still not good enough. My next draft was completed in November of that year, and this third try seemed to be the charmer. The response from friends was positive, and several film execs who read it were enthusiastic. Now I faced my biggest dilemma: I couldn't do a thing with it. Without film rights, I could not sell my adaptation of "Last Rung" or even show it around as my own. I again wrote to Stephen King, inquiring about obtaining the rights or at least an option on the story.

I did not receive a reply, but I knew that my inquiry was likely one of thousands that King receives from filmmakers wanting to make movies from his stories. I still didn't give up on "Last Rung" though, even as I returned to other projects, and I was heartened when my original short film was mentioned in the book *The Films of Stephen King* in 1994.

That same year, *The Shawshank Redemption* received critical acclaim and seven Academy Award nominations. The film's success was a personal thrill because I know Shawshank's screenwriter and director, Frank Darabont. (Frank also did a terrific job on the aforementioned short King film *The Woman in the Room*.) When Frank's book *The Shawshank Redemption: The Shooting Script* was published in 1996, it contained King's first mention of his "dollar deals," and he included *Last Rung* as an example. Eight years after its completion, I finally had confirmation that King had seen my film. Thanks to the King "network," I got the impression that the Man from Maine was generally pleased with my work.

Excited, I again wrote King about doing "Last Rung" as a feature, and this time I received a response from King's lawyer, who told me that King did not want to license the story "at the present time." I took this as a sign to listen to the theme of my script and let go.

Another year passed. Then, one day, a friend forwarded a posting he had found on the Stephen King Newsgroup on the Internet. It reported a rumor that King was allowing a Maine filmmaker to adapt "Last Rung" for Maine Public Television. My heart sank. If this were true, my quest was really over.

A few days later, the same friend sent me another posting, this one by Lucas Knight, the rumored "Last Rung" filmmaker, who was searching for *me*! Knight was trying to obtain a copy of our short film, which has never been available to the public. I replied immediately, and Lucas confirmed that the rumor was true. However, the deal with King was not for a feature-length version of "Last Rung": it would be another short adaptation, albeit a professional one.

At the end of 1997, Lucas and his partner were in preproduction and seeking funds to make their version of King's poignant tale.

Me? I still live in Los Angeles, and I still dream of writing movies for a living. In its various incarnations, "The Last Rung on the Ladder" has been a part of my life for more than a decade. I haven't worked on the feature since 1993, but I still hope it will see the screen someday.

As Red said in *The Shawshank Redemption*, "hope is a good thing, and no good thing ever dies."

I hope.

APPENDIX D

BOOKS ABOUT STEPHEN KING

If you owned any or all of these books, you would be well on your way to knowing a hell of a lot more about Stephen King and his work than you probably do now.

For around a hundred bucks or so, you can own every one of these titles, and it will be the best money you ever spent as a King fan.

For most King fans, there comes a time when a question arises that they absolutely must know the answer to. It could be anything from where King taught school (Hampden Academy) to what was his first published short story ("I Was a Teenage Grave Robber"). These books (as well as the one you hold in your hands) can answer those questions and will open up a whole new facet of the Stephen King universe to you, while also providing hours of entertaining reading.

So head on out to the bookstore. You'll be glad you did.

The Complete Stephen King Encyclopedia by Stephen J. Spignesi (1990, Contemporary Books, trade paperback)

> This was my first book about Stephen King, and frankly it is still the gold standard in terms of "one-stop shopping" for all your Stephen King research needs. It runs 750,000 words and is over eight hundred pages (*8 1/2 x 11 pages*) in length. The heart of the *Encyclopedia* (which was originally published in a limited edition as *The Shape Under the Sheet*) is an 18,000 word alphabetical concordance to King's work (both published and unpublished) organized into "People," "Places," and "Things" sections. The book also includes dozens of lengthy interviews with people from all realms of the Stephen King universe, including his secretary, sister-in-law, and brother (Dave King's first ever interview about his kid brother) as well as scholars, critics, film directors, book dealers, and fans. The entire run of *Castle Rock* is detailed issue by issue, and every film version of a King story is also covered in detail. The *Encyclopedia* also contains contributions from a wide range of writers,

including King's first collaborator, the journalist who has interviewed King more than anyone else, and several fellow horror writers. The book also contains fiction, poetry, indexes, photos, charts, and oddities, such as a comprehensive listing of all of the ways King has killed off his characters. I hope this review does not come off as too self-serving, but if you haven't seen this book and you are a King fan, then you will thank me for turning you on to it. Honest. This book is invaluable, but the 1990 edition is somewhat out of date. A new edition is in the planning stages, but the original will serve you well until the revised and expanded edition does come out.

The Stephen King Companion by George Beahm (1995, Andrews and McMeel, trade paperback)

George Beahm's first book about King and his work, *The Stephen King Companion* (recently updated) is the perfect introduction to the World of the King. An eclectic collection of interviews, book synopses, articles, and bibliographic information, this book provides a quick and easy initiation into the ever-expanding universe of Stephen King books, movies, and events.

Stephen King: America's Best-Loved Boogeyman by George Beahm (1998, Andrews and McMeel, trade paperback)

George Beahm's second book about King, this one a literary biography that looks at King's life and times and provides insight into the influences that made King the writer—and the man—he is today. Fascinating, if you are interested in King as a *person,* and most of his fans are.

Stephen King: The Art of Darkness by Douglas E. Winter (1984, Signet mass-market paperback)

An authorized look at King's life and work by one of King's closest friends, writer Douglas Winter. Doug's book has an authority that bespeaks his close relationship with King, and there are several exclusive interviews with King in *The Art of Darkness* that King granted specifically for this book. Invaluable if somewhat out of date at this point.

The Work of Stephen King by Michael R. Collings (1996, Borgo Press trade hardcover and trade paperback)

This is a five-hundred-page annotated bibliography of everything Stephen King has written *or* that has been written *about him,* complete through the end of 1994. It is an absolutely breathtaking work of scholarship and a resource that is invaluable in its scope and expertise.

Fangoria—Masters of the Dark: Stephen King and Clive Barker; Anthony Timpone, editor (1997, HarperPrism mass-market paperback)

An important collection of recent interviews with King, available in an inexpensive mass-market paperback edition.

APPENDIX E

SOURCES AND RESOURCES

Here is a listing of some of the people, places, and things Stephen King fans can turn to for help with their King needs. I personally know all the fine folks behind these organizations and publications and vouch 100 percent for their professionalism and integrity. You can deal with these people with total confidence, plus they're one hell of a great bunch of folks!

Betts Bookstore (a bookstore in Bangor, Maine, that specializes in Stephen King items)

Stuart Tinker
26 Main Street
Bangor, Me. 04401
Phone: 207-947-7052
E-mail: bettsbooks@aol.com

The Overlook Connection (a mail-order company that specializes in Stephen King items)

Dave Hinchberger
P.O. Box 526
Woodstock, Ga. 30188
Phone: 770-926-1762
Fax: 770-516-1469
E-mail: overlookcn@aol.com

Donald M. Grant, Publisher, Inc. (publisher of the limited editions of King's *Dark Tower* series)

19 Surrey Lane, P.O. Box 187
Hampton Falls, N.H. 03844
Orders: 800-476-0510
Order fax line: 603-778-7191

E-mail: dmgrant@aol.com
Web site: http://www.nh.ultra.net/~dmgrant

Popular Culture, Ink. (publisher of the first edition of *The Complete Stephen King Encyclopedia*)

P.O. Box 1839
Ann Arbor, Mich. 48106
Orders: 800-678-8828

Phantasmagoria (a Stephen King newsletter)

P.O. Box 3602
Williamsburg, Va. 23187
Phone: 757-221-0119
Fax: 757-221-0121
E-mail: geobeahm@aol.com
Web site: http://members.aol.com/geobeahm/index.html

The Magazine of Fantasy & Science Fiction

143 Cream Hill Road
West Cornwall, Conn. 06796

Entertainment Weekly

1675 Broadway
New York, N.Y. 10019

Playboy (back issues)

1-800-345-6066
http://www.playboy.com

Games

P.O. Box 184
Fort Washington, Pa. 19034

Waldenbooks (Walden-by-Mail)

1-800-322-2000, Dept. 453

SKEMERs (Stephen King E-mailers)

E-mail: skemers@aol.com

Dark Echo (an online horror magazine)

E-mail: darkecho@aol.com

Marvel Entertainment Group, Inc.

387 Park Avenue South
New York, N.Y. 10016

INDEX

1/01

GAYLORD S

ML